A GRAND
TOUR OF THE
ROMAN
EMPIRE

By the same authors

How to Manage Your Slaves
Release Your Inner Roman

A GRAND
TOUR OF THE
ROMAN
EMPIRE

MARCUS SIDONIUS FALX

with Jerry Toner

P

PROFILE BOOKS

First published in Great Britain in 2022 by
PROFILE BOOKS LTD
29 Cloth Fair
London EC1A 7JQ
www.profilebooks.com

1 3 5 7 9 10 8 6 4 2

Typeset in Bembo by MacGuru Ltd

Printed and bound in Great Britain by Clays Ltd, Elcograf S.p.A.

A CIP catalogue record for this book is available from the British Library.

ISBN 978 1 78125 575 9
eISBN 978 1 78283 217 1

FSC
www.fsc.org
MIX
Paper from
responsible sources
FSC® C018072

CONTENTS

AUTHOR'S NOTE

WHAT A WONDER is the Roman empire. Throughout its vast lands, stretching from Britannia in the north to Egypt in the south, from Hispania in the west to the Euphrates in the east, great cities glisten with fine marble and offer their citizens the utmost in public luxury. In the countryside, the fields flourish with an abundance of crops, and fecund herds graze the rich pastures. Everywhere, the population has boomed and prosperity abounds. I should know. My noble family's estates span the provinces of the empire, often acquired as rewards for our part in their conquest. When Philo of Byzantium long ago listed his Seven Wonders of the World, he had no clue of what was to come. These few sites have been outdone a hundred times by the glories of the Roman empire: its amphitheatres, its palaces, its aqueducts, its temples and its roads. No educated man should leave this world without having experienced them.

What would one wish for in a travelling companion on such a tour? A man of wit, charm and easy conversation, I would suggest. A man who can bear the occasional hardships encountered on the road and at sea with a calm and uncomplaining equanimity. A man

viii ·· A GRAND TOUR OF THE ROMAN EMPIRE

whose informed opinions could help while away the inevitable hours of delay with lively discussion on almost any subject, from the most serious matters of the day to the glories of the epic poets to the frivolities of gossip. What one would not choose is a Brittunculus – a nasty little Brit. A whingeing Brit, moreover, who has spent his entire life in the small town of Duroliponte and has a mind every bit as provincial as that suggests. A man whose classical education seems to have washed over him without leaving a trace and who prefers to decipher the scrawls and graffiti of the common plebs when he could be reading Virgil. A man who prefers beer to wine. Such a man is Jerry Toner. But for my guide to reach as wide an audience as it deserves, needs must. May the gods help me.

COMMENTATOR'S NOTE

TRAVEL AND TOURISM took off during the long centuries of the Roman peace, the *Pax Romana* of the empire, when travel was relatively safe and readily available and affordable, if not to a mass audience then to a much broader group than was historically the case. The huge grain ships heading to Rome to feed its under-employed crowds took with them hundreds of paying passengers, who slept out on the decks and prayed to the gods for their safe arrival. For the wealthy, making a tour of the highlights of Greece and Egypt was one of the benefits of empire, a way of deriving pleasure from places the Romans had conquered. But they were not only interested in seeing the sights. The accounts they wrote of their trips contained long excursions on the mythology connected with each place, its history, the logistics of their journey, and ruminations about all kinds of other issues. Falx's own text is of a similar vein and represents a kind of Baedeker of the ancient world. Needless to say, the fact that I have helped bring it to publication does not mean I approve of many of the views expressed within it.

The stability of the Roman empire also encouraged

many other forms of travel: imperial representatives and officials went where they were sent to perform local governmental tasks and oversee important projects, while soldiers moved to wherever they were stationed. Wealthy landowners would travel to inspect their estates. Trade and commerce thrived, and merchants transported their wares to markets throughout the empire, often settling down in the process. Artists and craftsmen went where the work was, and all kinds of street entertainers, fortune tellers and religious practitioners passed through towns in search of an audience. The rich sent their young to learn the skills of oratory at the great schools in Greece, while the sick went in search of cures at the renowned healing centres. The famed network of roads, while primarily for military use, also encouraged travel. It was as if the Roman empire were in perpetual motion. All these travellers took their cultures with them and the result was that many of the large cities acquired a new level of cosmopolitanism. People took their gods with them, too, and religions from the eastern part of the empire introduced new kinds of religious experience that were very different from those of the traditional pantheon.

Acting as Marcus Sidonius Falx's secretary during a long and gruelling tour of the vast Roman empire has been an experience I shall never forget. There have been highs: the great sites and shrines of the cities, the strange rituals, and the overwhelming diversity. But there have been many lows: the casual indifference towards the suffering of many, the overweening arrogance towards provincials, the unswerving belief in the superiority of

Rome and its values. Empire forced travel upon many. The crushing of revolts such as those of the Jews resulted in the displacement of whole peoples. Millions more slaves were shipped away from their homelands to wherever their owners decreed. But Falx merely reflects what we find in our sources. We hear so much more about what the Romans thought – wealthy Romans at that – than we do about those they ruled. As with so much of the Roman world, we find some material that is understandable, but a great deal also that stretches the imagination and makes us work hard to comprehend their world view. Looking at the evidence always makes me realise how much of the ancient world is lost to us.

Marcus is coy about his age but most of his views reflect those of the High Empire, that time praised by Gibbon as the period in the history of the world when the condition of the human race was most happy and prosperous. None of what Falx says is pure fiction. It is all based on a range of contemporary sources, although these have often been adapted to make them more easily accessible to a modern audience. I have added brief commentaries to his account at the end of each chapter to put some of his opinions into context and to counteract some of his unthinking biases. Alongside the suggested further reading at the end of the book, these will guide those who are interested in digging deeper to where they can find out more about the underlying primary sources, who wrote them and why, and to modern academic discussions.

CHAPTER I

A GRAND TOUR

THE EMPEROR HAD SUMMONED ME. Guards directed me to a broad terrace on the spur of the Palatine hill where he was walking in an agitated manner, followed by a gaggle of advisers. He is very tall and extremely pale, with an unshapely, hairy body. He also has a very thin neck and legs, and hollow eyes that sink below a broad forehead, above which his thinning hair sticks out in wisps. He is touchy about his baldness and it is forbidden to look down on him from any higher place. His face is naturally threatening but he works hard to make it all the more so by practising savage expressions in front of a mirror.

'Ah Falx!' he greeted me, 'Here is a man who will give me a straight answer. Tell me, Falx, what would you do to improve the empire?'

'O emperor, what a question is this,' I began, and, wishing to assure him of the impossibility of the task, added, 'as the proverb says, you are asking me to milk a he-goat!'

The emperor stopped as if he had been hit by a bolt from Jupiter. His entourage stared at me in horror at what I had said. How was I to know that the emperor's touchiness about his straggly hair and knock-kneed physique extended to a ban of any mention of goats! A lesser man would have faced execution.

'Get away from here,' he snarled with his most terrifying glare, 'and keep away – well away.'

I scuttled out of the palace. Unnerved, I have faced the barbarian hordes in battle, but I do not mind admitting that fear now made me sweat like the Tiber in full flow. I had offended the emperor and had been told to make myself scarce. It was time to lie low for a while.

I decided it was best for me to leave Rome and to do so quickly. I would travel first thing down to my villa at Baiae. But the emperor himself is known to enjoy holidaying at that seaside resort so I could hardly stay there for long. I considered my properties in north Africa, the large estates I had inherited from my uncle in Gaul, the olive farms in Hispania I had bought many years ago to import oil into Rome. All were suitably far away. And then there was so much of our great empire that I had never seen. I had studied in Athens as a young man but had not returned since. I had experienced the chaos of Alexandria for some weeks when sent on official business but had not had time to make the leisurely journey up the Nile to see the wonders of the pharaohs. And then there was my son, Titus, who was commanding forces up on the wall in the farthest-flung corner of icy Britannia. What better opportunity to surprise him and deliver in person those socks he is always asking my wife to send.

I realised that it was my chance to tour the empire. But a guidebook to help such a task was sorely lacking. I had read various travels guides to parts of Greece but they were mostly written by Greeks who were determined to try to revive the glories of their ancient past. With their endless tales of the Greeks' victories against the Persians, their detailed accounts of their local myths and customs, it is as if their present-day subservience to Rome does not exist. I decided that I would take this opportunity to write a guidebook for all the most memorable places and monuments throughout the whole empire, to be written in ten books. No one, not even a Greek, has ever attempted a grand tour of the entire Roman empire.

There is a great need for such a guide. Almost the whole world seems to be travelling back and forth across the empire. Why? Men travel for a whole range of reasons. Some go in search of education and spend years in Greece at the feet of philosophers. Many senators, as my father did, send their sons to Athens to hone the skills of oratory that will be so important to their careers in public life. What educated man is less than fluent in Greek, which he must master in order to adorn his speeches with a liberal scattering of apt quotes of the great bard, Homer? Others go looking for health. How many have made the long trek to Pergamum to consult the healing god Asclepius in his lavish sanctuary there. Aided by the attendants, they sleep in the temple precincts so that the god himself might visit in a dream and tell them what course of treatment to pursue. Or they go to consult with the great practitioners of Greek medicine, who can diagnose the humoral imbalances responsible for their illnesses.

Many travel for trade. Wherever you go, you see cargoes coming from as far off as southern Arabia and even India, in such numbers that their lands must have been stripped bare of spices. Nearer to home, the farmlands of Egypt and north Africa transport their rich harvests in the huge grain ships that are the lifeblood of the city of Rome. It is a wonder that there is space in the sea for so many ships.

Naturally, it is the common classes who travel for money. Those who can afford a life of leisure often make tours to explore the many interests that the empire has to offer. Human nature is such that we are curious about other peoples and places, and are keen to travel. Many make sea voyages, and endure long solitary journeys alone, simply to see some remote sight. For nature, self-conscious of her own beauty, made us natural admirers of her attractions. So people are eager to see with their own eyes anything special they have read or heard about. Of course, with some, this urge to travel becomes almost a sickness. Because they don't know what they want, are too fond of soft living, and yearn perpetually after something meaningful, which otherwise eludes them, they indulge in a pointless roaming across the earth's surface. Natural marvels, places where miracles have occurred, zoological curiosities, bizarre customs of far-off people – all are pursued with a desperate thirst for experience that no amount of such travel seems to slake.

These idle rich wander aimlessly, travel along distant shores, sometimes by sea, other times on land, always trying to calm some inner restlessness. 'Let's go to Campania!' they will say. But they will soon grow bored and long for wild places and head off for Lucania or the like. But, once there, they will pine for beauty and sophistication and rush down to Tarentum to enjoy its pleasant climate. And no sooner have they arrived than they will miss the noise and bustle of Rome and be overcome with a desire to see some bloodshed at the Colosseum. So one journey succeeds another, and one sight is changed for another. They seem to be fleeing from themselves.

It is the Roman empire that has made all of this travel possible. The immense majesty of the Roman peace and its excellent network of communications by both road and sea has generated an ease and security of travel that only serves to increase this wanderlust. We Romans have mapped out the world, bridged rivers, cut roads through mountains, and have filled wastelands with posting stations where officials can find an inn to stay and a stable to provide fresh horses. Yet hardly any of those non-Romans who wish to know about touring the jewels of the empire have any idea where to start. This guide will tell them all they need to know.

What glories shall we see? To begin with there is the architecture. Were all other knowledge of the Roman world to be lost, so many huge ruins would survive that it would be clear what a mighty civilisation had built them. The arches, bath houses, cupolas, bridges and aqueducts all tell of a prosperity that no previous age ever came close to matching and I cannot imagine that any human society will ever surpass. The so-called Seven Wonders of the World date from the time when Alexander had recently conquered the Persian empire, and reflect the narrow outlook of the Greeks: Alexandria, Rhodes, Olympia, Halicarnassus, Ephesus, Memphis and Babylon. But Roman prosperity and building skill have seen the continuous growth and embellishment of cities across the empire. There are now some 250 cities in Tarraconese Hispania alone. Even those founded by the Greeks, such as Alexandria, have blossomed under Roman rule. And everywhere, all these cities are captivated by one aim: to outdo their rivals and neighbours and to appear the loveliest of all. Even in those formerly barbarian regions of the north, there are triumphal arches, paved piazzas, marble temples and stone amphitheatres. They gleam in splendour and the whole world seems to have turned to pleasure and magnificence.

We shall see the graves of the heroes of old, such as the tomb of Achilles at Troy. We shall go in search of the heroes of more recent times and follow in Alexander's footsteps as he set off on his great trek into the Persian empire. We shall see the famed battle sites of the Persian wars, where the Athenians and their allies first drove back the Persian aggressor. And we shall visit places where other famous men have lived, sat and talked, such as the house of Socrates in Athens.

The gods will be at the heart of our journey. We shall experience the divine places where long ago the gods were born. We shall visit many important sanctuaries and shrines, which have gradually acquired vast arrays of priceless objects as gifts donated by grateful worshippers. Great art will be high on our agenda. Those two great masterpieces, Phidias's Zeus and Myron's bronze cow, will both feature. As will places of literary fame. We shall see the ruins of Troy and the beach where the Greeks first landed in their attempt to wrest back Helen. And we shall experience the beauty that only nature herself can offer, such as the vale of Tempe, where the river Peneus meanders through avenues of trees, with grassy-green banks, while birds sing from the treetops. In short, this guide will give you knowledge of peoples, their customs and their past; and of places, famous for their beauty, history or peculiarity.

You too will experience the benefits of the Roman empire. You will see how the world is more cultivated and richer than before and how every place is thriving. Fertile fields have replaced deserts, and cornfields have replaced forests. Swamps have been drained and there are now as many cities as there once were hovels. Every nook teems with civilised life. Roman domination has brought an end to those interminable wars between local tribes, who now cannot even remember a time when they had the ability to commit such reckless military follies.

To be ruled by us Romans is to find yourself under the power of superiors. We control a vast empire with a rule that is firm but not unkind. This happy experience has moved the whole world to hang on tight to Rome. The world would no more think of leaving Rome than a ship's crew would think of parting company with its pilot. Have you seen bats in a cave grabbing tightly to one another as they hang from the rocks? Thus does the world cling to Rome. All men pay their taxes to her with greater pleasure than some people would collect them from others. All the common people can appeal to the emperor for help. It is a state of affairs that is both pleasing and advantageous to rich and poor alike. Nobody ever considers an alternative and there are no dissenting voices.

It is as if the entire empire is on a perpetual holiday. The only people who deserve our pity are those few who still reside outside our empire. Let us pray that the gods grant that this empire and the great city of Rome flourish forever and only fall when stones float on water and blossom stops blooming in the spring. And let us pray that the great emperor and his sons be preserved and obtain blessings for all.

But, interrupting my day-dreaming, I realised that there was no time to waste. It was time to leave the city in case the emperor should decide to send his men after me. Traffic is banned in daylight in Rome so I had four of my slaves carry me in a curtained sedan chair until we were outside the city limits. There I transferred to a small wagon, whose wheels creaked viciously despite the application of extra animal fat to the axles to lubricate them, and in which I was able to stay out of sight under an awning.

It is an age-old tradition that travellers who set off on a journey, whether by land or water, pledge to fulfil some kind of vow on reaching their destination safely. The vow I took as I looked back at the gleaming towers of the great city was not the usual stupid and irrelevant sort. I simply vowed that, if I returned safely, I would dedicate my guide to the emperor in the hope of regaining his favour.

·· COMMENTARY ··

The description of the highly sensitive emperor is based on that of Caligula, who certainly seems to have been more touchy than most. Senators who fell out of imperial favour might, if they were lucky, have travel imposed upon them in the form of exile to some provincial backwater or isolated island, where they would hope that they might be recalled once the emperor's anger had calmed. Despite falling foul of the imperial temper, Falx has nothing but praise for the Roman empire, and his paean is based on the Greek orator Aelius Aristides' second-century CE *Panegyric to Rome*, which certainly has no room for any dissenting voices. Whether all of Rome's subject peoples saw their subordination as Falx does is hard to say as they left so few sources. Later Jewish sources express a resigned animosity towards an empire that had brutally suppressed their people on no less than three occasions. But many Christians, who we might imagine were hostile to Rome, did not fail to appreciate its material advantages and the description of the empire's boom is based on that of the Church Father, Tertullian (*On the Cloak* 2.7). We shall experience other counter views in later stages of the journey, but it is certainly true to say that the Roman peace made travel safer and more widespread. Much of this was associated with trade but there was also a growth in what we would call tourism of a variety of kinds. Falx's description of a rich set who flit about the empire is based on Seneca (*On the Tranquil*

Mind 2.13), who is dismissive of this vacuous group. Seneca's view cannot be taken as representative of wider opinion since he is positioning himself as a philosophical thinker in such texts. More likely, his view is an outlier, and most of the elite were happy to enjoy the pleasures of travel. To do so obviously required both leisure and money, and it was certainly not open to many outside the wealthiest classes, although more ordinary Romans, such as traders, could combine seeing the world with earning a living.

Making a grand tour of the sights was closely connected with empire, representing a kind of visual appropriation of Rome's conquests. Many powerful Romans went further and sought to express this urge by physically collecting and copying the great works of art they saw in the Greek world. Augustus adorned Rome with works such as Myron's Zeus, which he placed on the Capitoline hill, and the Aphrodite of Apelles, considered the greatest painter, which he placed in his forum. Most of this sculpture and painting was between two and four hundred years old so it is clear that the Romans were mostly interested in what we would call Old Masters. Great Art of this kind was also high on the tourist agenda. The three most famous works were probably Phidias's statue of Zeus in Olympia, Praxiteles' Aphrodite in Cnidus in Asia Minor, and the bronze cow by Myron on the acropolis in Athens. Much of this fine art was to be found in temples, just as it was later to be placed in Christian churches, as a result of donations by worshippers. Falx's decision to tour beyond the famous sites of the East was perhaps inspired by the travels of the emperor Hadrian, who spent over half his reign outside Italy. Unlike previous emperors who had largely relied on representatives to keep them informed about goings-on in the provinces, Hadrian wanted to see it first-hand and he visited almost every province of the empire, instigating various building projects, such as his famous wall in the north of Britannia.

It is not known for certain who first came up with the Seven Wonders of the World. Antipater of Sidon listed seven great monuments he had seen, in about 100 BCE, but included the walls of Babylon instead of the light-house at Alexandria. At roughly the same time, Philo of Byzantium wrote a short description of the seven sights most worth seeing in the world. Other lists also existed and their proliferation is itself best seen as an index of the growth in ancient tourism in the Hellenistic world. Most of the lists focused on ancient man-made build-ings, such as the pyramids and the Temple of Artemis at Ephesus, with only two more contemporary edifices being included: the Pharos lighthouse and the Colossus at Rhodes. This latter was the last of the seven to be completed, soon after 280 BCE, but was destroyed in an earthquake in 225 BCE, meaning that all seven coexisted for not much more than half a century (if, that is, the hanging gardens of Babylon ever existed at all).

CHAPTER II

THE BAY OF NAPLES

LIKE ANY TRAVELLER HEADING SOUTH from Rome, I set out on the Via Appia, which passes over the Alban hills before turning straight for the fertile plains of Campania. I was making for my villa at that most charming seaside resort, Baiae. There I would work out the itinerary for my tour and do some rudimentary logistical planning. A holiday is like a small military campaign and requires a comparable level of organisation if it is to succeed. Once the necessary plans were made, I would depart from the port at Puteoli, on the Bay of Naples.

The Via Appia is a fine road. Generally it is far quicker and indeed more comfortable to make a journey of any distance by sea. But the Via Appia is paved and broad and a carriage can make good headway without leaving the weary traveller black and blue from the bumpiness of the ride. I had arranged for a lighter carriage to meet us a few miles from Rome, once I felt it was safe to sit out in the open. Soon after, we faced the usual onslaught of beggars at Aricia, which is notorious for the large crowd of them who wait there because the steep hill means that carriages have to slow to a crawl. This gives them the opportunity to mob travellers and surround their vehicles with loud pleading. The only way to get rid of them is to throw a handful of small coins on to the road behind. By the time they have fought over them, you are able to put some distance between you and them and they move on to the next carriage. They are a cheeky bunch and they always blow kisses after the coaches as they speed away down the other side of the hill.

At Formiae, we turned right on to Via Domitiana and followed the coast and its inland lagoons down towards Cumae. Here, the road encounters a mountain but passes through it in a tunnel that is wide enough for two teams of horses going in opposite directions to pass each other comfortably. Windows have been cut out at many places, which allows the light of day to be brought down from the surface of the mountain along shafts that are of considerable depth. The tunnel is still gloomy, though, and the dust is so bad that it is necessary to cover your mouth and nose with a cloth.

I slept as we travelled and by the morning of the following day we were approaching Baiae. The whole coastline is riddled with holes down beneath the ground level, which are full of streams and of fire, and this makes the hot water spout up wherever it can. Some of these hot springs are salt water, others pure and drinkable. There are some small lakes that have the taste of seawater but in them even people who cannot swim do not sink, but float on the surface like wood. Since we were in a hurry, we did not travel on to Neapolis. If you have time, you should go there by continuing on the Via Domitiana, which has been possible since the emperor Trajan extended it from Puteoli. Neapolis was founded as a Greek city and it retains a Hellenic feel. There are very many traces of Greek culture preserved there – gymnasia, exercise areas for youths, brotherhoods – and there are Greek names everywhere even though the people are now Romans. They still hold a sacred contest every four years, in the manner of the Olympic Games in Greece though on a smaller scale and with a focus on the arts, especially music. It is very famous, not much less than those held in Greece, and even the emperor Augustus attended it shortly before his death.

Neapolis has springs of hot water and bathing establishments that are not inferior to those at Baiae, although they are far less busy. It is a city of idle relaxation. It is also full of people who have tired of life in Rome and want to find a more restful existence. They go there in search of a little peace and quiet but then fall in love with the place and make it their permanent abode. The weather is good but, it has to be said, changeable. The land is rich, made fertile by the fatty substance contained in the volcanic ash that enriches the soil because of the nearby volcano Vesuvius, which means that the fresh produce is of the highest quality. The seafood is naturally also exceptional. If you take a walk by the edge of the winding shore, where the waves spatter your shoes on the sand, you will see boys playing dice among the beached fishing boats and you can direct your slaves to select whatever fish you wish to eat for your supper.

Baiae. The most beautiful resort in the world, where villa upon villa, palace upon palace has been built, one after another, along its golden shore and upwards among its ring of green hills. Some are even built out into the sea. These villas are surrounded by their gardens, which are neatly laid out with rows of myrtle and plane trees and cropped hedges, all of which provide numerous shady spots away from the heat of the summer sun. As is the case all along the Bay of Naples, hot sulphurous springs bubble out of the rocks and, at Baiae, these feed into baths built for the purpose of catching them, and in which wallow the wealthy of Rome. Some come seeking cures for their ailments, others come looking for pleasure. Both are to be found aplenty. The air is clear and salubrious, and along the seashore you will find oyster beds to ensure that this delicacy is at its freshest.

Baiae is by nature beautiful but human artifice has contrived to make it even more so. The sea is formed into an inland lake into which a narrow channel flows. Dozens of boats bob on the calm waters of this natural harbour: some small fishing boats, others mighty galleys of the emperor. Many emperors have tried to outdo their predecessors and their gorgeous palaces have set a limit of the possibilities of luxury. The sound of parties fills the air, and songs and music ring out across the waters almost all day long. A downside of this is that it is not uncommon for you to have to swerve out of the way of some drunken reveller staggering home. And if you fall in with the wrong sort, Baiae, for all its beauty, is the home of vice. Wives are treated like common property and it is certainly not a place for the virtuous woman. Rich wasters blow their inheritances on pleasure. It is said that anyone who bathes in the waters falls in love and it is certainly true that many men who went to Baiae in search of a cure left with a broken heart. Some of these types are extraordinarily soft. If they manage a walk around the bay they think they have equalled the marches of Alexander or of Julius Caesar, or, if they sail in the brightly coloured boats from Lake Avernus to Puteoli, they see it as an adventure as great as the Golden Fleece, especially if it is in the hot season. Puteoli has quieter pleasures but it is possible to live at Baiae without songs on boats and without profligacy at banquets. I come here for rest from the bustle and work of Rome, and I bask in the sun, take a siesta, saunter along the shore and bathe, before delighting in the local food.

What is more beautiful than the sea? The best villas sit close to the water's edge. As you walk through my own you are greeted with multiple views of the ocean. There is a dining room built out on to the rocks so that a light spray enters the room if the wind is from the south-west. The sea can be seen from three sides through the folding doors and the full-length windows. In another room, one large window provides a broad seascape. The warm seawater swimming pool also has a sea view, and there is a window in an upstairs room that looks out along the coast. At sunset the shadows of the wooded hills fall across the water and the whole house seems to swim in the crystal surface of the sea. From the front, it is possible to look over the bay towards Misenum, where the emperor Tiberius often stayed at his own seaside palace and where he eventually died, and towards the Portus Julius, where the imperial fleet is based and from where Pliny the Elder was driven by his thirst for knowledge to set sail to watch the eruption of Vesuvius close up, only to perish in the attempt. How mighty is the beauty of the sea, the view of its hugeness, its many fair islands and delightful coastlines. It is an inexhaustible source of pleasure. But perhaps the greatest joy is a short sail along the coast followed by a walk along the shore.

If you are of sufficiently high status you may be invited to visit the ultimate villa: that of the emperor Hadrian at Tibur. How colossal it is, four times as large as the Palatine hill in Rome. It contains two palaces and many reconstructions of the famous beauty spots the emperor had visited on his own tour of the empire. You might imagine yourself in Greece as you walk through a Lyceum, an Academy, a colonnade, a vale of Tempe, and even a Hades. In truth, it is both the height of good taste and the lowest vulgarity.

When I arrived at my villa, the housekeeper was shocked to see me. Usually I would send word ahead and he would have everything prepared in advance. Now he was running about shouting out a stream of orders to his team of slaves. One of my tasks in my short stay here would be to write to the caretakers of my other properties to warn them to expect me. Once we had settled, and I had bathed and eaten, I turned my mind to my route.

Like any tourist, I wanted antiquity above all else and so determined to head eastwards first. Greece is the root of so much of our own civilisation that it is the obvious place to start. From there we would head across the Aegean, down the coast towards Judea, before setting sail for Egypt and its extraordinary ancient sights. Our travels would then head west along Africa to Hispania before we would turn north towards the provinces of Gaul and Britannia, and completing the tour with a return journey down the Rhine, past the hairy barbarians on the further bank, and through north Italy back to Rome. This route would enable us to take in almost all the major wonders of the Roman world in all its variety without requiring an excessive amount of overland travel. Journeying by boat is so much more civilised, especially in the summer months, when it is safer too.

On land we would be able to use the Cursus Publicus, the State Post. This was set up by the emperor Augustus to enable speedy communications for his messengers across the empire by means of the excellent road network. There are also river boats on the main navigable routes to expedite the journeys further. Only those carrying a diploma signed by the emperor, his agent or a provincial governor are permitted to use the service. I have such a diploma. Every thirty miles or so there is located a mansio, an inn, where the imperial representative and his party can take a meal, stay overnight, change horses, and have damage to wheels fixed. The regular change of horses means that it is possible to cover about five miles an hour, or about fifty miles per day, although, as we would be in no hurry, we would simply hop from inn to inn. It is possible to cover over one hundred miles per day if travelling overnight, as Julius Caesar once did, or indeed as did Icelus, who informed

Galba in Hispania about Nero's death in Rome only seven days after its occurrence. It takes at least five days to sail from Ostia, the port at Rome, to the Spanish coast so he must have covered the 300-mile land part of the journey in under two days. The swiftest journey I know of is that of the emperor Tiberius, who travelled from Ticinum in Italy to Germany, a distance of 200 miles, in only twenty-four hours. I had no intentions of equalling such record-breaking feats. Normally I would stay overnight when travelling to Baiae, at a lodge I keep specially for the purpose. It is basic but perfectly comfortable and has a barn in which the slaves can sleep. Even this single stretch of overnight travel had left me exhausted.

Sea travel is far swifter, although the unpredictability of the weather means that the sailing season runs only from spring to early autumn, from 5 March to 11 November usually. On that first date, the feast of the Ship of Isis, the patron goddess of sailors, takes place all over the Mediterranean, with a ship being consecrated in her honour. Then all the ships that have been in dry berth for the winter are wheeled down to their harbours and put in the sea. There are always some ships that continue to ply the oceans during the winter, particularly those going on official business, such as carrying documents or transporting prisoners. Or indeed those being sent into exile, like the poor poet Ovid who was forced to set sail for the Black Sea on a stormy December day. But for any casual traveller, the possibility of shipwreck in the winter months is too high to make it worth the risk.

We would need a map. I looked out my special travel

map. This is a long piece of vellum, about one foot wide and twenty-two feet long. Clearly this is not meant to represent the actual shape of the empire. I do not need to be told that the Nile does not run from west to east, for example, as it appears to on my map. Rather, the map provides a picture of the State Post in a manner that makes it easy to use. It marks out where the inns are located and places them along lines representing the roads. These link various cities and are marked with the distance in miles between them. The inns are represented by different symbols according to their quality. A sign of a building with a courtyard means that it is a high-class inn, whereas a drawing of a simple box house with a single peaked roof means that the traveller can expect a modest establishment at best. If there is no symbol at all, all expectations should be laid aside because the inn will be of the most basic kind. These inns are not exclusively for those who have permission to use the State Post but such guests have priority and are required to be put up without charge. The expense of providing such services is not inconsiderable and falls open the locality in which the inn sits, with the exception of Italy where it is paid for by the treasury.

We would travel primarily by four-wheeled carriage. There are plenty of these that can be hired from local guilds across the empire, and they sit in ranks at the gates and main streets of all the larger cities. It is always tempting to take a faster two-wheeled cab but these are more likely to crash. The slaves and the provisions travel behind in other carriages and wagons and can catch us up if they need longer or if we wish to go ahead to the next inn. I did once on an impulse travel in the style of a poor man. Wanting to enjoy a simple pleasure, I carried all my luggage myself on my wagon, and took so few slaves that only one extra carriage was sufficient. I slept on the ground, with only a mattress under me and a cloak on top. Meals were simple affairs and took less than an hour to prepare. I drove in a peasant's wagon, drawn slowly by mules led by a slave walking barefoot. I realised how superfluous was all the paraphernalia of life. But then I was passed by a beautiful swift carriage and was seized by a surge of envy, an envy that was made all the stronger when those wealthy passers-by laughed at me. I felt ashamed that people would think that a Falx should own such a poor vehicle. And I swore I would never travel in such a manner again.

Even so, I refrain from some of the worst excesses that you see on the road. I know a man called Milo who took all his singing boys with him on a journey to Lanuvium along with a whole retinue of slaves. Then there is Julius Caesar, who had portable mosaic floors carted with him on his campaigns. Mark Antony's journeys were like a travelling circus, what with his huge gilded carriage, drawn by lions. Of course, some emperors have gone far beyond this. Nero maintained a suite of a thousand carriages, his mules were shod with silver shoes, and his liverymen dressed in scarlet. His wife, Poppaea, had her horses wear golden harnesses and always took 500 asses with her whenever she travelled so that she could bathe in their milk every day. You see wealthy parvenus imitating this imperial excess. Some travel with Numidian outriders or have runners clear the way ahead. Or they use those fat little Gaulish horses to pull the wagons at the same time as taking more docile horses to ride on. I have even seen oxen and mules draped in purple trappings and with silver bridles and bits. Carriages are often fitted with curtains of silk or decorated with works of art. Or the master brings his mistress in a carriage of her own. Or has his favourite boy sit next to him, his face covered by a mask so that the sun's harsh rays might not harm his delicate face.

Some innovations are, however, very useful to have on the journey. Papyrus scrolls are far too cumbersome to read while travelling so I recommend the more compact codex books with leaves of parchment held within them. I always take a shorthand writer with me so that I can dictate letters while travelling, which he can write up longhand once we have stopped at our destination. I also let him wear long sleeves in winter so that he can keep his hands warm and take his notes better. Sleeping carriages are very useful if you have a long journey to make, one requiring overnight travel. Fitted out with mattresses and warm blankets they are surprisingly comfy. Movable seats are a useful addition that allow you to move out of the sun or move into a place where there is a cooling breeze. If you like to play dice to pass the time, you can always have a gaming board fixed to the carriage, as the emperor Claudius did.

I decided to travel light. My wife would stay behind to look after my affairs. While regrettable, her absence would reduce the baggage considerably. I would need only the essentials. I took a selection of cloaks: short light ones for hot weather, wool and leather ones with hoods for when it rained, and long woollen ones for the cold. I packed my two-inch miniature sundial, made of bronze and designed for use across the empire. Then there was kitchenware for the slaves to cook with, table-ware, towels, bedding, heavy shoes, and a broad hat to keep off the sun. I would need oil for washing, and myrrh to rub on as a lotion. And weapons to be carried by some of the slaves in case of attack by robbers. For added security, I split my money between several trusted home-bred slaves who carried it in bags on a chord around the neck. I would have to take gifts for when staying with friends, acquaintances and friends of friends, such as jars of olives from my own estates, honey, and amphorae of wine.

The advantage in travelling with only the essentials was that it meant I needed the bare minimum of slaves, twenty or so at most. I took my steward to manage all the daily affairs, such as the organisation of the slaves and the purchasing of provisions as required. I took my favourite messenger boy, Hermes, who could run off quickly to carry out whatever errand was required of him. Then there was the head chef and his team of apprentices, including a butcher and a sausage-maker. We would need to entertain at various points on the journey and it would not do to be without a good cook. Then there was the barber, a cobbler, my wardrobe master, and my own personal attendant, none of whom could we do without. Then, of course, there were 'the boys', as I like to call the unskilled slaves, who do all the loading and unloading that such a venture involves, as well as waiting at table, acting as kitchen hands and so on. Even with this group, I made sure that the steward hand-picked a group of his most trusted underlings since there are many opportunities on a long trip for the malcontent to run away.

By the next morning we were ready to leave. We set off along the coast towards Puteoli from where we would join a merchant ship heading towards Greece. As we trundled along, I gazed across to the island of Capri, where an earlier, somewhat difficult emperor had built for himself a retreat where he could indulge his many sexual desires. It is a beautiful island despite bearing the shame of that emperor's debauchery. Puteoli itself is a city adorned with an excellent harbour and has many hot springs because of its proximity to Vesuvius. These contribute greatly to the healing of the sick but also provide huge pleasure and enjoyment to the healthy. Puteoli is also famous for its earth, which, when mixed with lime and then added to water, makes a concrete that can set even under water. There are four types – black, white, grey and red – but all are equally efficacious. It has brought great wealth to the area and allowed the construction of buildings that far supersede those of the Greeks.

Puteoli is the scene of great rejoicing when the Alexandrian ships arrive, by which I mean those boats which are usually sent ahead to announce the coming of the grain fleet in autumn. These smaller vessels carry mail and other small cargo from Egypt. The locals are always glad to see them, because it means that the grain will soon arrive safely and nobody will go hungry in the winter, and all the rabble of Puteoli stand on the docks to watch them come in. The Alexandrian boats are easily recognisable by the very trim of their sails. Only they are allowed to keep their topsails spread out when approaching the harbour so as to maintain their speed, and these stick out conspicuously even when there is a crowd of other boats alongside them at sea.

Puteoli is a huge, safe port. Goods pass through there in vast quantities in transit to Rome. Once unloaded, cargo is disbursed among smaller ships and taken up the coast towards the capital itself. The city's inhabitants come from all over the empire – Greeks and Jews, Egyptians and Syrians – all drawn to the port by their trade with Rome. In the harbour itself, on the pedestal of a colossal statue of the emperor Tiberius, are represented fourteen cities in Asia, among them Ephesus and Sardes, all of which were severely damaged by an earthquake during his reign and which he helped to restore. The town councillors at Puteoli put up the statue in the emperor's honour because they all hailed from these far-off cities. While everybody in my party was bustling about and hurrying to the waterfront to look at the ships, I took the opportunity to locate an inn where we might stay until we managed to secure our passage aboard a merchant vessel heading towards Greece.

I found a place called The Camel not far from the docks. Outside a board promised friendly service and creature comforts and proclaimed, 'Here your host, Septumanus, offers meals and rooms. Anyone coming in will be the better for it. Come stay here, stranger!' I entered the small central bar area. It was a greasy tavern. The smoke from the kitchen filled the room, and the smell of burnt sausages was oppressive. Most of the seats were taken by a motley collection of sailors, muleteers and stevedores, and, what with the steam and clatter of pots and pans from the kitchen, I had to speak loudly to make myself heard to the owner. Unlike most of his customers, he did at least speak Latin. He assured me that the mattresses were comfy and that his price was all inclusive and would cover board for the boys, who would sleep outside in the yard to keep an eye on our luggage. It was cheap and, since I planned only to be here for a single night, I decided it would do.

Leaving the slaves to arrange everything, I set off to the harbour to find a ship. Asking a few sailors, I was soon pointed towards a small merchant vessel and I approached it in order to find the captain and make a booking. He was sitting on the deck.

'Will you take me and my party to Greece?' I called.

'Aye, sir, I will do that. But not today. The wind is poor and 'tis month-end, never an auspicious time to set sail. We shall leave tomorrow once the winds and the omens are good.'

This was splendid news. I returned to my retinue and set them about making preparations for our imminent departure. The journey would take four to five days. We had brought tents for the slaves to sleep in on deck, while I would have one of the cabins. The ship had a galley with a hearth and I sent the cook to buy provisions: white bread for me and dark bread for the slaves; wine for me and wine vinegar for the slaves, which can also be mixed with water to make an everyday drink for everyone. Then there was meat, fruit, cabbage, oil, garum, honey and sausage, plus leeks for the slaves, as well as fish both fresh and dried. Soon everything was ready and we headed to our beds for the night, in anticipation of an early departure.

My room would have been better suited to a mule. The pillows were stuffed with reeds instead of feathers, and were so full of fleas and bugs that they almost seemed to move of their own accord. Large spiders hung from the beams and every so often a lizard would drop from the ceiling. The walls had been scratched with various messages from previous occupants: 'I pissed in the bed, I admit it. I'm sorry. Why? you ask. Well, there wasn't a chamber pot.' At least it was only for a night.

The following morning I got up early, barely having slept because of the endless scratching. I had expected the ship's captain to send his herald to summon us for the sailing but nobody had arrived. I went back to the harbour.

'So, captain, are we to depart? The winds seem favourable.'

'Sail?! On a day such as this,' he replied. 'Why, I heard a crow croaking in the rigging this morning. It would be madness to set sail with an omen such as that.'

They are a superstitious bunch, sailors, and I had learned long ago that it was best to humour them. I went back to the inn and informed my retinue of the delay. I spent the morning dictating notes to my secretary. In the afternoon I went for a walk around the area near the inn and ended up reading some of the scrawls that seemed to cover almost every wall. What a load of rubbish they are. There is nothing written in them that is either useful or pleasing – only so-and-so 'remembers' so-and-so, and 'wishes him the best', and is 'the best of his mates', and many things of equal ridiculousness. Much of it is very puerile: 'Lesbianus, you shit and you write "Hello, every-one!"', I mean, what is the point of that? Or the endless claims about their alleged sexual prowess. A certain Gaius Valerius Venustus, soldier of the First Praetorian Cohort, in the century of Rufus, claimed to be the greatest of fuckers. Another claimed that, 'Here I screwed lots of girls'. Who do they think is reading this stuff? Some of it is at least practical. There was one advertising a missing bronze urn from a shop and offering a reward of 65 sesterces to anyone who returned it, more if the thief were caught. But most of it was just silly: 'The all-night boozers want Vatia to be Aedile.' Who cares what they think? As for the wisdom of 'The one who buggers a fire burns his penis', do we really need to be told this? Or else it is full of the most aggressive ill-mannered cursing: 'Chios, I hope your piles become so sore again that they hurt more than ever before.' Charming. The reality is that you will find this kind of stuff all over walls and pillars wherever you travel. You might admire some but most you will just laugh at. And you should be careful that it does not harm you imperceptibly by instilling in you the habit of nosiness. It makes you think that you should be interested in other people's affairs when, in fact, their problems should not concern you. And just as you would not let your hunting dog pursue every scent, so you should not blunt your intellect by looking at this worthless nonsense and read something of value instead. I took out my copy of the *Odyssey*.

I slept fitfully the second night and was most disturbed to have the following dream. I dreamed that either side of my head was shaved. Its meaning was clear: we would be shipwrecked. For men shave after they have been involved in a shipwreck since in the storm they offer their hair as a gift to the gods should they be saved. I was less than pleased when soon after dawn the captain sent us a message that we would be departing soon. I paid for him to make an extra sacrifice to ensure that the omens were not as my dream had portended. The sheep's liver was clear and, somewhat nervously, I mounted the gangplank, only to sneeze loudly. The captain turned white. 'It is a dreadful omen to sneeze when boarding a boat,' he wailed. I'd had enough. 'Will a gold coin change your mind?' I asked. 'The winds are so favourable, sir,' he declared, 'and the message from the sheep was so clear I am sure this is some mischievous minor deity that is toying with us.' And off we sailed.

The trade wind, the Etesian, was blowing from the north. The big-bellied ship was not built for speed or agility and so, with the help of a harbour pilot, the captain used its small square sail at the front to manoeuvre out of the harbour. Once out at sea, however, the ship, with its square mainsail fully out and its triangular topsail angled to catch the upper winds, made good speed. I sat on a chair on the poop deck from where I could get the clearest view of the coastline, and, over the noise of the wind and the waves striking against the hull of the boat, chatted with the skipper as he directed the crew to steer by moving the tiller bars and steering oars on each rear flank. My Grand Tour was under way.

·· COMMENTARY ··

The Bay of Naples is ringed with hot volcanic springs and became very fashionable among the Roman elite, who would escape the capital's heat and dust by retiring there to their summer villas. Baiae was the most chic resort and several emperors kept palaces there. Hadrian died at Baiae in 117 CE. Seneca is critical of the pleasure-seeking behaviour that went on at the resort but, as with his view of jet-set travellers, we should be careful not to see his views as standard. The presence of the emperors lent Baiae a huge amount of cachet and it is clear that Rome's smartest set were desperate to be seen there. The luxury villas they built reflected the most refined and most expensive tastes, and were carefully constructed to provide views of the water from different rooms and from different angles. Pliny the Younger gives an account of his holiday retreat at Laurentum that emphasises how proud he was of it and what extraordinary attention to detail went into the planning of every nook and vista. Villas were often a means for the richest Romans to display their wealth in a highly conspicuous manner, whether in the form of art or plants or aquatic life, and the collecting of expensive fish in special pools was a popular enough activity to draw Cicero's ire (*Letters to Atticus* 1.18.6).

The beggars mobbing travellers at Aricia comes from Juvenal (*Satire* 4.117). It is impossible to know whether they were blowing their kisses ironically or not, but the fact that they were using the local terrain to their advantage suggests that they were well aware that they were effectively forcing travellers to be generous towards them. The comments on Naples are based on those of Strabo (*Geography* 5.4.8), who wrongly believed that volcanic ash contained a fatty substance that enriched the soil.

Falx's travel map is based on the Peutinger Map, a medieval copy of a Roman original. Its distorted dimensions make it seem as if it were simply not a very good map, but it was not designed to accurately reflect the physical layout of the Roman empire. It was a practical shorthand that helped the traveller plan their journey by representing the communications network, in a similar way to the London Underground map, which helps tourists traverse the capital while bearing only a vague likeness to the geography of the city above ground. The pictorial guide to the quality of the resting establishments on the route also made it easy for the traveller to plan according to both their tastes and their capacity to cope with the discomfort of covering long distances by road.

Many of the practicalities of planning a journey can be found in the fourth-century account left by Theophanes (see John Matthews, *The Journey of Theophanes: Travel, Business, and Daily Life in the Roman East*, 2006). Theophanes's journal offers an extraordinary quantity of detail about his trip, which saw him and his entourage travel from Egypt to Antioch and back again. We are told where they stayed each night, what provisions were bought and how much was paid for them, and who they entertained and in what fashion. Theophanes never actually states how many slaves he took with him but the quantities of food and wine that were bought suggest that the number must have been substantial. For the wealthy, slaves were an indispensable part of any trip, needed to make it as comfortable and civilised as possible. Seneca was once seized with an impulse to travel in the manner of a poor man but soon gave up when ashamed to be seen in such a state (*Moral Letters* 87). The fourth-century CE Christian bishop, Synesius, expressed a similar desire to make a journey on foot but his family were opposed to it because those he met on his trip would laugh at him (*Letters* 109).

Inns were commonplace but mostly seem to have been fairly basic. They certainly had a mixed reputation (see Jerry Toner, *Popular Culture in Ancient Rome*, Polity, 2009). Falx's dismissive comments on popular graffiti are to be found in Plutarch ('On Being a Busybody' 520e), Horace (*Satire* 1.5), and Pliny the Younger (*Letters* 8.8). Plutarch's astonishment at the banality of the writings might suggest that he had never come across graffiti before or that it was rare, but anyone who has been to Pompeii will have seen how widespread the phenomenon was (there are about as many pieces of graffiti surviving in Pompeii as there were citizens). Interestingly, this suggests that some kind of basic literacy was fairly commonplace, even if only among the artisan class. It also shows that the authors of these graffiti had very different literary interests than those found in elite texts, although there are a number of quotes of Virgil so not all graffiti was of a crude kind. (On graffiti, see Kristina Milnor, *Graffiti and the Literary Landscape in Roman Pompeii*, Oxford University Press, 2014, and Peter Keegan, *Graffiti in Antiquity*,

Routledge, 2014.) The various examples quoted here are all from Pompeii: *CIL* 4.4957, *CIL* 4.1904, *CIL* 4.10070, *CIL* 4.581, *CIL* 4.2175, *CIL* 4.64, *CIL* 4.1820, *CIL* 4.1882.

Falx's dream of shipwreck comes from Artemidorus's *The Interpretation of Dreams* (1.30) where it is taken as read that a shaved head was an indication that the individual had survived some dangerous situation by dedicating his or her hair to a deity in return for survival. The dangers of travel, particularly by sea, meant that a vast range of superstitions grew up around ships. The religious calendar forbade setting sail on certain business days but there were also others which were widely thought to be ill-omened, such as 24 August and 5 October, and the month-end was generally viewed with suspicion. The frequency with which such superstitions crop up in Artemidorus's manual suggests that these were often the source of what we in the modern world would call 'anxiety dreams'. One interesting example of such omens is the story told by Cicero (*On Divination* 40) about the fabulously rich Triumvir, Marcus Crassus. Desperate to emulate the military achievements of Pompey and Caesar, he was about to set sail on an expedition against Parthia when a man selling figs from Caunus on the quayside cried out 'Cauneas' to advertise his wares. This was heard as saying, in Latin, 'Cave ne eas!', meaning 'Beware – don't go!', and is evidence that the Latin 'v' was pronounced similarly to a modern 'w', since otherwise the phrase would not run together so well. Needless to say, Crassus ignored the warning and was killed in the campaign.

‣ CHAPTER III ‣

AMONG THE GREEKS

M Y DREAM TURNED OUT to have been the
work of some malevolent spirit, wandering the
world, unhappy no doubt at its fate, and inflicting misleading portents on those poor mortals who happen
upon its path. The winds were fair, the waters calm, and
within a few days we could see the west coast of the Peloponnese coming into view. We were approaching the
cradle of our civilisation: Greece. That land of ancient
fame, where every inch of ground has some mythical,
historical or artistic association. Whose cities have long
attracted visitors from all over the world. Ever since
our general, Aemilius Paulus, took a rest after having
defeated the Macedonians in a summer campaign, and
went on a tour of Greece, we Romans have loved to
follow in his footsteps. Passing through Thessaly he made
his way to Delphi, home of the famed oracle. Here he
offered sacrifices to Apollo and placed statues of himself
on some unfinished columns in the temple entrance in
order to commemorate his victory. He went on to visit

the most famous cities, among them Athens, Corinth and Sparta, and the most beautiful temples, including those at Olympia and Epidaurus.

I cannot deny that our conquest of Greece left many places desolated. But the long steady peace since then has seen Greece recover some of its lost glory, even if it can never regain the heights that it once attained. Yet I confess that there is something all the more attractive about a Greece that is but a shadow of its former self. Once thriving cities such as Thebes, which at one time held hegemony over all the Greek city states, now lie largely uninhabited, and sheep graze among the marble remnants of its gymnasium that jut out from the grass. Out in the country, I have encountered herdsmen who have never seen a city and know nothing of life outside their collection of meagre huts, as if Greece has returned to the simplicity of its ancient past.

We disembarked as close as we could to our first destination, Olympia. Like all educated Romans, I speak Greek fluently. Indeed, several of my slaves are Greek, and I arranged for them to hire large carriages for the overland journey that lay before us. I chose for myself an essedum, a large and elaborate horse-drawn passenger carriage, which has a driver and a slave walking at the bridle to lead the animals along. It is not the quickest means of travel, particularly as the yoke has a tendency to ride up and press on the horses' windpipes if they pull too hard, making them choke, but it is far more comfortable. The wagon was fitted for sleeping, having a large mattress laid out in the back, and was covered with a leather canopy to give protection from sun and rain alike. The wagon also carried a commode for my personal use. Everyone else would have to go behind a roadside tomb.

Olympia lies in a wide valley, with the sanctuary bounded by walls and to the north by Mount Kronos. As is the case with Delphi, a jumble of buildings located among the olive and plane trees covers the site. The temples of Zeus and Hera are the most important, but there are over seventy temples in total, to say nothing of the treasure houses, altars and countless statues dedicated to dozens of deities.

We had come to see not just these famous buildings but the even more famous games, which take place every four years in the eastern part of the site. The Olympics are the most important of the many games that happen in Greece, with the other most significant being the Pythian, the Isthmian and the Nemean. We call them games but they are really festivals held in honour of the gods. One of the ways to honour the god of the festival is to make an offering of an outstanding athletic performance and it is these contests which are most avidly watched by the huge crowds that attend. Other festivals focus on artistic performances, such as singing or dancing. There are also numerous local festivals, such as the Dionysia in Athens, which is held each year in March, with competitions between tragedians and comedians. But all the festivals provide a wide variety of attractions for the visitor, such as the famous architecture, the excited crowds, the pageantry, the rich showing off – it all makes for a tremendous event. The organisers invite the most famous entrants they can afford, with charioteers, actors and flautists being paid handsomely to travel and compete. People come from all over Greece and beyond for the five days of the Olympics and delight in the running, boxing and chariot-racing.

The site is filled to overflowing. Even those who have been exiled from their cities can attend the festivals. Moving around you will find yourself surrounded by countless peddlers hawking whatever it is they happen to have, and traders of all kinds. There are plenty of pimps hiring out their prostitutes and they often do a circuit of festivals throughout the year. You will also encounter more educational pastimes, and you will find it difficult to escape from the noise of the wretched philosophers and their disciples, all shouting and reviling one another. Many authors will be reading aloud their stupid works, and many poets reciting their dreadful poems, while onlookers applaud those they like. Jugglers will show off their tricks, fortune tellers will interpret the future for those looking to find out who will win the contests, and lawyers will charge a fortune for their usual misleading judgements.

Before making our way to the stadium, we fought through the crowds to the Temple of Zeus, in whose honour the games are held. Inside stands Phidias's gigantic statue of the god, over forty feet in height. Carved panels of ivory represent the deity's flesh and sheets of gold leaf his clothes, hair and armour. Precious stones are used to create the god's eyes. It is hard work being a tourist: the pressing crowds, the scorching summer heat, the hassle from beggars, the lack of baths. There is no shelter when it rains. There is the overwhelming noise and clamour of the crowds. But when you balance all these discomforts with the magnificence of the spectacle, you understand that they are worth bearing. And when you gaze upon Phidias's sublime statue, you realise that it would be wrong to die without having seen such things.

The greatest excitement is to be found in the stadium where the athletic contests take place. I sent a slave very early in the morning to keep a place for me so that I had a good view. My favourite is the stade, a race in which the runners sprint from one end of the stadium to the other. It is the ultimate test of speed. I am less keen on the long jump, although it is undeniably skilful the way in which the athletes use stone weights to increase the length of their jumps, gripping them until nearly reaching the ground then throwing them backwards to generate a last bit of extra distance. The pankration is a cross between boxing and wrestling, except that almost anything goes. There are no holds barred. The contestants kick and punch and try to choke their opponents, or knee them in the head or even gouge their eyes. In one famous contest, the judges found it hard to decide who was the victor because both men had died from their injuries. Eventually they decided to award the crown to the body that had *not* had its eyes gouged out. It is undoubtedly the toughest of sports, a fact reflected in the Greeks' belief that it had its origins as a re-enactment of the fight between Theseus and the Minotaur.

The chariot racing takes place in the hippodrome and is always thrilling. I can never see it without thinking of the disgraceful example set by the emperor Nero. From youth Nero had been a fan of all things Greek. He loved poetry and music and even established the first Greek games in the city of Rome, the Neronia, named, naturally, after their founder, which focused on these arts. Some years later he made his own tour of Greece. Even the Olympic Games were postponed for two years so that he could make an appearance in them. Even though Olympia does not normally hold music competitions it was decided to hold such contests in the emperor's honour. He won all the crowns. He also won the ten-horse chariot race, with the judges wisely awarding him first prize in spite of the fact that he fell off.

You may also wish to watch the Hera Games. These are the races in which only unmarried girls may participate. They are divided into three categories by age, with the youngest competing first, and, unlike in the men's events, the girls do not run naked but rather wear a knee-length tunic that leaves their right shoulder bare. The length of their races is also reduced by one sixth of the length of the stadium. The winning girl receives an olive crown and a portion of the cow that is sacrificed to the goddess. She is also permitted to put up a portrait of herself in the Temple of Hera, for whom the race is run. The games date back to ancient times. They say that Hippodameia inaugurated them in gratitude to Hera for her marriage to King Pelops, whose father Tantalus founded the house of Atreus.

The temple of Hera is a must. Not only is there the beauty of the building itself, but inside sit all manner of priceless objects that have been dedicated to the goddess by grateful worshippers. There is a statue of Hera sitting on a throne with a bearded Zeus standing by her, but these are crude works of art. Far more sophisticated are the statues of the five Hesperides by Theocles, and of Athene wearing a helmet and carrying a spear and shield by Medon, both of which are fashioned of ivory and gold, as well as a marble Hermes carrying the baby Dionysus, a work of Praxiteles. Be careful not to miss the beautiful chest of Cypselus. Made of cedar and embellished with figures of ivory and gold, it was in this chest that Cypselus, the tyrant of Corinth, was hidden by his mother when the rival Bacchidae clan were anxious to discover him after his birth. His descendants donated the chest in gratitude for their ancestor's survival. The temple contains many other offerings, far too numerous for me to describe in detail.

Such art is one of the glories of Greece and it attracts a great many travellers from across the seas. It is, of course, possible to see some original works in Rome and Italy, particularly those that were plundered during the conquest of Greece, and there are also many copies to be seen in villas and public spaces. But the originals still in situ are valued the highest and are universally known among educated and cultivated men. People make the long journey to Thespiae solely to lay eyes on the Cupid by Praxiteles, and to Cnidos for the same artist's Venus.

The great works of the most famous painters are a core part of any tour. The first to gain fame was Apollodorus of Athens, who began the practice of painting objects as they really appeared with a brush. His work *Ajax Struck by Lightning* can be seen at Pergamum to this day. Prior to him, there is no painting by any artist that can now be seen that has the power of riveting the eye. Next came Zeuxis of Heraclea, an artist whom even Apollodorus described as having stolen all the skill from others for himself. Zeuxis became so rich that he went so far as to parade himself at Olympia with his name embroidered on his garments in gold letters. Later in his life he decided to give his art away for free, since, he claimed, it was all priceless. So he gave his *Alcmena* to the people of Agrigentum. He also painted a picture of Penelope, in which the peculiar character of that women almost comes to life, and a figure of an athlete, with which he was so pleased that he wrote beneath it the line that has since become synonymous with him: that it would be easier to find fault with him than to imitate him. His *Jupiter Seated on his Throne*, with the other gods standing around him, is a magnificent work, as is his *Infant Hercules Strangling the Dragons*. It has to be said that many criticise Zeuxis for making the heads of his figures and their gestures out of proportion but he was so scrupulously careful when painting, that I cannot agree. Once, when he was about to paint a picture for the people of Agrigentum, to be consecrated there in the Temple of Juno, he had the young women of the place stripped for examination in order to adopt in his picture the most commendable points of each. His closest rival was Parrhasius of Ephesus, who once entered into a competition with Zeuxis. Zeuxis painted some grapes so naturally that birds flew towards the picture. Parrhasius, on the other hand, painted a curtain with such accuracy that Zeuxis, overcome with excitement at the judgement of the birds, arrogantly demanded that the curtain should be drawn aside to let the picture be seen. When he realised his error, he accepted that Parrhasius had won, since he himself had deceived only birds whereas Parrhasius had tricked an artist. Zeuxis's image of Helen can be seen in Rome, in the Portico of Philippus.

But it is Apelles of Cos, in my view, who has surpassed all other painters before and since. Indeed, I would say that single-handedly he contributed more to painting than all the others put together: he even went so far as to publish some treatises on the principles of the art. His artistic merit lies in his work's charm and gracefulness, though he claimed, in fact, that his greatest skill was knowing when to stop – a memorable caution, which reminds us that perfectionism can produce bad results. Alexander the Great, who banned all other artists from painting him, often visited Apelles's studio. Alexander even commissioned him to paint a nude of his favourite mistress, Pancaste, but in the course of the work the painter fell in love with her. When Alexander realised this, far from being angry, he made him a gift of her.

His portraits are extraordinarily lifelike. A man who was able to divine the future by examining the features of the face once looked at a picture and was able to accurately name the year of the subject's death. When asked to paint a portrait of King Antigonus, who had lost an eye, he invented a method of concealing the defect by painting him in profile. Among his works, too, there are some figures representing individuals at the point of death. But it is not easy to say which of his productions

are the best. His *Venus Rising from the Sea* was consecrated by Emperor Augustus in the temple dedicated to
his father, Julius Caesar. He painted also, in the Temple of
Diana at Ephesus, *Alexander the Great Wielding the Thun-
derbolts*, a picture for which he received twenty talents of
gold. The fingers have all the appearance of projecting
from the surface, and the lightning seems to be darting
from the picture. You will also find works of his at Samos,
Rhodes and Alexandria. His many artistic inventions in
painterly techniques have been enormously influential
but there was one skill which no other painter has been
able to imitate. When his works were finished, he used
to cover them with a black varnish, of such remarkable
thinness, that it both gave more vividness and softness of
tone to the underlying colours, while preserving them
from contact with dust and dirt, but its existence could
only be detected by a person who got close enough to
touch it.

From Olympia, we were heading now across the
Peloponnese to the famous city of Sparta, a city whose
citizens had little interest in the soft arts of painting.
It is an arduous journey, especially in the heat of high
summer and, prior to setting out you should make sure
that you have stocked up on supplies. You should buy
loaves of bread and take plenty of vegetables, such as
gourds, cucumbers, lettuces and leeks – whatever is in
season. Buy eggs, olives, olive oil, pickled and fresh fish,
and cheese. Wine is for me a daily necessity to be taken
with meals or simply to be enjoyed on its own. I also recommend the herb-flavoured wine known as absinthion,
which makes a very pleasant aperitif. Other necessities

include firewood for cooking as you will not always be able to find lodgings for the night.

Fruit is always in plentiful supply in the summer months. Figs, both fresh and dried, apricots, plums, melons, apples and peaches should all be easy to obtain, and cheap. Grapes will be ripe by mid-July. As for meat, pork or goat are widely available, but you should salt anything which you do not intend to eat immediately. Keep the tenderest meat for your own consumption. Smoked sausages or meatballs are a welcome addition to the table, as are boiled trotters. Allow for the slaves to receive the occasional cut of meat along with their coarse bread. Generally, slaves should be fed only wheat, wine vinegar, olives, garum, olive oil and salt, but there will be many occasions where they can benefit from the leftovers from your table or any excess supplies you have bought. I find that allowing the cook to distribute any surplus food to the household slaves according to their rank is a useful way of rewarding them for their continued good service. Pilfering, however, should never go unpunished as you will otherwise soon find that you yourself are having to eat the rough bread. Occasionally while travelling I will even dine with my senior slaves as a way of rewarding them, though I recommend that you keep this as a rare treat. Make sure that you bring enough herbs and spices to complement the meat on your travels and sufficient pulses to make sure that nobody goes hungry. I sometimes have snails served to the boys. But I would generally avoid shellfish in the summer months as the danger of illness is too great, although I am partial to mussel rissoles if bought close to the sea.

Regarding sickness during travel, I suggest packing powdered antimony, which serves a variety of medicinal purposes. Stomach upsets are common and barley soup is a well-tried remedy that is easily made while on the road. Beetroot makes an effective laxative should the dry heat make you constipated. Absinthion also makes an excellent precautionary tonic and, I find, keeps the innards clear from illness. Mulberries act as a remedy for any complaints of the mouth.

Sparta is a city made famous not by the magnificence of its buildings but by its discipline and its institutions. Each year the Spartan boys are flogged to toughen them up and it is still possible to watch this. The boys will have their backs torn by rods without uttering a groan. Boys sometimes die without uttering any complaint. It is all great training for their life of military service. I myself have seen at Sparta troops of young men fight with each other. They are incredibly earnest and will use not just their fists, but will kick, bite, scratch and gouge, and they seem to prefer to die rather than lose the contest.

Near Sparta we were shown the place where Penelope made up her mind to marry Odysseus. As a younger man, I was inclined to count these legends as foolish, but having travelled widely I have developed a more thoughtful view of them, which is this. In the days of old, those Greeks who were considered wise spoke their sayings not in a straightforward way but in riddles. The legends of antiquity, therefore, are the hand-me-downs of Greek wisdom and should be accepted as a tradition that provides their version of the truth. There are many such heroic relics to be found in Greece, but those associated with the Trojan wars have the greatest value. In Rhodes there is a goblet given by Helen to the Temple of Athene at Lindos, said to be the size of her breast. In Euboea sits a ship dedicated by Agamemnon to the god Artemis. The sceptre of Agamemnon, forged by Hephaistos for Zeus, can be seen at Chaeroneia, and his shield and sword in the Temple of Apollo in Sicyon, not far from Sparta, where you can also see Odysseus's cloak and the armour and oars of the Argonauts. The heroes of old also went westwards and relics can be found in Italy and beyond. In Rome, of course, lies the ship of Aeneas. In Capua you will find the loving-cup of Nestor; at Beneventum the huge tusks of the Calydonian boar, slain by Diomede; and in Gades, in Hispania, Teucer's golden belt. There are also divine relics. In Phocis, if you have time to travel north from Corinth, you can see the clay from which Prometheus first made men, in front of his temple there. The remains actually smell like human skin. I have heard that in the Caucasus mountains one can see the rock to which Prometheus was bound.

You should also make time for the many places of interest with links to the great men of more recent eras. The armour of Masistius, who led the Persian cavalry at the battle of Plataea, is kept in a temple at Athens, together with the sword of Mardonius, although I have some doubts about whether that is genuine. While in Sparta, be sure to see the lance of King Agesilaos. And above all, wherever you travel in the East, take the opportunity to revel in the proximity to all things connected with Alexander the Great. His spear, for instance, and the harness that he used on his great white charger,

Bucephalus, can be found in Arcadia. Many items associated with him have found their way to Rome. A candelabrum in the shape of a fruit tree, which was taken
as booty by Alexander when he captured Thebes, was
dedicated by him to Apollo at Cumae, and can now be
seen in the Temple of Apollo on the Palatine. The four
statues, which supported Alexander's own tent, can also
be seen in Rome: two in front of the Temple of Mars
Ultor, and two in front of the Regia, where the Pontifex
Maximus lives.

Speaking of statues, do not miss, while you are in
Sparta, the two remarkable statues that foretold what
would happen to the men whose likenesses they were.
The first is that of Hiero the Spartan, who died in the
battle of Leuctra, that crushing defeat which ended Sparta's domination of Greece. Just before Hiero died, the
eyes fell out of his statue, and the blind carving can be
seen to this day. The second is that of the Spartan king,
Lysander, who had done so much to establish that domination. Immediately before that same battle, Lysander's
image started to grow a beard of grass, completely covering his face and thereby erasing it, in the same way that
the defeat eradicated the Spartan presence across Greece.
We should not, of course, be surprised that statues were
able to predict such things. Aristotle used to say that
Homer is the only poet whose words move because they
are so vigorous, but the same is true of stone carvings
that have been offered to the gods. They are not simply
insensible stone. They are filled with divine spirit and
possess their god's knowledge of the future.

The journey from Sparta towards Corinth and Athens

is one of tranquil beauty. Arcadia is the land of the god Pan, whose retinue of nymphs and other spirits of nature inhabit every grove and idyll. It is also the home of the great plane tree at Caphyae, which was planted either by Menelaus or Agamemnon. There are many other famous trees in the empire that are well worth a detour. One of the largest planes is to be found in Lycia, its hollow trunk measuring over eighty feet in circumference. The consul Licinius Mucianus once dined inside it with eighteen guests, and as he rested after the banquet, he acknowledged that this was a far finer view than could be had in the gaudy marble dining rooms of Rome. And at Gortyn in Crete, you can visit the evergreen plane under which Zeus embraced Europa. It is perfectly natural for us to venerate certain trees. In olden times, trees were the temples of the gods and even today simple folk still dedicate tall trees to deities. So visit the ancient willow at Samos, the oak at Dodona, the olive on the Athenian acropolis, the lotus tree in the forum in Rome, which is older than the city itself, or the 220-foot high pine on Mount Ida. What is more amazing than the sight of a tree with full bright foliage on a green-grey trunk, with murmuring brooks at its feet, refreshing successive generations of men?

I had been in Arcadia before. As a young man, drunk with the joys of Greek culture, I had wandered through its green pastures and leafy groves, and it is striking how little has changed. A few shepherds and goatherds lead simple lives tending their flocks against a backdrop as wild as it is attractive. It is a bucolic existence. A life free from the cares of the modern world. I sometimes think

I shall retire here. In the shade of a beech tree, I shall sit, a happy old man, amid the familiar streams and sacred springs, and enjoy the cool.

I headed next for Corinth but called in at Epidaurus on the way. This would be an unremarkable city were it not for the magnificent temple of Asclepius, which has become full to bursting point with the many relics and offerings made to the god by the sick in gratitude for their cure. The sacred sanatorium sits in a secluded spot, surrounded by both mountains and a high perimeter wall, inside which a woodland area allows patients to rest in the shade. In the same area stand a number of sacrificial buildings so that the ill can communicate with the healing god. Recently, the emperor Antoninus Pius extended the sanctuary and his imperial patronage has only added to the popularity and prestige of the place.

I attempted to visit the main temple but had to wait for it to open. Here I encountered another of the perennial problems of the traveller: being accosted by some fellow tourists as if you were an old friend and being unable to shake them off for the entire visit. Two elderly ladies in their fifties decided that I was just the person to accompany them on their tour.

'Oh what lovely statues,' they cried, 'Can you tell us who carved them?'

'The artists were the sons of Praxiteles. Can't you see those letters on the base?'

'Oh my eyesight isn't what it was. May the gods be kind to them for their lovely work. Look at that statue of a girl looking up to an apple. You would think she would faint if she didn't get it.'

'And, by the Fates,' added the other old woman, 'see how that little boy is strangling the goose! If it wasn't stone standing before us, you would think it was about to speak.'

'Oh and this one looks as if it is actually walking! You can tell at once who it is meant to be.'

Inside the sanctuary their wonderment only increased.

'What works of art!' they exclaimed when confronted by the paintings of Apelles. 'Look at that naked boy – if I scratched him, I swear I would leave a mark. He has flesh on him that seems to quiver with life.'

'And that man with the hooked nose, and the one with the snub nose – aren't they the living day! And that ox – if it weren't so unladylike, I would scream, the way one of its eyes is glaring at me so!'

'Why, a man who has seen Apelles's works, without being properly amazed, ought to be hung up and beaten like clothes in a laundry!'

I took advantage of the sanctuary to make my escape: 'O Great One, be favourable to these women for their good offerings and, if they have husbands, to them even more so.'

I then left them instructing their poor slave girl in how to cut up their sacrificial chicken.

'Cut the bird up carefully, girl, and remember to give the thigh to the priest and place the honey-cake in the serpent's grotto, and say the appropriate prayers. We can take the rest home for supper …'

Corinth, before its destruction by our general Mummius, was a glorious city. The citadel and the isthmus presented a striking spectacle, with the citadel inside the walls rising to a great height, with streams flowing everywhere, and the isthmus separating by a narrow belt of land two seas, one to the east and the other to the west. The city was later refounded by Julius Caesar as a Roman colony and became both the capital of the province of Achaia and the home of the governor's residence. It grew rich and populous once again. The city may lack the seductive charm of old Athens, but it is alive with the sound of business and trade. Its location is even more beautiful than that of Athens. From the top of the citadel there is a stunning view northwards over the Bay of Crisa to the snow-covered peak of Mount Parnassus. Many fine new buildings have been erected. Of particular note are the colonnade running from the harbour of Lechaeum to the citadel, and the Temple of Capitoline Jupiter. The emperor Hadrian built a vast aqueduct from the nearby mountains and also established public baths. Owing to its place on the isthmus, the city has two harbours, one for each sea. Whatever direction the wind is coming from, ships are able to sail into the one and out of the other, which makes it a great place for traders to meet. This fact, and its status as a colony settled by retired Roman soldiers, means that the city is only half Greek. You will find as many gladiatorial combats and animal hunts as you would in Italy and you would be well advised to attend these since you will find them harder to come by as you travel further east and into Egypt. Corinth is also full of book dealers, making it a good place to stock up on reading material for the journey ahead.

Corinth is such a metropolitan city and so full of visitors that it suffers from that other perennial problem of touring: tour guides. They will accost you and promise to show you all the sights for only a modest fee but then rattle off their prearranged programme, expounding on every last inscription, and completely ignoring you even if you beg them to shut up. The one I hired gave me an interminable tour of the thirty-seven statues of Lysander and his officers, erected near the entrance to the sacred precinct after their victory at Aegospotami, when the Spartan fleet crushed that of the Athenians at the end of the Peloponnesian War, forcing me to admire the patina and explaining in the minutest detail all the techniques used in their production. The patina is indeed remarkable since it is unlike verdigris or rust, with the bronze exhibiting a shiny deep-blue tinge, which seems somehow particularly appropriate for these maritime commanders. I made the mistake of asking how this blue tint was acquired and the guide went into a long and tedious story of how a fire once consumed a house containing some gold and silver and a great store of copper, and how, when these were melted and fused together, the resulting alloy had this special patina which characterises Corinthian bronze to this day. Then another tour guide, who was addressing his party nearby, interrupted to claim that the true origin of the colour was that a bronze worker in Corinth once discovered a hoard of gold, but was scared that he would be found out if he took it all at once. He therefore stole a little at a time and added it to his mix of bronze so that he could recover it later, but the wondrous colour that resulted meant that he was able to sell it for a great price. Frankly, I suspect that both stories are a load of nonsense.

Leave time to visit one or two of the battlefields of the Persian Wars. Marathon, situated only a day's run from Athens for Pheidippides, is probably the most easily accessible. Poor Pheidippides. That hero who, when the Persians landed at Marathon, ran all the way to Sparta in only two days to seek their help, only to be rejected. He ran back to Athens in a further two days before heading for the battlefield from where he returned to the city to announce the victory over the Persians. 'We have won!' he cried and then collapsed and died. You will undoubtedly need some of his endurance as you make your tour round the empire, but the sight of Marathon will leave you filled with energy. On the plain where the heroic Greeks fought, you will see the tombs of the fallen and the marble trophy that was set up to honour the victory. The ruins of temples burned by the Persians can still be seen.

Athens is the jewel of Greece. Who would not admire the loveliness of the ground stretching from the acropolis down to the town and the coasts, with the backdrop of the mountains? It is true that the city suffered grievously during its capture by Sulla but her quiet ruins display a sublime beauty. As you survey the famous backdrop of the Parthenon and consider the public spaces where so many great men once walked, envy herself must weep at what a city she once was. I had been here before. I knew all about it. As a boorish youth, I came here and studied. Athens, in those days, was still a city without aqueducts. In her narrow, quiet streets men walked and spoke as they had done in Socrates's day. Centuries of youth could be felt in the airs around her pediments and pillars. I was charmed by the magic of Pericles's city, its glory undimmed by half a millennium, its youth eternal.

The roads into Athens are particularly bumpy and you should make sure to arrive in daylight and sufficiently early to have time to find a place to stay. You should certainly avoid the harbour area after dark. I had been given a recommendation of an inn close to one of the city gates but my directions had stated only that it was the third tavern inside the gate and this was an establishment of a different name. I stopped someone and asked if he knew of the place.

'You know that big house,' he answered, 'the one that belongs to Cratinus, the millionaire? Well, when you get past that, go straight down the street to your left, then when you get to the Temple of Diana go right. Then just before you get to the town gate, right by a watering pond, you'll find a little bakery and, opposite it, a carpenter's shop. That's where it is.'

Try as we might, we failed to find it. It was still early and the city was crowded so it gave me an excellent opportunity to watch the common people going about their business. They are a loyal bunch and pictures of the emperor could be seen on money-changers' tables, on stalls, in shops, hanging in the eaves, in entrance halls, in windows – in fact everywhere. It is striking how individuals are able to go about their work even in the middle of a very great crowd. The man who is teaching a pupil to play a flute devotes himself to that, often conducting his lessons in the very street, and the crowd does not distract him at all, nor the din made by all the passers-by. And likewise, the dance teacher is engrossed in his work, being utterly heedless of those who are fighting and selling and doing all manner of other things, and so is the harpist and the painter. But here is the most extreme case of all: the school teachers sit in the streets with their pupils, and nothing stops them in this great throng from continuing their lessons. I remember once seeing, while walking through the agora, many people on one spot and each one doing something different: one playing the flute, another dancing, another doing a juggler's trick, another reading a poem aloud, another singing, and another telling some story or myth, and yet not a single one of them prevented anyone else from attending to his own business and doing the work that he had in hand.

This pleasant scene was interrupted by a crash. The driver of a vehicle, while trying to pass others, hit one of them so hard that it overturned, and a slave was badly injured. Immediately there was a tumultuous argument about whether the first driver was liable for the injuries to the slave or just for the damage to the cart. I left them to fight it out.

Athens is always busy but it is at its most crowded during the various religious festivals. Note that the Eleusinian Mysteries attract Roman visitors more than any other festival. You will need to find a good inn since you are likely to stay for several days if you want to see all the sights. In a city like Athens you have considerable choice. Those attached to large houses are often decent since they have generally been set up by the property owner through a freedmen acting as agent. It is a profitable business that I myself do with various of my properties.

Taverns, incidentally, are often named after animals – one of mine is called the Elephant and Pygmy – and I can, off the top of my head, recall staying at places such as The Snake and The Great Eagle.

I passed quickly by one place called The Cock. In front of it, a woman wearing a Greek headdress was dancing drunkenly, waving castanets in an almost threatening manner. 'Come on in,' she called to me, 'and rest your weary ass. I promise you some cool shade under a lush tree. And a fine meal of cheese, yellow plums, mulberries, grapes, gourds, chestnuts and apples, wine of this year's vintage, wreaths of violets, roses, lilies and folk music. Ceres and Bacchus shall be your friends, Amor too if you want it.'

And she let off a loud cackle that would have scared off a hardened legionary. I decided to ask a local. I approached an old woman selling fresh vegetables. 'Excuse me, ma'am,' I said, 'you wouldn't happen to know a good place to stay, would you?' She promptly got up and led the way. She seemed an honest sort. But, just as we entered a narrow side road, this streetwise woman threw back a grubby curtain and announced: 'You ought to stay here!' I was presented with a line of naked prostitutes with some would-be customers prowling around them. I realised that I'd been led right into a whorehouse. I cursed the woman's tricks and dashed out of the doorway. You will find that many inns double up as brothels. You can assume that any young woman serving in a tavern will be prepared to offer other services if you desire them. When I sell slave girls I sometimes stipulate in the contract that they cannot be used for prostitution and always specify that working in a tavern counts as such. Given that most innkeepers are little more than pimps, it is hardly surprising that they have a bad reputation. And rightly so, on the whole. They lie about their premises, they cheat you about the prices, and they water down the wine. I have heard of many instances where unscrupulous innkeepers have served up human flesh to their unsuspecting clientele, including one where it only became apparent when a finger bone was found in a dish. Mind you, I have also heard that human meat is actually quite tasty, with a succulence and taste reminiscent of pork and that many who have dined on it have been totally unaware of any difference.

After much wandering around, I approached a small establishment called The Olive, just off one of the main avenues leading up to the agora. The innkeeper's wife was standing at the front, and, as we approached, immediately began to smile and make ingratiating gestures as these people always do. We entered the room where the usual chairs stood closely packed around small tables. A number of low-class men were playing dice. But the counters had marble tops and a small shrine to the household gods stood at one end and, given that it was by now starting to grow dark, I decided we would have to give it a go. The landlord was dealing with a client who was leaving.

'Here is your bill, sir. You had one sextarius of wine, half a sesterce worth of bread, one sesterce worth of relishes. Is that correct?'

'That's right.'

'You had a girl for two sesterces?'

'Yes, that's right.'

'And a sesterce worth of hay for your mule?'

'That damn mule will be the ruin of me!'

Meanwhile, having agreed terms, the innkeeper's wife showed me to my room. She went on and on about guests who leave without paying their bills.

'We once had a guest who ate up sixteen loaves, would you believe. And twenty pieces of boiled beef, at half a sesterce a piece. Lots of garlic, too. What else was there? I've not yet mentioned the pickled fish, have I? Oh no, and the new cheese, the wretch. Then, when I'd figured out the price, he bellowed in my face, drew his sword and went mad. We were all terrified. Then he just ran off, but not before he had grabbed one of our rugs as well.'

I asked her whether she had contacted the local centurion but she shook her head. 'What would be the point? He would soon have been far away. How I'd love to take a rock and smash his teeth out and take a scythe and slit that throat which ate up my tripe, and then hurl his lifeless corpse into the deepest pit.' I assured her that I had no intention of doing anything like that, and, at the merest suggestion of it, she stopped and leaned towards me, hissing, 'I have put a curse on him and will do the same to any others that dare to steal from me. Let the gods deal with them!'

The room had a small flat bed and no windows so that it was almost pitch-black until a small oil lamp was brought in. The lack of sunlight meant that it was pleasantly cool despite the summer heat. I tried to inspect the mattress for bedbugs but the light was poor and, frankly, it was too late in the day to change my mind now. My slaves set up my commode in the corner.

I went down to the bar area to eat, and I ordered some wine mixed with warm water. Moving into the back room, I was greeted by various sayings, presented on the wall, of a somewhat 'philosophical' nature, clearly something of a local speciality, except that these gave thoughtful advice on movements of the bowel: 'Thales advises those who shit hard to push hard', said one; 'Cunning Chilon taught how to fart silently', said another. From the main room, a man who had clearly drunk far too much could be heard slagging off the emperor – I told the innkeeper to shut him up or I would have him arrested. The main dish on offer was lamb's lips and, with its heavy seasoning, was just about passable. By now the gamblers were starting to get rowdy and what had started as a pleasant game was clearly going to end up in a fight. The landlord tried to throw them out but they were having none of it. I decided it was time to retire. As I lay under my cloak and blew out the lamp, I muttered, 'Behave yourselves O bedbugs'.

Athens possesses many wonders: the acropolis, the harbour, the walls connecting the city with the Piraeus and the dockyards, memorials of great commanders, statues of gods and men. Waking early, I started with the acropolis, and began by sacrificing to the patron goddess of that place, Athene. There is only one entry to the acropolis, which is set high on a precipice and surrounded by strong walls. The gateway has a roof of white marble, and even today is unrivalled for the beauty and size of its stones. On the right of the gateway is a temple of Wingless Victory. From this point the sea is visible, and here it was that, according to legend, Aegeus threw himself down to his death. If you recall the story, the ship that carried the young people to Crete began the voyage with black sails. Theseus, who was sailing on an adventure against the Minotaur, had told his father beforehand that he would use white sails if he should return victorious. But the loss of Ariadne had made him forget the signal. So Aegeus, when he saw the black sails, thought that his son was dead and threw himself over the cliff edge. There is a sanctuary dedicated to him near this spot. On the citadel sits the most perfect Parthenon – what need I say about this most famous of temples? – and the equally well-known bronze cow by Myron and the portrait of Phidias on the shield of Athene. Simply gaze in awe.

I visited Socrates's house and followed this with a nostalgic trip to the Lyceum, where I had myself been a student. I was pleasantly surprised to find that nothing had changed. Some philosophers and their students were walking up and down the colonnades discussing the nature of knowledge.

'But what do you mean by saying that we do not learn, and that what we call learning is recollection? Can you instruct me that this is so?' asked a student.

'It is no easy matter, but I shall try. Call over one of your slaves, one who can speak Greek.'

The slave boy came over.

'Tell me, boy, do you know that a square figure looks like this?' and he drew one in the sand.

'I do.'

'Now, a square figure has four equal sides, doesn't it?'

'Certainly.'

'And if you draw a line through the middle of each side, they are equal too, aren't they?'

'Yes.'

'And a shape of this sort may be larger or smaller?'

'To be sure.'

'Now if this side were two feet and that one also two, how many square feet would the whole be? Or let me put it thus: if one side was two feet long, and the other only one foot, of course the space would be two feet times one?'

'Yes.'

'But as that side is also two feet long, it must be two times two feet?'

'It is.'

'Then the space is two times two feet?'

'Yes.'

'Well, how many are twice two feet? Count and tell me.'

'Four.'

'And could there be another square twice the size of this, with all its sides equal like this one?'

'Yes.'

'Then how many square feet would it be?'

'Eight.'

'Now, try and tell me how long each side of that figure would be. This one is two feet long: how long will be the side of a square which is double in size?'

'Clearly, it will be double.'

'Do you observe, I am not teaching the boy anything, but merely asking him each time? And now he supposes that he knows about the line required to make a figure of eight square feet.'

'Well, does he know?'

'Certainly not.'

'He just supposes it, from the double size required?'

'Yes.'

'Now watch his progress in recollecting, by the proper use of memory ...'

And so it went on. It was an old routine, but it never failed.

The emperor Hadrian loved Greece as much as any man and brought new vigour to Athens, constructing a new zone on the south-eastern side. The highlight of this is the colossal Temple of Zeus with its 120 columns, but he also erected a library with another 120 marble pillars and a gymnasium with a hundred more. He built an aqueduct to bring fresh water from Cephisia to the new city. Athens is still the greatest of Greek cities and the most beautiful of all. Nature provided her harbours and her acropolis. Art gave her the greatest temples, the masterpieces of sculpture, and the best libraries. Athens outstrips all other cities and a visit there uplifts the soul. The light is stronger and fuller, as though Athene herself takes a veil from the eyes of the visitor. All around there is so much beauty that walking has the feeling of being a dance of joy or a happy dream.

Strolling through the agora you will find all kinds of souvenirs to take home as mementoes and gifts. Miniature replicas of the Parthenon are very popular as are glass vials with pictures of all the city's chief sites identified by labels. The miniature temples are available at a range of prices, with silver being the costliest and terracotta the cheapest. Athens specialises in producing elaborate stone coffins and you should consider having one made to your liking and shipped back to your family tomb. If you leave it to your heirs to choose, you never know what monstrosity they will inflict upon your spirit.

·· COMMENTARY ··

Travel guides were widely used in antiquity, with the first known being a guide to towns and monuments of Attica written by Diodorus in the fourth century BCE. The only one that survives complete is the ten-volume guide to Greece, written in c. 160–180 CE, by a Greek called Pausanias. These ancient travel books shared some similarities with our modern equivalents: factual information, an eye for the unusual, and an invocation of the emotions and associations elicited in the author. But there were some profound differences. Pausanias also reported on the various mythological, religious and folkloric traditions and stories associated with places, with some long excursions on seemingly irrelevant topics. For the ancients, there was no distinction between the legendary and historical past and so relaying the myths linked to a place was part of the required background reading for any serious traveller. The heroes of old, celebrated in epic poems such as the *Iliad*, *Odyssey* and *Aeneid*, were just as well known as historical figures, and relics associated with them were accorded a high value. The ancients also seem to have largely accepted that these relics were genuine, in the same way that relics associated with Jesus and Christian saints were revered in the later medieval world. Tradition was seen as the equal, if not the superior, of history. Pausanias had another agenda. His interest lay in recovering Greece's great past, both mythical and historical, and in ignoring its present-day subordination. His guide reads as if the Romans had never conquered Greece. Rome has been written out.

The ancient tourist was in search of antiquity so it was natural to head eastwards. For the wealthy Romans who made tours of places such as Greece and Egypt, their desire to reach back to the distant past can be seen as reflecting something of a chip on their shoulder about Rome's relative youth. Seeing old masters and ancient architecture was a way to link their own empire to the great realms that had come before them. It was also a way to make clear that the Romans had become sufficiently cultured to deserve to be in charge of such an empire. It is hard for us to understand quite how great was the awe in which educated Romans held the Greek cultural achievement. It was to Greece that Roman artists turned for inspiration and precedent, hoping to find in the past the basis for a Roman artistic flowering. As Pausanias shows, the Greek elite never accepted defeat in the cultural sphere, and, in the period known as the Second Sophistic (dating from roughly 60–230 CE), they seemed to attain a position of cultural dominance within the Roman empire through their skill in rhetoric and performance. It is, of course, possible to interpret this emphasis on culture as a form of escapism that allowed educated Greeks to forget the realities of their military and political domination by the Romans and focus instead on a fantasy world where they were still in the ascendency.

Temples were a core part of any tour. In the same way that churches and cathedrals became repositories for all manner of works of art, so ancient shrines gradually acquired a whole range of special objects donated to them as grateful offerings to the gods to which they were dedicated. These objects were valuable for their historical associations, cost or beauty, or for their quality of workmanship. Visitors to temples were therefore engaged in several layers of activity: seeing the architecture, experiencing the special location of the temple, making a religious offering, and appreciating the art and artefacts inside. The description of the Temple of Hera at Olympia is based on Pausanias (5.17–20), who often goes into extensive descriptions of the individual works of art, seemingly to emphasise the degree of Greek artistic skill. Pliny the Elder's *Natural History* (35.26) contains a lengthy discussion of the merits of various different painters and underscores the fact that what Romans wanted in art was these Greek old masters. While these fine artists had indeed been innovative in their day, it is their age which seems to have made them most appealing to a Roman eye. A section of a play written by Herondas mocks the tourists who go to temples to gawp at the art they know nothing about (*Mime* 4).

The festivals of Greece were one of its key tourist attractions and appealed to a whole range of tastes, both sporting and artistic. From early in Greek history, groups of neighbouring city states began to hold collective religious ceremonies, financed at state expense. The religious significance was such that a sacred truce was held for a month around the Olympic Games, to allow for warring states to have time to travel to and from the festival before returning to continue hostilities. The focus of each was a particular god that they worshipped in common and the event would take place at a location dedicated to that deity. The Greeks believed that the gods could be worshipped through actions, including high-quality performances of athletics or the production of works of art, and contests were held to judge which of these was deemed to have won and thereby honoured the god the most. The four largest of these 'agonistic' festivals – the Olympic, Pythian, Isthmian and Nemean games – grew to such a size that they became truly Pan-Hellenic and Greeks would travel from everywhere to attend them. Of these 'majors', the Olympics were ranked highest, and were held every four years in honour of Zeus at the shrine of Olympia. Situated in the north-west corner of the Peloponnese, the location had certainly not been chosen for ease of access, particularly given that the games were held during the heat of summer. The events were initiated by a formal procession and included a sacrifice and a banquet. There were many other more local festivals. The Dionysia were held each March in Athens to worship Dionysus, and featured competitive dramatic performances for which tragedians such as Aeschylus, Sophocles and Euripides wrote. The popularity of these festivals often resulted in significant public resources being directed towards extensive new buildings in order to accommodate the growing number of visitors.

The sheer number of attendees must have created an almost overwhelming experience. Thousands, perhaps tens of thousands, crammed into Olympia for the five days of the festival. Some of these were embassies sent from city states at public expense. Mostly they were private individuals making the trip out of a pious desire to pay homage to the god. But other attractions also enticed them. The pageantry, the thrill of the contests, the famous temples and the artwork they contained all enhanced the experience. The Temple of Zeus contained the sculptor Phidias's colossal statue of the god, and was a 'must-see' for any visitor, while the size of the crowds meant that a variety of service providers, such as hawkers, tour guides and prostitutes, also poured into the site. It is clear that there was something of a 'party atmosphere', although the crowds, heat and lack of amenities also made it a physically demanding trip (Epictetus, *Discourses* 1.6.26). The description of the crowd is from Dio Chrysostom (*Oration* 8.9), who details the huge and varied crowd at the Isthmian Games (the street scene in Athens is based on his *Oration* 20.9–10). Pausanias (5.16) gives an account of the games of Hera and the various contests held for girls. The fact that Spartan girls received the same tough, physical education as their male counterparts meant that a majority of the participants of the Heraean Games seem to have been Spartan women. Cicero describes a rather gruesome form of 'dark' tourism, where people would visit Sparta to watch the traditional whippings meted out to the boys, some of whom even died in the ordeal (*Tusculan Disputations* 2.34). It is rather pitiful to think of the poor Spartan children continuing to be raised in such a brutal way long after their city had become a military irrelevance.

The problem of asking for directions given the lack of street names comes from Terence's play *The Brothers* (581–4) and the description of all the imperial images from Fronto (*Letters to Caesar* 4.12). The philosophy lesson is taken from the famous passage from Plato's *Meno*, where Socrates elicits recalled knowledge of geometry from a slave boy (*Meno* 81a–86b). The female tavern keeper was something of a trope, which can be best seen in *The Innkeeper* (Copa), once attributed to Virgil. Galen (K12:254) describes human flesh as tasting like pork and how butchers had been caught selling it to unwitting customers.

· CHAPTER IV ·

EPHESUS TO ANTIOCH

TRAVELLING BY SEA is no light matter, even in the summer. Some of the smaller, open ships make heavy weather of the most straightforward crossing. Having been held up at Puteoli, I was keen to find a decent berth for the trip across the Aegean Sea towards the jewels of the Greek cities in Asia: Ephesus, Smyrna and Pergamum. Ephesus stands out even among these bright stars. Yet Smyrna is the most beautiful.

It was easy to obtain a passage from the Piraeus, the great harbour at Athens. Soon we were standing aboard a good-sized trader, bound for Rhodes, swept along by a good westerly. I sat on the top deck beside the captain to admire the passing islands while he told me countless stories of the gods and heroes associated with each place. Like all Greeks, he seemed happiest when at sea, never steadier than when dealing with the pitching and rolling of a ship ploughing through the cresting waves of a favourable wind. As a Roman, I have learned to cope with the sea but I do not love it as a Greek does.

For me, it is never natural to stand above the water and peer into the murky fathoms that wait to swallow you up should your ship sink.

The variety of sea life that fills the oceans is quite extraordinary. It is also the case that the largest animals are to be found in the sea. You may well ask why this is so. The evident cause is the superabundance of moisture with which they are supplied, allowing them to grow at an uninhibited rate. Such is the variety in the sea that you can even find animals that resemble objects, for example the sword fish, the saw fish and the cucumber fish, which looks so like a real cucumber both in colour and smell that it is hard to believe it is not the same thing. Given this, why should we be surprised to see a shell from which a horse's head can be seen protruding?

The largest sea creatures are in fact to be found in the Indian Ocean, and in the river Ganges, for example, you can see eels three hundred feet long. At sea, it is usually about the time of the solstices that these monsters are to be seen. For at that time of year, these regions suffer from huge whirlwinds and great rains, and the sea is so stirred up that the creatures are driven up from the very bottom of the ocean to the surface. At other times there are great shoals of tunny fish blocking the sea. Alexander the Great's fleet was only able to make progress through them by advancing against them in battle order. His soldiers also reported that the Gedrosi, who live on the banks of the river Arabis, are in the habit of making the doors of their houses with the jaw bones of huge fish, and also use them as rafters in their roofs.

The whale is the largest sea animal that lives in our

sea. The orca, which is extremely hostile to the whale, can also be seen. This animal is hard to describe but it resembles an enormous mass of flesh armed with teeth, and it attacks the whale and tears at its young with razor-sharp teeth. It will also attack the females as soon as they give birth and are at their weakest, piercing them through the side just as a war galley in full sail slices through the side of an enemy ship. The whale knows its only hope is to flee, and when they do so en masse, pursued by the frenzied orcas, it is as if the sea has been stirred up in a great fury against itself, even though there is hardly a breath of wind to be felt in the air.

An orca was once seen in the port of Ostia, where it was attacked by the emperor Claudius. He was having his new harbour constructed and the animal had been attracted by some oxhides that had fallen overboard. Caesar ordered a great number of nets to be extended at the mouth of the harbour, from shore to shore, while he himself went there with the praetorian cohorts, and so treated the watching crowds on the shore to a rare spectacle. The boats attacked the monster and the soldiers on board showered spears upon it. But several boats were sunk by the showers of water sprayed over them by the creature in its death throes.

The fastest sea animal is the dolphin. Indeed it is faster than any bird and can accelerate more quickly than an arrow. It is this that sometimes lets us witness the most amazing sight. If a dolphin goes down to the very depths in pursuit of a fish and then darts upwards so as to breathe, it will sometimes leap out of the water with such speed that it will fly right over the sails of a passing ship. Dolphins generally travel in pairs and they suckle their young at the teat. So great is their affection for their young that they stay with them for years. Dolphins live for about thirty years, a fact that has been ascertained by cutting marks on their tails each year by way of an experiment.

The most remarkable thing about the dolphin is not only that it is capable of loving man but that it loves music as well. It can be charmed by any instrument but especially by the notes of a water-organ. It will come right up to ships and race them, flying by even when the ship is in full sail. In the reign of the emperor Augustus, a dolphin in the Lucrine Lake fell in love with the child of a certain poor man, who used to entice him to the shore with pieces of bread. Whenever the boy appeared, the dolphin would fly to the surface, and after feeding from his hand, would offer him his back for a ride. This happened for several years, until the boy happened to fall ill and die. The dolphin, however, still came to the spot, with a sorrowful air and showing every sign of deep grief, until at last he died of sorrow, something about which nobody had any doubt.

I told this to the captain and he told me of an even more remarkable event. In the city of Hippo in north Africa, there is a large pool of seawater that is connected to the open sea by only a small channel. Here the locals love to fish, sail and swim, especially the boys. They love to show off by swimming out as far as possible, and the winner is the one who leaves the shore furthest behind. In one of these contests one boy, more daring than the rest, kept swimming on and on. A dolphin met him, and first swam in front of the boy, then behind him, then round him, then came up beneath him to carry him, threw him off, and again came under him, and carried the terrified boy first out to the open sea, and then back to dry land and to his amazed playmates. The story spread through the city, and every one flocked to the spot to gaze upon the boy, as if he were a kind of miracle, and they crowded around him to ask him questions, hear the tale, and have him tell it over and over again.

The next day, the boys swam out again, watched this time by a great crowd on the beach. But the boy was less daring this time. The dolphin returned and tried to get him to come out further by leaping out of the sea, diving and twisting. This was repeated on the next day, and the day after, until the men of the place, who were all hardy sailors, began to feel ashamed that they were too scared to swim out. They approached the dolphin, played with him, and even got close enough to stroke him. The boy who was the hero of the first adventure now felt confident enough to leap on the dolphin's back and was carried out to sea and brought back again. Boy and animal seemed to grow attached to each other. Neither showed fear of the other and thereby the boy grew bolder and the dolphin ever more tame. The animal would even come on to the beach, and, after drying himself on the sand and soaking up the heat of the sun, would roll back again into the sea. Even the proconsul of Africa, Octavius Avitus, came to see, and was moved by some absurd superstition to pour perfume on the dolphin as he lay on the beach. The strange smell

so disturbed the animal that he fled out to sea and dis-
appeared for several days. Eventually he returned but
in a listless and seemingly downhearted state. He soon
recovered his strength, however, and resumed his former
playfulness with the boy. The dolphin's fame grew and
soon all the nearby magistrates were flocking to see the
sight. They would travel to the town and stay, all of
which, of course, was done at the expense of the locals
who were obliged to entertain such important guests.
Not only that but the town transformed from a sleepy
little fishing port into a fashionable resort. In the end,
the locals decided that it had to stop. So it was decided
to kill the dolphin.

'You will no doubt bewail such a sad ending,' finished the captain, 'but there is not a bit of fiction in it
and all the details are true.'

It is hard not to pass the myriad islands of the Aegean
without thinking of the harsh exiles that have been
meted out to those who have displeased their emperor.
Augustus even banished his own daughter to such a
place because of her sexual promiscuity. Such a fate
might await me if the emperor has not forgotten the
insult that he perceived from my words. The best to
be hoped for in exile is to be condemned to one of the
larger and more hospitable islands, such as Andros or
Naxos, where you will be more likely to have visitors.
But this was no time to dwell on such unpleasantness.
There were too many fine things to see and places to
visit to allow melancholy to cloud the tour. Delos is
perhaps worth a visit if you have time since it contains
many historical sights. The island was the home of the

treasury of Athens's League of Cities, before the Athenians grew greedy and took the money back to Athens, revealing this supposedly voluntary league for what it actually was – the Athenian empire. Above all the palm seized by Latona when giving birth to Apollo is still on display, as well as the famous horn altar built by Apollo as a boy. Of the other islands, Chios, Samos and Lesbos are also worth seeing. Mytilene, the capital of Lesbos, is in particular a beautiful city, in its regularity, architecture and location.

But we were headed for splendid Rhodes, whose tall towers were clearly visible when we were still far out at sea. We approached her harbour. It was crowded with ships from all over the eastern provinces and the breakwaters extended far out into the water. From afar, there were so many masts in the dockyards that it looked like a field of corn swaying in the breeze. As we neared, we could see displayed prominently in the harbour the figureheads from enemy ships that had been kept as trophies, memorials to Rhodes's great victories of old when it was free. Behind the harbour, the city rose up the hillside in a great semicircle. We made first for the acropolis, famed for its cool gardens and parks, pausing on the broad, straight main avenue only to grab a snack from one of many cookshops that lined it. From the summit, we had a clear view over the closely packed city. I hired a guide who took me around the many temples, which are crammed to the rafters with high-quality statues and paintings. The guide claimed that Rhodes contains more than three thousand statues. The climate is hot but the city's location on the edge of a beautiful island lends it a quality of cool elegance that has attracted many Romans over the years. It was here that the future emperor Tiberius studied astrology for seven years. His house, like his villa in Capri, stood at the edge of a steep cliff, from which he would hurl any companions he suspected of plotting against him.

The earthquake hit suddenly. We were sitting in our inn when the buildings started to creak and large cracks appeared in the walls. We instinctively did what everyone does when the earth starts to move: we threw ourselves outside, abandoning our possessions and entrusting our survival to the public spaces. Sure enough, several buildings collapsed, although our inn managed to stay standing. Before long, stories were circulating of strange omens that had accompanied the quake: a flock of hundreds of sheep had been killed, statues were cracked. Some people were so deranged that after the tremors had subsided they wandered about unable to help themselves. Some men died of fright. We saw bodies being pulled out of one of the collapsed buildings. Two young boys were carried out along with a man who it turned out had been their teacher and had tried to protect them. Some had been crushed by falling debris. Others were buried up to their necks, and might not have survived if the earthquake had been more serious. As it was, people were able to help them. A couple of corpses hung impaled upon the sharp points of the projecting timbers of one fallen building. Many were imprisoned unhurt within the slanting roofs of houses that had fallen over them. Thankfully, there had not been an outbreak of fire, which so often accompanies

such disasters, when the oil lamps and ovens in buildings set fire to the timbers that fall upon them. Thankfully, also, it had happened in broad daylight, when most
people were out and about rather than asleep inside and
so less likely to escape the falling debris.

Earthquakes are a common phenomenon in the east.
I have experienced several such tremors in the past but
have been spared anything disastrous. I have perceived
that there are two different types: those with a counter-
acting shock in the opposite direction, in which pillars
may be seen righting themselves and split walls come
back together in their original position; and a second
form, which brings destruction like a battering ram. This
quake was minor and short-lived. Soon, those whose
buildings had been most affected were busy buttressing
and shoring them up with cedar beams. They had experienced it all before.

Later that evening further slight tremors could be felt,
accompanied by a deep, growling noise that sounded
like thunder issuing from the bowels of the earth. Not
only that, but the surrounding air grew dim with the
vaporous exhalations of a smoky haze rising from an
unknown source, and gleamed with a dull radiance. I
must confess I was quite overcome with fear, consider-
ing the faintness of the tremors. Looking back, I think
my terror was down to the fact that it seemed reasonable
to expect the same thing to happen again, only worse.
Whatever the reason, I decided it was time to move on.

We hopped up the coast via a small, local trading
ship whose Ephesian captain shared our desire to leave
Rhodes and return to his home city. It was comical to

hear him criticise the Rhodians for the earth that resembles the sea in its motion. As if Ephesus does not suffer earthquakes! But the Ephesians have much to be proud of. Their city is the capital of the province, is rich in commerce and is, quite simply, one of largest and most beautiful cities of the empire.

The famous Temple of Artemis draws visitors from all over the empire. But Ephesus is also a bustling port with a channel leading out to the sea and a harbour basin. The captain had claimed that a hundred and fifty thousand people inhabit the city, and walking through its streets it is impossible to believe otherwise. First, you will want to visit the Temple of Artemis, which took 120 years to build and contains more than 100 marble pillars, each 56 feet high. It is advisable to get up early and visit before the crowds of visitors descend. There are, in fact, plenty of other, newer, buildings worth investigating, such as the temples of Domitian and of Hadrian. Celsus Polemaeanus, recently a governor of Roman Asia, paid for the construction of a wonderful library from his own money. It holds almost twelve thousand scrolls on any subject you could possibly imagine and is cleverly designed to face east so that readers can make the best use of the morning light. Damianus of Ephesus not long ago paid for a long colonnade to link the Temple of Diana with the city, so that worshippers could reach the temple without getting wet when it rained, while in the temple sanctuary he built a vast hall for sacrificial banquets, decorated with rich marble. The locals honoured him for what they called his 'contempt of money'. There is a huge theatre, able to seat twenty-five thousand and said by many to be the largest in the empire, where gladiatorial combats are staged as well as plays. So much business takes place in the city that there are two marketplaces, one for private commerce, the other reserved for official matters. There are a number of large bath houses where you can unwind after your long journey.

When such building is undertaken, it is usually entrusted to special commissioners whose job it is to specify the contract, listen to the competing architects describe their designs, accept the most attractive tender for the work, and then oversee its completion. Any sizeable project, such as baths or an aqueduct, will require imperial approval. Part of the city revenues used to pay for such works comes from the fees charged to people elected to priesthoods or local offices and magistracies. These fees vary according to the importance of the place and the office. An important position, such as an aedileship, might cost you more than 20,000 sesterces in a place the size of Ephesus. But even this constitutes the bare minimum and office holders are expected to spend lavishly on the enhancement of their city and the entertainment of its citizens. Indeed, you will find that in every city, whatever its size, throughout the empire, astonishing sums are spent voluntarily by the leading citizens for the benefit of the community, and the buildings erected by such private munificence often surpass the municipal ones in both size and importance. Their reward is a glory that lasts longer than bronze. The names of the leading benefactors are immortalised in prominent inscriptions on the buildings they fund, while during their lifetime they will receive public orations, wreaths, and statues in their honour. The Greeks are fanatical when it comes to their own cities, something that the emperors have been happy to foster since it leads the town councils and wealthy individuals to go to extraordinary lengths to beautify their cities in direct competition with their neighbouring rivals.

The grandest buildings are familiar enough: temples, porticoes, theatres, amphitheatres and bridges. But there are many less ostentatious private benefactions that all contribute to the improvement of the city: laying stone paving slabs for the streets, the erection of sundials and drinking fountains, and the setting up of booths in the marketplace. And there are some that go off the scale in terms of their grandiosity. A few examples will suffice. At Thagaste in Numidia, a Roman knight built a portico costing 300,000 sesterces. Crinas the physician had walls built in his native city for nearly 10 million. Gaius Julius Quadratus, proconsul of Asia, was described by locals as a divine agent sent to rejuvenate Pergamum.

But before I describe Pergamum I must direct you to the fairest city of all those fine cities along that coast, Smyrna, a place almost always called 'The Beautiful'. The streets used to be dirty, since the city lacked drainage, but the benefits of Roman rule have led to significant enlargement of the municipal facilities. Like a huge amphitheatre, Smyrna spreads up the surrounding hillsides from the shore, and from the heights there is the most wonderful panoramic view of the sea. The city itself has such charm that it seems to have been born not made, like some natural extension to the environment that surrounds it. The climate is perfect. In the hotter months, it is cooled by the winds from the west and in winter it is kept mild by the proximity of the sea. It is blessed with so many attractions: gymnasia for exercise; public places where one can stroll and chat; theatres at which to enjoy the highest quality productions; and countless elegant temples and their precincts in which to thank the gods for such a city. Baths abound, an almost constant supply of spectacles distracts the urban plebs, and there are pleasant walks covered from the heat of the sun, as well as plentiful springs and water wells to slake your thirst. The city is laid out with broad, straight streets and numerous squares, with pavements fashioned from the local marble and double-storied arcades full of stalls and shops. One notable feature is the presence of many schools, which serve to educate, to the highest level, not just the locals but visitors from all across the empire. Great teachers in all the sciences are always in residence. The famous sophist, Scopelianus, chose Smyrna as his base because, he claimed, it was the chief muse of all the Ionian cities, 'the bridge on which their strings were set'. In sum, it is a city that combines the best of Greek and Roman cultures, a place where work and leisure are in perfect balance, a place where anyone would be delighted to dwell.

I had planned to linger in Smyrna for some days but I had begun to suffer from bouts of blurred vision and my bowel movements had become dry and constricted. I therefore decided that it was opportune for me to travel to Pergamum and visit the famous shrine of the healing god, Asclepius. I will not dwell on the details of the journey. I set out at noon, had my luggage sent ahead

with the slaves, and about sunset reached an inn by the
river Hermus. But the rooms were insufferably hot and
so we pressed on. Late at night we reached Larissa, but
the inn there was even worse, and it was midnight before
we reached the next town, only to find that everywhere
was locked up. So we travelled on even further and the
cocks were crowing by the time we arrived at Myrina,
where we caught up with the slaves, who were actually
in the process of getting ready to set out on their journey
for the day ahead. I tried to rest for a while on a bed in
the hallway before journeying on to Elaea, where tiredness forced me to stop and rest for the night at a basic
but acceptable inn. Next day, we reached Pergamum.

Pergamum is an ancient city that has been reborn
under the empire. Trajan laid out an entire new section
at the foot of the acropolis, and the regeneration was
such a success that Hadrian promoted it to the rank
of metropolis. An ambitious building programme followed, with a new forum, huge temples, a theatre, a
stadium and an amphitheatre all being added. It was at
this time that the shrine of Asclepius was also developed into the massive complex that it forms today.
This sanctuary is now rightly famous throughout the
empire and attracts many thousands of visitors seeking
to benefit from the god's healing powers. It lies a couple
of miles from the city centre and I decided not to waste
time looking for somewhere to stay but instead headed
straight there. While making our way, we came across
a small statue to Hercules set up in a cave. Here it is
possible to consult the god by means of throwing some
dice, and I felt compelled to do so, no doubt as a result

of the god's influence. I prayed to him in front of his image, then picked up four dice, a plentiful supply of which are placed in a dish on a table by the statue. I threw them on to the table and noted the result: two ones, a three and a four. For every throw there is an explanation inscribed on a stone tablet. The god said to me, 'Why do you hurry? Stay calm, for the time is not yet ripe. If you relax a little, you will achieve success.' I immediately understood. We returned to the city and located a salubrious inn. I then visited the baths and took a light meal of dried fish and figs before going to bed early. Ascelpius would wait till the morning.

The sanctuary is approached along a long colonnade. There is an impressive array of facilities, including a large theatre, a circular treatment centre, a healing spring and a library. I began by bathing in the waters of the sacred spring and then retired to the temple where attendants led me to a couch in a dormitory where I could sleep and be visited by the god in my dreams. But the god did not grace me with a visit. On the following day I bathed again and then slept. I dreamed that my food had not digested properly. I consulted the priest as to the meaning of this and he advised me to take an emetic. I vomited in the evening. The god ordered me to do many strange things. I had to go to the sea and when the harbour waves were swollen by the south wind and ships were almost in distress, I had to sail across to the opposite side, after eating honey and acorns, and then vomit. I was foolish to question the god. For my vision soon returned to normal and my bowels recovered their regularity. Out of gratitude, I set up a small plaque at the entrance to the shrine thanking the god for my cure and praising his greatness, along with a pair of terracotta eyes to represent my healed vision.

There are many such healing sites across the empire and a visit can easily be combined with your tour. Sea travel in itself is very good for conditions of the lungs and, indeed, any change of air is good for all manner of lingering illnesses. My own doctor particularly recommends a change of climate as a cure for repeated headaches, dropsy and complaints of the bladder. Those who are sick in the lungs and spit blood are advised to live in pine-tree woods or in mountainous regions close to the sea. The proximity of cattle to supply fresh milk is also recommended. Anticyra in the Gulf of Crisa is the best place to obtain medicinal preparations, since it is here where the best hellebore grows, which makes the most effective emetic.

Temples, as we have seen, are not simply places of worship. In addition to the fine art within, the precinct grounds are often extensive and provide parks for the sacred animals and birds to live in. Visitors can experience the beautiful wooded glades of such holy areas and the cool, pure air. The exceptional Temple of Aphrodite at Cnidos is surrounded by orchards of fruit trees, planted solely for the beauty of their bloom. Myrtles, laurels, towering cypresses and planes all thrive, supporting vines that grow up from them and from which bunches of grapes hang. In the summer months, the air hums with the noise of grasshoppers, and seats are placed within this idyllic scene in order to accommodate the feasts of supplicants to the goddess. At the Temple of Apollo, too, at Gryneum, not far from Pergamum, there is a splendid park of trees planted specially for their wondrous scent. Surrounding the temple of the Syrian goddess at Hierapolis, close to the river Euphrates, there is a large park for the sacred oxen, horses, eagles, bears and lions and, at a more basic level, you will often find flocks of sacred geese being kept near temples. There is, incidentally, a ravine near this temple, out of which sulphurous fumes emanate and kill any man who breathes them, with the exception of eunuchs. A small viewing platform has been built to enable the visitor to better see the fumes, since it is believed that the ravine is in fact a gateway to the underworld, such as there is at Lake Avernus near Cumae.

Freaks of nature and other curiosities are also often housed in temples. In that same temple at Hierapolis you can see huge elephant tusks, along with examples of strange barbarian costumes and jewellery that were brought back as loot by Dionysus from his expedition to India. The skin and jaw bone of a huge snake, 120 feet long, killed by catapults in the first Punic War, used to be kept in a temple in Rome. Similarly, the emperor Hadrian gave an Indian snake to the Temple of Zeus that he built in Athens, and the skin of a bear he had personally killed to the Temple of Eros at Thespiae. A skeleton of a whale is on display at the Temple of Asclepius at Sicyon. In the Temple of Concord in Rome, Augustus exhibited four elephants that had been carved out of a colossal single block of black obsidian. And Julius Caesar made an offering to the Temple of Mother Venus of a breastplate made entirely of British pearls. Back in

Smryna, there is a distorting mirror. At Erythrae stand two amphorae fashioned from remarkably thin clay. On the acropolis in Athens sits a huge bronze ball beside the statue of Athene, used as a test for athletes to see who can move it. In Athens, too, in the Temple of Asclepius you can see a Sarmatian breastplate made from horses' hooves. Trajan gave a bison's horn cased in gold, part of the booty of the war with the Getae, to the Temple of Zeus in Antioch. I have also heard of a candelabrum in front of a temple of Venus that cannot be extinguished by wind or rain.

The beauty of these temples, their contents and their environments, drives us to face the dangers of travel by land and sea. Greedily, too, we yearn to see the ancient stones that once housed the angry heroes who moved Homer to sing his verses. Troy, the mother of Rome, is where such hunger can best be satisfied. Troy, that glorious place that fell alongside Hector, from which Aeneas led a group of refugees across the sea to found Rome, and where Achilles's body lies.

Troy is tax-free. The Romans awarded this special status out of respect for their mother-city and it has allowed her to prosper anew. Once I had found lodgings, I went out immediately to savour the special atmosphere of the place. As I strolled through the town, I was filled with an extraordinary pleasure. Here I was in the city of heroes. As I walked round the streets I found myself reciting the many verses of Homer I had learned as a child, as if renewing my acquaintance with the heroes of old. My reverie was interrupted when several men rushed up to me, all offering to take me on a guided tour for only a small fee, and promising to show me all the sites associated with the Homeric heroes. I chose one, who seemed less garrulous than the rest, and off we went in search of Troy's glorious past.

He began by taking us down to the beach where the Greek ships under wide-ruling Agamemnon's command first landed in the expedition to recover the wife of his brother, Menelaus, famed for his spear-throwing. Ten long years saw them besiege the city to no avail before the ruse of the wooden horse allowed them to trick their way into Troy and bring about its destruction. I sacrificed to bright-eyed Athene and poured libations to the dead heroes. The guide took me to the gravestone of fleet-footed Achilles, whose rage hurled so many sturdy souls down to the house of Hades and made their corpses carrion for the dogs and birds, and I anointed it with oil. I ran a race beside it with some of the other tourists who were there, naked, as is the custom, and then crowned the tomb with garlands, pronouncing the hero happy in having lived so glorious a life. The guide asked me if I wished to see the lyre of Paris. But, like Alexander the Great, I had no interest in seeing the instrument of a man so cowardly that he shunned the duel in favour of the safety conferred by bow and arrow. At the tomb of horse-taming Hector we found an epigram written by Germanicus, nephew of the emperor Tiberius.

Guides are known to make things up and you should be careful not to believe everything they say. At one point the guide told the story of how the city of Canopus in Egypt was named after Canopus, the pilot of Menelaus, master of the war cry. The guide claimed that Canopus was bitten by a serpent and died and that flaming-haired Menelaus erected a monument to him at one of the mouths of the river Nile where the town later developed. When I pointed out that I had once learned from an Egyptian priest that the word meant 'golden ground' and had been used for ten thousand years before the landing of Menelaus, cherished by Zeus, he simply retorted that his version had been handed down in tradition since the days of Troy and asked who I would rather believe, him or an Egyptian priest. I decided that it was tactful not to reply. Guides are themselves well aware that what they are saying is untrue but continue to peddle their myths because that is what they believe their public wish to hear. Indeed, if all the legends were banished from Greece, guides would starve, for the truth is often hard to swallow.

Dutiful tourists that we were, we carefully listened to all our guide's stories. We traipsed behind him to every place of combat, to where the Greeks had positioned their encampment, and to the cave where Paris had delivered his judgement in the beauty contest that had started the whole war. Every nook in Troy is said to be the chamber of Helen or the place from which Paris fired his fateful arrow at speedy Achilles. On this stone, our guide opined, old Priam watched the corpse of his son Hector, he of the shining helmet, being dragged behind the chariot of his cruel conqueror, Achilles, breaker of men. I wandered through some high grass and was warned not to disturb the ashes of Hector. We stumbled across a few scattered stones and were informed that this was the altar where King Priam fell.

An aeon is too short to visit all the glories that Troy has to offer. But it was time to move on and we journeyed back to the sea with the aim of finding a berth on a ship bound for Antioch. We found a small coastal trader that was planning to set sail that evening, since the night was clear and the stars by which the pilot could steer were all visible. The passengers all prayed to the stars before we set off, imploring them to lead us safely back to dry land.

I had given some thought to making a circuit of the Black Sea. There are undoubtedly some places worth visiting here, such as the site on Mount Theches, in Trebizond, where Xenophon first caught sight of the waves with rapturous shouts of 'The Sea! The Sea!', when he and his band of ten thousand Greeks travelled back from their invasion of Persia under King Cyrus. And on the far side of the waters is that grim town of Tomis to which poor Ovid was banished by decree of the emperor Augustus, having offended him either with one of his poems or with his misbehaviour, and where no one spoke Latin and his genius was left to languish and wither. But to make such a journey entails a significant detour and when much greater treasure lies in the opposite direction the delay is hard to justify.

And so we sailed, and by morning we had only the breezes that blow early in the day from the mouths of the rivers. These breezes were indeed cool, as Homer himself says, but they were not sufficiently strong for the pilot, who wished to make good speed. A calm soon followed, and the pilot ordered his crew to use oars so that we made some progress. Soon after clouds built up, and before long they brought on a violent storm and a strong headwind. We had a narrow escape. The squall produced such a swell of the sea that the water appeared almost hollow, and caused a deluge of water to break not only over that part of the ship where the benches of the rowers were placed, but also over the part that is between them and the upper deck. Everyone was called to help. But as fast as we pumped out the water, more crashed in upon us. Thankfully, the oarsmen were still able to row and, with great difficulty, we made our way to a small harbour on the coast. It was one of those ancient, Greek settlements with a temple to Athene from which it drew its name. There is a ruined castle at this place, and the port can contain only a handful of boats, but it is sufficient to provide shelter from a storm. Several other ships tried to squeeze into the same harbour and we admitted as many as we could. Those who could not fit in tried to ground themselves on nearby beaches. One ship, whose pilot must have been a novice, foolishly exposed its flank to the wind and the swell almost immediately drove it on to the rocks where it was wrecked.

The storm blew for the rest of the day and into the night, with much thunder and lightning, but by dawn all was calm. The sailors of the wrecked ship had all made it ashore and were able to recover the sails and nautical instruments, and had also scraped off the wax from the hull. They had to be swift because the inhabitants of the area, like all coastal inhabitants, see a wreck as some kind of common property, which of course it is not. The law is perfectly clear that the ship and its contents remain the property of the shipowner. The emperor Hadrian even stated that those who owned land on the seashore were responsible for making sure that nothing was stolen from the wreck of a ship that had been badly damaged or broken up. But such wrecks provide an easy opportunity for locals to benefit from an entrepreneur's misfortune. They no doubt consider that trade is a high-risk business and that investors can afford a few losses alongside the rich pickings they make when their ships and their cargoes dock safely. That is one thing. But I have heard that some fishermen even try actively to wreck ships by showing lights at night in order to trick a ship's crew into thinking they are approaching a port when in fact they are being lured on to rocks. And I have also heard of shipwrecked sailors and passengers being sold into slavery by local inhabitants, who should be their saviours but act more like pirates.

From that point, we were blessed with perfect weather coupled with a helpful wind that drove us swiftly along our course. We followed the coast of Asia Minor, first to the south, then in an easterly direction. Who could travel here without his mind turning to Alexander the Great and his heroic conquest of the Persian empire? It would be possible to do an Alexander tour on its own. There is the ancient oak under which his tent had been pitched before the Battle of Chaeroneia. At Tyre, one can visit a spring where Alexander dreamed he captured a satyr, a dream interpreted as referring to the capture of the city. We decided to pay the captain extra to stop at Issus so that we could enjoy the site of one of Alexander's victories.

When Alexander had set out on his epic adventure into Asia, he moved quickly to take all the coastal cities in the hope of neutralising the massively superior Persian fleet. Report reached him that the Persian king, Darius, was amassing a huge army in Babylon, and that he planned to move to the Gulf of Issus where he could meet up with his fleet for supplies and then harry the Greeks by landing troops behind enemy lines. Alexander, realising the threat, moved his army to Issus, where he confronted the Persian army. We walked the battlefield and tried to understand how the battle itself had played out. Darius had formed his line with his heavy cavalry concentrated by the coast on his right. Next he placed his Greek mercenaries and then his Persian infantry, which were so numerous as to stretch into the foothills of the mountains at the far end of the coastal plain. Darius positioned himself in the centre with his royal cavalry guard. The Greeks faced him across a river.

The battle did not start well for the Macedonians. The centre of their phalanx had to advance across a river and up a fortified bank against well-trained Greek mercenaries, and they suffered heavy casualties as a result. As many as one hundred and twenty officers died here and Alexander was forced to retreat. The Persian cavalry charged the Greek cavalry and Alexander's heavily outnumbered Thessalians struggled to cope against the multiple charges of the Persian horse. But it was Alexander's right wing where the crucial stage of the battle took place. Alexander made a brave attack on foot and then, with a cavalry charge against Darius, broke the Persian line. He attacked the king himself and caused him such alarm that he fled the battlefield. Allowing Darius to flee, Alexander wheeled round and attacked the mercenaries from behind. Once they had fled, the rest of the Persian forces also turned heel and ran, following the example of their own commander-in-chief. The Macedonian cavalry pursued the fleeing Persians for as long as the daylight lasted and killed so many thousands that when Alexander and his bodyguards came to a ravine, they were easily able to cross it on the piled up bodies of the dead.

I had noticed while walking the battlefield that there were a considerable number of locusts everywhere. But since the wind was calm and the ship's captain in no hurry to move on we decided to venture into the nearby town to have a meal and to look at whatever sights of interest there might be. This was an error.

The region had been hit by a plague of locusts that had stripped bare all the crops. Those who could had fled, leaving those unable to make the arduous journey to starve. The town was full of the elderly, the young and the sick, who had gone into the town to try to live by begging. At first, before we realised the gravity of the situation, we gave out a number of small coins but once it became clear that the whole town was in strife we stopped. It was a grim scene. There were children and infants bleating in the streets. Some of their mothers had died, others had been abandoned by their parents, who could not bear to have no food to give them when they begged for it. Some were attempting to sell their dearest possessions, such as gold ornaments, and one could have bought them at well below their value if one wished. I could see no bread for sale, only a few turnips, some cabbage or mallow, all at vastly inflated prices. It is despicable how the sellers in the marketplace, as soon as food is scarce, hide their goods in order to make a fortune by profiteering.

I saw some people eating vetches, while others roamed the streets, picking out and eating the dung-spattered roots and leaves of vegetables. I even saw some chewing small wisps of hay and recklessly eating certain pernicious herbs. And well-born women, whose clothing advertised them as such, could be seen begging shamelessly in the marketplace. The starving cried out for morsels of bread with their last gasps, and the dead lay in the midst of the streets and alleys, naked and unburied. Their corpses were being gnawed at by dogs and some old men went about trying to kill the animals fearing that they would acquire a taste for human flesh and start devouring the living. There was no good to be had by staying in such a place. We returned swiftly to the boat and encouraged the captain to set sail now that some light breeze had picked up. Upon hearing about the tribulations the area was suffering, he immediately agreed, fearing that the place was in the grip of demons.

Antioch, the capital of Syria, is the rival of Alexandria in size, splendour and wealth, and it was here that we were headed. Sitting on the river Orontes, Antioch is perhaps the third-largest city in the empire, after Rome itself and Alexandria. As many as a quarter of a million inhabitants have the good fortune to dwell here. It has two principal streets, both of which are colonnaded to keep off the sun and rain, and they cross in the centre.

The longest is thirty-six stades in length and both are lit up at night. The city's aqueducts bring the sweetest water from the nearby hills and its markets are filled with exotic goods that have come via the caravans to Palmyra. The city has a monumental elegance and offers every amenity you would expect from such a metropolis, but on an even grander scale than you can imagine. Squares, colonnades, forum, basilica, temples, aqueducts and fountains, public and private baths, granaries and markets, theatre and amphitheatre, and statues and inscriptions are everywhere to be seen.

The first and greatest praise of a city is the excellence of its land, which is like the keel on a ship in that all the other planks are fastened to it. Antioch is indeed blessed with fine, fertile soil, and it is ringed by mountains. It is a city of such greatness that it is no surprise that it was founded by Alexander. After the battle at Issus and the flight of Darius, Alexander came to this region and pitched his tent near the spring, where there is now a shrine. Refreshing himself after his toils he drank the cold, clear water of the spring, and its sweetness tasted almost like mother's milk, so much so that he named the spring after his mother. He immediately adorned the place with a fountain and then began to build a city, since he had found a spot that was almost the equal of his own greatness.

When I judge a city's society, I consider whether the different parts are harmonious, like a musical composition, and so form a complete whole. If we begin by looking at Antioch's senate, since the whole structure of the city is based upon this, it is immediately clear that we are dealing with a great city. It is composed of men whose fathers, grandfathers and even great-grandfathers were all senators, men who have learned from the knowledge of their ancestors. By means of their skill in the tribune and their services in lawsuits they are made judges, and deliver justice to the people of the province. Through their wisdom, Antioch has grown to become the leading city of Asia.

The porticoes have the appearance of rivers that flow for the greatest distance through the city, while the side streets seem like canals drawn from them. Some of the side streets, which face towards the mountain, lead to the charms of the slopes, often ending in elegant gardens. Others, which face the other way, lead to the banks of the river Orontes. There is also the new part of the city, which stands on an island formed by the flow of the river. It is round, and an unbroken wall surrounds it like a crown. From the four arches at the entrances, four pairs of porticoes proceed, stretching out towards each quarter of the city, as in a statue of the four-handed Apollo. Three of these pairs run as far as the wall and are joined to it, while the fourth is shorter but is the more beautiful since it runs towards the palace. This palace occupies almost a quarter of the whole island. From its colonnades by the wall there is a view worthy of the emperor, with the river flowing below and the suburbs providing a feast for the eyes on all sides. The palace itself is in no way inferior to any other and is indeed far superior to many, especially in beauty, divided as it is into so many chambers and colonnades and halls that even those who are well accustomed to it become lost as they go from door to door.

The two halves of the city are split by the river but
united by five strong bridges. Thus the water divides
the city in two, but the bridges do not allow it to be
separated, joining the younger to the older, like a colt
to its mother. As you pass through the many porticoes,
numerous elaborate private houses are to be seen mixed
among the public buildings, such as temples and baths.
Who could not admire the baths? Some are fitted for the
winter by being sheltered from the harsh winds, others
designed for the summer and so airy that they seem to
have been built in the sky. The city is always filled with
construction activity: some buildings are being torn
down, some are half completed, while others are having
their foundations laid. Everywhere you go, you hear the
cries of those urging on the workmen.

The markets are full to the brim and the supply of
goods for sale is extraordinary and seems inexhaustible.
Those who do their shopping early in the morning get
nothing more than those who wait till the evening. The
markets are always busy and nightfall does not reduce
the level of activity. The whole city seems always to be
full of a great cacophony of noise. So the traveller who
draws near when it has grown dark in the last stage of his
journey is able to push on to the city in good spirits, safe
in the knowledge that he will easily find good lodgings
and a fine supper even if he arrives at night. Once here,
you can both bathe and dine more magnificently than
men invited to feasts of victory in most places. Everything is available, and there is no need for your slaves to
rush about in search of produce, because they only have
to listen out for the cries of the peddlers selling their

wares. The city has an almost festival atmosphere and half the population seem to be on holiday at any one time. It is certainly a place that brings great comforts and pleasures after the toils of the road and the sea. Indeed, people here appear to know that in Antioch they have, while still living, all the things that the poets promise to the righteous dead.

The city is surrounded by graceful villas with colonnades, galleries and balconies, the windows and gates tastefully decorated with stone carvings, gardens and baths. In the grounds stand stables, vats and oil presses hewn into the rocks, and sepulchral chambers, with pillared entrances and filled with sarcophagi. It was in one of these suburban villas that we were staying, in the guest rooms of a cousin of an old friend. The rooms were located on the ground floor and had their own entrance. They consisted of a dining room and bedroom, so that I was free to come and go without entering the peristyle. As is usual in such instances, I was invited to dine with my host on the first night, when I was able to give him one of the gifts I had brought for this purpose, in this case a painting. Subsequently we were supplied with poultry, eggs, herbs, fruits and other produce of the country to eat in our rooms. The slaves bunked with the household slaves in a barn.

Taking an evening stroll by the light of the oil lamps hanging in the open-fronted shops, I hired a boy to carry a torch so that we were able to look at some of the side streets, since the daytime ban on traffic means that the main streets were busy. At one point we were forced to squeeze into a doorway to avoid being crushed under an overladen ox-cart. The boy's lantern had a horn cover to generate a beam of light. Coming to a square, I was disturbed to see a large gathering of lower-class men. Such meetings can only ever end in trouble. Sure enough, it turned out to be a group of bakers who were shouting and arguing as various of them tried to speak. They seemed to be unhappy about supplying the city's bread under the terms of their current contract and were threatening not to bake any more. Sadly, the urban masses are the same wherever you go. They are constantly being thrown into disorder and chaos by the reckless among them, who are always looking to stir them up into rioting. I have seen crowds of angry people complaining about tax or the price of grain commit blasphemy and throw stones at pictures of the emperor and smash them on the ground. They have even thrown statues of the imperial family down and dragged them through the city while, as is usual on such occasions, hurling at them every insult they could think of. It is a disgrace.

·· COMMENTARY ··

Pliny's *Natural History* is a remarkable compendium of Roman knowledge of the natural world and contains a long catalogue of various sea creatures from the different oceans, not all of which is accurate. The very desire of Pliny to catalogue the world can be seen as an expression of the same urge to exploit Rome's imperial possessions as that which drove tourists to visit the great sites of Greece and Egypt. The strange tale of the dolphin being killed because it became too popular can be found in a letter from Pliny's nephew, Pliny the Younger (9.33; see Pliny *Natural History* Book 9 for more dolphin tales). The fact that the attraction drew the elite to the resort, including various magistrates and even the proconsul himself, underlines how spontaneous travel for the purposes of leisure was primarily the preserve of the upper echelons of Roman society. That they expected to be put up and entertained in their accustomed style shows that tourism in this era could inflict harm on the local community just as it can today, but for some very different reasons.

Earthquakes were relatively frequent events in the eastern half of the empire. Rhodes was seriously damaged by one in *c.*150 CE. The reference to sheep being killed and statues cracking comes from Seneca (*Questions about Nature* 6.1.1–5), who describes the impact of the earthquake of 62 CE that struck the region of Campania and severely damaged the ill-fated town of Pompeii. Such texts give us a graphic insight into the terror that an unexpected natural disaster could generate in the ancient world. A tombstone of 120 CE from Asia Minor records the death in an earthquake in Nicomedia, in what is now north-west Turkey, of two young boys, Dexiphanes, aged five, Thrason, aged four, and their slave teacher, Hermes, who was twenty-five and died alongside them. A carved image shows Hermes with a hand on the shoulder of each to console them, because 'during the collapse he held them both in this way'. The boys' father set up the gravestone out of gratitude for the support that his slave had shown his sons during what was a terrifying final ordeal (*CIG* 3293). The reaction of people in seeking open ground is found in texts such as Agathias (*Histories* 5.3). Doing so was a sensible strategy in most ancient towns because the urban layout usually incorporated a variety of open spaces, such as a forum, a circus, gardens and a wide main street. The account of the famine is based on Eusebius (*History of the Church* 9.8) and *The Chronicle of Pseudo-Joshua the Stylite* (38–42). The degree of almost morbid curiosity these texts show for the suffering of the poor is noticeably different from disaster narratives written by earlier historians. The difference, of course, was that these later authors were Christian and so saw the poor, and recognised their suffering, in a way that classical writers did not. The Christianisation of the Roman empire in the fourth century may therefore have helped alleviate the plight of the poorest through disaster relief and everyday alms-giving, although we should remember that pagan emperors had always made generous gifts to their citizens and helped to rebuild areas stricken by catastrophe. It may be, however, that the focus on the poor found in Christian texts represents no more than a rhetorical shift, carried out at least in part in order to conceal the establishment of the church as the state's religion, along with all the riches that that brought with it. On disasters in general, including earthquakes and famines, see Jerry Toner, *Roman Disasters*, Polity, 2013.

The cult of Asclepius was widely popular, with the

centres at Pergamum and Epidaurus being the largest and most famous. Treatment involved sleepovers in the temple, so that the god could make known his thoughts via dreams, followed by dream interpretation, as well as rituals and group activities, all carried out within the institutional framework of the Asclepion. At Epidaurus, short narratives of these divine cures were engraved and set in a wall. One, for example, from the fourth century BCE, reads: 'A man who had his toe healed by a serpent. He was taken outside by the temple servants with a malignant sore on his toe and set upon a seat. While he slept a snake [a symbol of the god] crawled out of the shrine and licked his toe. The patient woke up and was healed. He said that in a dream he had seen a beautiful youth put a drug on his toe.' Aelius Aristides, in the second century, had a lifelong devotion to this practice, and he kept a comprehensive journal of his treatments. It is a relentless account of thorough, some say neurotic, attention to every physical detail of his life (see his *Oration* 27.1–8 for an account of his journey from his sickbed in Smyrna to the Aslcepion at Pergamum). The god ordering him to sail across a stormy harbour while eating honey and acorns, and then vomiting, is from *Sacred Tales* (1.65). Aristides is completely unfazed by these divine commands, and when on another occasion the god commanded him to bathe naked in snow, he 'gladly obeyed' (4.11). There was no simple dichotomy between these religious treatments and ancient medicine. Physicians worked at the temples of Asclepius, and the great doctor Galen, who served as the Roman emperor Marcus Aurelius's personal physician and is known to have written more than 350 medical treatises, set out on his career following a dream in which Asclepius appeared to his father. Nor was there any straightforward opposition between medicine and faith-based healing. Aristides tells us how certain dreams appeared to him at the time when a physician had arrived to treat him. Aristides has no doubt whose advice to follow. The doctor would only be able to help him 'as much as he knows how'. And the doctor, when he heard about the dreams, being 'a sensible man', also yielded to the god. They both recognised the 'true and proper doctor' and did what he commanded. The result was that his night was 'wholly endurable and everything was without pain' (*Sacred Tales* 1.57).

Long-winded guides were a common bugbear for tourists (see Plutarch 'On the Oracles at Delphi' 395a–400f on a guide at Delphi; and Lucian *Amores* 8–9). The description of the Black Sea is based on Arrian's *Sailing Around the Black Sea*, as is the account of the near shipwreck. The laws concerning shipwreck can be found in *Digest* (47.9) and make it clear that many coastal inhabitants saw a wreck as a stroke of good luck from which they could benefit. Libanius's *Oration* 11 in praise of Antioch is the source of much of the account of that city. The dispute with the bakers, which took place in Ephesus in the second century, is found in the inscription *SEG* 4.512, and underscores the political nature of bread supply in antiquity. The description of popular riots in which imperial imagery was attacked is based on Sozomen's *History of the Church* 7.23. However popular the Roman emperors would like to have thought they were — and have us believe it, too — we should always remember that the ordinary people were able to push back, especially when the government had failed in one of its primary duties of ensuring a ready supply of affordable food.

CHAPTER V

JUDEA AND BEYOND

THE SECURITY OF THE EMPIRE allows us to travel at a speed the ancients could only dream of. With a good wind, merchant ships can travel from Rhodes to Alexandria in only four days, and even to travel the length of the Nile takes only ten. Italy to Egypt takes a mere seven days from the south, nine from Puteoli. Ostia to Hispania can be done in five days, to Narbonese Gaul in four, and to Africa in just three, with a strong tail wind. Alexandrian ships are the swiftest and have the best and most experienced captains. But on a tour such as this, speed is not of the essence. It is a more leisurely form of travel with stops and detours built into the itinerary. Still, you would not want to spend too long making the trip. A merchant ship taking the scenic route round Greece, Asia Minor and Syria will take one hundred days to travel from Italy to Beirut because it is making so many stops on the way.

We sauntered down the coast. At Byblos, I entertained the local magistrate and splashed out on some snow from the heights of Lebanon to cool our wine. The largest cities in Phoenicia are Sidon and Tyre, which contain numerous fine private villas and houses, some as many as six storeys high. As you travel around the empire, you cannot help but be struck by how Roman control has created a drive towards architectural unity. Everywhere there are villas, temples, baths, theatres, amphitheatres, aqueducts and triumphal arches, all set in the uniform layout of a symmetrical city that resembles an army camp in its regularity.

We soon arrived in Judea. Judea is an extensive province. The part that borders Syria is called Galilee, while the part that is nearest to Arabia and Egypt has the name of Perea. Perea is separated from Galilee by the river Jordan and is covered with rugged mountains. The Jordan is a delightful river and almost seems keen to linger among the inhabitants of its banks as it meanders its way along its course until, with great reluctance, it flows into the gloomy and pestilential waters of the Asphalt Lake. This is a curious body of water into which no body will sink, even those of bulls and camels. To the west of this noxious lake live the Esseni, a people who live apart from all others and are all the more marvellous for that. They have no women and so know nothing about sexual desire. They have no money and their only companions are palm trees. Day after day, however, many strangers join them, presumably because they have grown weary of the miseries of life. In this way, even though they do not procreate, these people are able to prolong their existence almost eternally. Jerusalem is by far the most famous city of the region. Like most of the others, when it recklessly sought to throw off Roman rule, it was reduced to a heap of ashes. There are no Jews now in Jerusalem.

The causes of this resistance are unclear. Having been quickly and successfully pacified, the province became a constant source of strife. Jews and Greeks seemed always to be at each others' throats, and the Jews, with their strange worship of a single god, resented it when emperors expected them to put up statues in their honour. The emperor Gaius went so far as to order a statue of himself to be erected in the Jewish Temple in Jerusalem, a command that the governor of Syria, Publius Petronius, failed to carry out for fear of provoking a rebellion. A few years after, two brothers led an uprising in Galilee, but this was soon suppressed and the pair were executed. But this was by no means the end of the trouble.

The Jews continued to complain about Roman rule, especially the level of tax. They were also incensed when Greeks sacrificed birds in front of one of the Jewish temples and the Romans did nothing about their complaints. This led to protests and attacks upon Roman citizens. The army intervened but the local garrison was attacked and many troops were killed before they abandoned Jerusalem. Sensing an opportunity to throw off Roman rule, many other cities joined the rebellion. On hearing the news, the legate of Syria, Cestius Gallus, marched south to restore order. Despite some early successes, his legion was ambushed and massacred.

The most fearsome of the Jewish rebels were known as the Sicarii, so called because they kept knives concealed about their clothing so that they could retain an element of surprise when they attacked Roman soldiers. During the collapse of order in Jerusalem, they were keen to break into the archives to destroy the bonds of the moneylenders and so bring an end to debt collection, knowing that this would make them popular among the masses. Their success meant that many other outlaws came from the countryside into the city and joined them, after which there was no atrocity left undone.

The general Vespasian was sent to crush the revolt, with his son Titus as his second-in-command. Armed with four legions, he moved into Galilee, but to begin with he did not seek to attack Jerusalem where the majority of the rebels were based since it was well-protected by strong walls and other defences. Instead the Roman forces dealt with the smaller rebellious towns and cities, destroying enemy forces and punishing the local populations for supporting them. Soon they controlled all of Galilee. With many rebels fleeing to Jerusalem, the city became a hotbed of political factionalism. Various different leaders took control only to be replaced. There was then a long pause, since the death of the emperor Nero had given Vespasian the opportunity to compete for the throne, something which he did successfully after a year-long civil war. He was now in a position to hand over full command to his son, Titus.

Titus laid siege to Jerusalem. He placed three legions on the western side of the city and the fourth on the Mount of Olives to the east. Within three weeks, Roman forces had succeeded in breaching the two outer walls of the city's defences. But the Jews resisted strongly and prevented Titus from breaking through the third and strongest wall. For seven long months, the Romans besieged the city. The Jewish Zealots inside lacked the discipline of regular soldiers and infighting broke out again. At one point they destroyed the food stocks in the city, a drastic measure thought to have been undertaken either to enlist their god's intervention on their behalf or as a stratagem to make the defenders more desperate and so more likely to succeed in repelling the Roman army. Titus, meanwhile, had his engineers build ramparts and a circuit wall around the city to starve out the population more effectively. And effective it was. Inside the city, the Jews went hungry and some were forced to eat their own roasted children to survive.

The Romans offered to negotiate a surrender but the Zealots wounded the messenger sent to speak to them. Fighting resumed and, during this, the Jewish Temple, which Titus had ordered his troops to spare, was set on fire when the Jews in the north-western approach to the building used fire to try to stop the Roman advance. Soon the building was ablaze and the fire burned out of control. The flames quickly spread throughout the rest of the city and the legionaries poured in. They were almost drunk with a lust for vengeance after the long siege and many were trampled by their own side and so died as miserably as the defeated. Everywhere there was panic and slaughter. Most of the victims were unarmed citizens, butchered wherever they were caught. The altar of the Temple was piled high with corpses, while down the steps of the sanctuary poured a river of blood.

The remaining resistance was soon mopped up. Some of the Jews escaped through sewers and hidden tunnels, while others made a final stand in the upper city. The Roman forces were held up sufficiently that they were compelled to build siege engines to break into this last redoubt. The delay was short-lived, however, and the city was soon under Roman control. All of the surviving citizens were captured. Those men of fighting age and the elderly were killed. The remaining 97,000 were enslaved. Of these, many thousands were condemned to fight as gladiators or were fed to the beasts in games celebrating the Roman victory. Many others were employed in building the Flavian amphitheatre in Rome. The booty from the Temple itself was taken back to Rome and exhibited at a magnificent triumph, an event that was commemorated on the arch dedicated to Titus. Titus ordered that the city should not be entirely demolished but that the main towers and the western wall should be left standing in order to demonstrate to posterity how well-fortified a city his brave forces had captured. These can still be seen today. This was the end to which Jerusalem came on account of the madness of its revolutionaries, a city of great magnificence and even greater fame. Indeed the whole of Judea was laid to waste. The trees had all been cut down and everything of beauty was destroyed.

The few remaining rebels holed up in Masada, which is a fortress on a rock. It is a lengthy detour to visit here and I am not sure it is worth it unless you are interested in siege warfare. Lofty and to all appearances impregnable, the fortress can only be reached by a single pathway, known as the snake, because it is too narrow for men to walk side by side. The Sicarii had seized it at the start of the revolt and, after the fall of Jerusalem, they found themselves joined by many refugees. The Roman governor of Judea, Lucius Flavius Silva, was dispatched to dislodge them, taking with him a legion and many Jewish prisoners of war to carry out the building work. He began by circling Masada with a wall before starting to build a huge ramp up against the western face of the rock. Thousands of tonnes of stones and earth were moved by the slaves and, bit by bit, the ramp moved up towards the top.

By the spring of the next year the ramp was finished. A giant siege tower was constructed so that a battering ram could be used against the wall and it was slowly dragged up the ramp. With volleys of blazing torches the Roman forces finally breached the wall but, upon entering it, found it to be a graveyard. The Jewish rebels had all killed each other, since their religion forbids suicide, preferring a glorious death to a life of servitude. Only two women had survived, by hiding inside a cistern along with five children, and they recounted to the Romans what had happened. When they started their revolt, the Jews had hoped that all their people beyond the Euphrates would join with them but at the end there were only 960 Jewish Zealots left at Masada.

Judea is a depressing place. As if this crushing defeat was not enough, the Jews revolted not once but twice more. The first of these rebellions took place largely in the many cities in north Africa where Jewish populations lived but where they resented both Greek and Roman interference in their affairs and took advantage of the emperor Trajan's absence on campaign to revolt.

The Jews in the region of Cyrene put a certain Andreas at their head, and killed many Romans and Greeks. They would eat the flesh of their victims, make belts for themselves of their entrails, anoint themselves with their blood, and wear their skins for clothing. Many victims were sawn in two, from the head downwards, or they were thrown to wild beasts or were forced to fight as gladiators. In all, two hundred and twenty thousand perished. In Egypt, too, the Jews perpetrated many similar outrages, as they also did in Cyprus, under the leadership of a certain Artemion. There, two hundred and forty thousand died and for this reason no Jew may set foot on that island, and even if one of them is driven upon its shores by a storm he is put to death. Among others who subdued the Jews was the general Lusius Quietus, who was sent by Trajan to carry out this task.

Still the Jews rebelled. One of them, called Simon, claimed to be their Messiah, a divine hero who could drive out the Romans. At first the Romans took no notice of him and his rebels used to meet secretly in underground passages, which they pierced from above at intervals to let in air and light. Soon, however, all Judea had been stirred up, and the Jews everywhere were showing signs of unrest, gathering together and attacking Roman citizens. Many Jews from outside the province were also joining them. In response, Trajan's successor, Hadrian, sent against them his best generals. First of these was Julius Severus, who was dispatched from Britannia, where he was governor. Severus did not dare to attack his enemy in open battle because they were so numerous and desperate. Instead, by intercepting small groups, and by depriving them of food and besieging them, he was able, rather slowly, to be sure, but with comparatively little danger, to crush, exhaust and exterminate them. Very few of them in fact survived. Fifty of their most important outposts and 985 of their most famous villages were razed to the ground. Some 580,000 men were slain in the various raids and battles, and the number of those that perished by famine, disease and fire was too great to count. In this way, nearly the whole of Judea was desolated. The Jews were forewarned of this outcome by omens. Before the rebellion, the tomb of Solomon, which the Jews regard as an object of veneration, collapsed, and many wolves and hyenas rushed howling into their cities.

Hadrian had had enough of this rebellious people and he attempted to eradicate them. He banned the Jews from using their calendar, burned their religious books, and executed their scholars. Circumcision was forbidden. On the site of their temple, which lay in ruins from their first revolt, he erected two statues, one of Jupiter, the other of himself. He refounded Jerusalem as the Roman city of Aelia Capitolina, in reference to himself and Jupiter, and he barred Jews from entering the city apart from on one day a year. And so that he did not have to even use the name Judea, he renamed the province Palestine.

This is the city you will find on your visit. It is a typical Roman city now, with a grid layout, although there are two pairs of intersecting main roads, the cardines running from north to south and the decumani from east to west, because the Temple Mount required a main road to run either side of it. These broad streets are lined with colonnades and shops of all kinds. For obvious reasons the city was not re-walled. You will find the main forum at the junction of the main cardo and decumanus, adjacent to which is the huge temple to Venus. Hadrian built a triple-arched gateway as an entrance to the eastern forum, which is well worth a visit if you are looking to buy souvenirs of your visit.

The ban on Jews entering Jerusalem extends to the Christian Jews. You are likely to encounter various such groups making their own tour of other sites in the region that they consider to be sacred. Near Hebron they visit the graves of the grandsons of a man called Abraham. Or they travel to a town called Bethlehem as this is where the man they believe to be a god was born. I have heard it said that they even visit an ark on a mountainside in Armenia.

You may also come across members of this strange sect in less pleasant circumstances. While travelling south towards Egypt we passed a group of Christians who, along the side of the main road, had just been cru-cified and were far from death. One of them began to hurl abuse at us, saying that 'implacable wrath shall fall upon the men of Rome' and that 'heaven will deliver justice' and that the Romans would pay for their cursed arrogance and would themselves be enslaved. I left him to his lunatic ravings. I asked another of the criminals what offence he had committed and he replied that he was a slave who had run away from his master.

'Why did you do such a thing?'

'Because he beat me for no reason every day.'

It is a sad fact that some masters mistreat their slaves but that in no way condones such behaviour. My own slaves entreated me to take pity on him and, for the sake of household harmony, I did so. I therefore left one of them behind to break the man's legs and thus put a quick end to his suffering.

The Jews were scattered far and wide after their final defeat. War often causes populations to flee, or they may be moved by the authorities in order to repopulate those areas left desolated by conflict. But it is money that drives most people to travel in peacetime. Trade is the lifeblood of the empire's lower classes and has been made possible by the security delivered by the Roman state, particularly in this eastern corner of the empire. It was our first emperor, Augustus, who opened up a trade route to the Orient when he conquered Egypt, and when its final queen, Cleopatra, held an asp to her breast. New shipping lanes were quickly found, from the Red Sea ports of Myos Hormos and Berenike to Arabia, east Africa and India. It was an Egyptian sailor, Hippalos, who, during the time of Nero, discovered the south-west monsoon wind to India that was then named after him. What had previously been beyond exotic now became commonplace, as incenses from Arabia, spices from India and silks from beyond all flowed unimpeded into the empire. From these ports, the goods are transferred to the town of Coptos on the Nile by means of camel, an arduous journey across the desert that takes six to twelve days, but one thought well worth it for the profits involved. The caravans traverse the hot sands at night in order to avoid the excessive heat of the daytime sun, navigating by the stars, and they rest by day. Roman soldiers have even dug wells and cisterns along the routes to provide water to these traders, so important are the goods they ferry.

The merchant ships that sail east carry archers on board to protect themselves against pirates. It takes them a month to reach the town of Ocelis at the most southerly point of the Red Sea, from where it is another forty days sailing to make the coast of Malabar. Once loaded, the ships make the return journey by means of the north-easterly monsoon wind as far as the Red Sea, and then with the help of the south wind back to Berenice. I have heard it from a ship's captain, who claimed to have made the trip several times, that the journey from Alexandria to India took three months there and three months back. The captain thought that I was looking to get involved in the business, and to finance the purchase of a cargo for transport to India or Arabia in return for a share of the profits on his return. He was wrong, however. Such high-risk ventures appeal to ambitious freedmen, I find, and there is in fact an excellent return available in funding smaller, local trips. But I pass on his information in case it appeals to you.

The coast below Berenice is that of the Fish-eaters, who live in scattered caves in the narrow valleys. Further inland are the Berbers, and beyond them the wild Flesh-eaters and Calf-eaters. Each tribe is governed by a chief. Below the Calf-eaters there is a little market town on the shore, after sailing about four thousand stades from Berenice, called Ptolemais of the Hunts, from which the hunters started for the interior under the dynasty of the Ptolemies. In this market town you will find the true land tortoise, which is white and has a small shell. You can also find some ivory. But the place has no harbour and can only be accessed by small boats. In these regions there is great appetite for cloth made in Egypt and poor-quality cloaks dyed in colours, as well as articles of flint glass, brass and linen. Metals, such as soft sheets of copper, which are used to make cooking utensils and ankle bracelets for women, and iron, which is used to make spears for elephant hunting, are also much in demand.

Beyond this place, where the coast turns towards the south, there is the Cape of Spices, a sudden promontory, at the very end of the Berber coast. The anchorage is dangerous at times because of the swell, and you should note that a sign of an approaching storm is that the deep water becomes more turbid and changes its colour. When this happens, all the vessels run to another larger promontory called Taba, which offers safe shelter. In the market here you should buy cinnamon, which is available in many varieties, and frankincense, as well as slaves of the better sort. Navigation is dangerous along this whole coast of Arabia, which is without harbours and has bad anchorages because of the many rocks. Beyond here is the town of Muza, about twelve thousand stades from Berenice. The whole place is crowded with Arab shipowners and seafarers, and buzzes with commerce.

Beyond here, the land recedes considerably and there is a very deep bay. This is frankincense country, mountainous and forbidding, wrapped in thick clouds and fog. The trees from which the incense is collected are not of great height or thickness but produce it in drops on the bark. The frankincense is gathered by the king's slaves and those who are sentenced to do so as a punishment. These places are very unhealthy, even to those sailing along the coast, and are almost always fatal to those working there, who also often perish from want of food. The bay has a large promontory facing eastwards, called Syagrus, on which sits a fort for the purpose of defending the harbour and the warehouse where the frankincense is stored. Opposite here, well out at sea, you will find an island called Dioscorida. This is large and contains both desert and marsh, and it is full of crocodiles, snakes and great lizards, which can be eaten and their fat melted to be used instead of olive oil. No fruit, vines or grain grow on the island. The few inhabitants live on the north coast, and consist of a mixture of Arab, Indian and Greek traders. The island is the best place for tortoises, including the true sea tortoise, the land tortoise, the white tortoise, and the mountain tortoise, which is largest of all and has the thickest shell that can be made into caskets, small plates and that sort of ware. A harbour called Moscha lies beyond this bay and you should winter there if the season is late.

As you sail along the coast, which turns northward near the entrance of the Persian Sea, you'll encounter many islands, known as the Calaei, along the shore. Be careful, as the inhabitants are a treacherous, uncivilised lot. Not far beyond, diving for pearls is widespread, but the quality is inferior to those from India. Six days further on, you will come to a Persian market town called Ommana. Many ships come here loaded with copper, sandalwood, teak timbers and ebony. It is a good place to buy dates.

Beyond the gulf of Baraca is the beginning of India. That part of India, which faces the east, runs in a straight line for a distance of 1,875 miles until it comes to a bend, at which point the Indian Ocean begins. Here the coast takes a turn to the south and continues to run in that direction for a distance of 2,475 miles, as far as the river Indus, the boundary of India on the west. In this region, the appearance of the heavens and the stars is totally changed. There are two summers in the year, and two harvests. The followers of Alexander the Great state in their writings that there were no fewer than five thousand cities in that portion of India that they conquered, not one of which was smaller than that of Cos, and that India forms one third of the whole earth, with an innumerably large population. The rivers are huge. It is stated that even when sailing six hundred stades per day Alexander the Great was still unable to reach the mouth of the river Indus in less than five months. And it is a well-known fact that this river is not as large as the Ganges. In his treatise on India, Seneca says that there are sixty-five rivers in total.

India is a fertile country, yielding wheat and rice, sesame oil and clarified butter, as well as cotton and the Indian clothes that are made from it. Very many cattle are pastured there, and the men are of great stature and black. You can still see traces of Alexander the Great's expedition, such as ancient shrines, remains of forts and great wells. The entrance to the town of Barygaza is very hard to navigate for those coming from the ocean. On

the right side lie rocks and on the left projects a promontory that causes a strong current. Because of this, native
fishermen in the king's service are stationed at the very
entrance in large boats called trappaga, and they will
pilot you into a safe anchorage. You will find that the
whole of India has many rivers that are strongly tidal
depending on the moon. For this reason, entering estuaries is very dangerous for the inexperienced. The rush
of waters at the incoming tide is irresistible, and anchors
cannot hold, with the result that even large ships are
caught up by the force of it, turned broadside and then
driven ashore.

It was in these regions that Alexander set out for the
Ganges, and you will still find ancient drachma coins
being used, with inscriptions in Greek letters and the
symbols of those who reigned after Alexander. Near
here, in the city of Ozene, you will be able to buy agate,
cloth and spikenard. The local people are keen on Italian
wine. Beyond here, the land contains all kinds of wild
beasts: leopards, tigers, elephants, enormous serpents,
hyenas and baboons of many sorts. The market towns
contain great quantities of pepper, but also pearls, diamonds and sapphires. You should set off from Egypt in
July if you plan to sail here. Beyond the town of Bacare
lies the Dark Red Mountain. The first place you come
to is called Balita, which has a fine harbour. Beyond
this is Comari, where men come who wish to dedicate
themselves to the local goddess for the rest of their lives,
and bathe and live in celibacy as she herself is said to have
once done. From Comari, head south to Colchi, where
you will find the pearl fisheries, which are worked by

condemned criminals. Beyond this point there are many barbarous tribes, among them the Cirrhadae, a savage race of men with flattened noses, and the Horse-faces and the Long-faces, who are said to be cannibals. After this comes the river Ganges, which rises and falls in the same way as the Nile, and on its bank is a market town that has the same name as the river. Here you can buy malabathrum, spikenard and pearls, and cottons of the finest quality.

Beyond India, there is a very great inland country called Thinae, from which raw silk, silk yarn and silk cloth are brought in caravans through Bactria to Barygaza, and are also exported by way of the river Ganges. This far-off land is not easy to access. The regions further on are difficult to attain either on account of their excessive winters and great cold, or are beyond reach because of some divine influence.

Trade with such places has transformed how we dress. In the old days, men wore homespun wool, and only wealthy women wore expensive cloth such as linen. Now you see men wearing linen tunics every-where. And they choose only those clothes made from the finest linen from Egypt, Syria and Cilicia. Silk used to be mixed with linen or cotton to produce a light, almost transparent material, which was worn only by women. Now it is not uncommon to see men dressed in garments of pure silk. The traders who make these journeys never sail with an empty hull and take with them Roman delights to sell and exchange as they go. They have a sharp eye for quality and know exactly in what goods each of these foreign lands specialises.

They are patient, too. The voyage down to Rhapta, for example, which takes its name from the sewed boats they use, is quite safe but can be time-consuming, since waiting for the right winds can make a round-trip last as long as two years. But it is worth it because this is the best source of elephant tusks and rhinoceros horn for use in medicines. What luxuries come from Africa: hippopotamus skins, tortoiseshell, monkeys and black slaves can all be found in the empire's marketplaces. And what myrrhs and frankincenses come from Arabia to make even the most stinking old goat smell of purity. The voyage to India on the monsoon winds is more dangerous but can be even more profitable. A trader returning from those far-off climes comes laden with spices, cinnamon, nard, malabathrum, and above all pepper. And with heaps of precious gemstones, too, such as sapphires, diamonds, agate, onyx and pearls, to say nothing of the fine cottons.

Whether all this luxury is doing us any good is another matter. Do we really need pepper? What I find most remarkable about this spice is that it is so popular. Some plants have a pleasant taste or a charming appearance, but pepper has only its bitterness to recommend it. And for that people travel all the way to India and, what is more, are prepared to pay handsomely to buy it. Quite how much depends on the quality and the variety. A pound of the long pepper from northern India, which is the hottest type, costs fifteen denarii. The white and black sort from south India fetch seven and fourteen denarii respectively. People waste money by sprinkling pepper liberally into their dishes and even use it to spice up their drinks, and it also has a medicinal application. There is even a specially constructed warehouse for it in Rome, where thousands of pounds of the stuff are stored, safe from the mice whom it would be better used to feed. I often wonder if the traders who first sailed to India used this worthless substance as ballast on their return journeys, and then duped the inhabitants of the Roman empire into thinking that it was a rare and valuable commodity. The result is that gold and silver flows out of the empire like a vast shining river, as traders take million upon million of denarii to pay for their transactions, sapping our strength and transferring it to the East. How right we are to tax these luxury imports, meaning that the state at least derives some benefit from the profligacies of its most wasteful citizens.

On sailing for Egypt, since we were leaving the province, we were approached by the customs officials at the port demanding to know what goods we had to declare and asking for a list of them. They are a dishonest breed and were almost drooling at the sight of our extensive baggage. It is unpleasant how they poke their noses in everywhere, running their hands not just through open items but inside bags as well. They are, of course, entitled to examine the baggage and confiscate all undeclared goods, which can be bought back but at a price they determine. Travel items are not taxable. You are also exempt if you cross the provincial frontier to attend a festival, but you will need to be carrying religious symbols to prove this to be true. Declared goods are taxed at rates of one fiftieth and one twentieth of their value. Luxury items are taxed at one quarter of their value. They are not allowed to search women, a fact which some exploit by secreting valuables about their person. Be warned that slaves will be freed if you try to sneak them through as members of your family rather than as possessions. All of these matters can usually be fixed if you know the right person. Naturally, the emperor had long ago granted me and my family the privilege of tax-free travel and it was a great pleasure to see the disappointment, indeed pain, on the officials' faces when I produced the appropriate documentation. Should you ever wish to insult a customs official, you might try saying the following: garrotter, thief, coffin-nail, oppressor of the poor, crusher, pariah or indeed any other vile term that comes to mind.

·· COMMENTARY ··

For all Falx's certainty that Roman rule brought significant benefits to its subjects, the resistance put up by the Jews shows that we should not assume that the conquered peoples of the empire agreed. Initially pacified under Augustus, the province of Judea become a repeated source of trouble for the later emperors. The causes of this unrest were not simply Roman domination but included the imposition of Roman law, conflict with Greek inhabitants, who had spread all over the eastern Mediterranean after the conquests of Alexander and whom the Romans were suspected of favouring, and concerns about the status of the Jewish religion in a pagan empire.

The account of the first Jewish War is based on that of Josephus (*War Against the Jews*), whose detailed account is the only one to survive. Josephus was a high-status Jew from Jerusalem, who was initially a commander of Jewish forces against Rome. Captured and enslaved by Vespasian, he adopted the emperor's name, Flavius, upon being freed. He became a Roman citizen and then accompanied Titus on the later part of the campaign, serving as an adviser and interpreter. His account is, therefore, first-hand. Unbiased it is not. His text absolves Titus of any blame for the destruction of the Temple in Jerusalem when it is far from obvious that this was the case. His claim that over a million people, mostly Jews, were killed during the city's siege also seems to be an exaggeration. His account, however, does give a clear sense of the passion with which the Jewish fighters hated their Roman oppressors. It was a passion that resurfaced in two further revolts. Dio Cassius gives brief accounts of these (*History of Rome* 68.32 and 69.13–14). It is unclear whether Hadrian's anti-Jewish legislation preceded the final revolt, and thereby helped cause it, or followed it and reflected imperial exasperation at this problematic people. The three Jewish–Roman conflicts had a significant impact on the Jews, killing vast numbers, and transforming them into a scattered and persecuted minority. Evidently, travel in the Roman world was not always the result of peaceable tourism and trade but was forced on millions as a result of Roman military suppression, which left them as refugees. The Jews of the diaspora now became the norm, with the demographic centres of Judaism moving from Judea to Galilee and small communities across the Mediterranean. Unsurprisingly, hostility towards the Romans persisted and can be seen in texts such as the *Sibylline Oracles* (not to be confused with the *Sibylline Books* of the Roman state), which contain various prophesies of doom about Rome (for example: 3.45–62, 350–5, 356–80; 5.155–78, 386–433). Rome was commonly referred to by later Jews as 'the evil empire'. But the crushing defeats also led many Jews to become more passively quietistic in their opposition to Rome, with one text bemoaning, 'You go into the country and you meet a bailiff; you come back to town and bump into a tax-collector; you go home and find your sons and daughters starving' (Simeon ben Laish, B Sanhedrin 98, 6). See N. de Lange, 'Jewish Attitudes to the Roman Empire', in P. D. A. Garnsey and C. R. Whittaker (eds), *Imperialism in the Ancient World*, Cambridge University Press, 1978, pp. 255–81.

Christians were included in the ban on Jerusalem, as the Romans did not see them as a separate group, but this changed with the conversion to Christianity of the emperor Constantine in 312 CE. Constantine wanted to rediscover the Jerusalem that Jesus had known and to do this had to clear the rubble from the hill of the crucifixion and uncover the cave where Jesus's body was believed to have been placed. Towards the end of her life, Constantine's mother, Helena, made a religious tour of the Holy Land and found what she believed to be remains of the True Cross at a site where the emperor ordered the construction of the Church of the Holy

Sepulchre. Other churches were also built on holy sites discovered by Helena. Soon Christian pilgrims were flocking to Jerusalem in a form of religiously motivated travel that closely resembled the festival visits of the pagan world. These pilgrims wanted to see the famous buildings and places they knew from the Bible but also sought to explore what Christian faith meant to the individual believer in a way that was similar to the search for self-understanding found in earlier pagan travel texts. Christian pilgrims also had a strong desire to see physical relics associated with the saints and martyrs and, in combination with that, sought the miraculous events they hoped such holy objects might induce. Often this would be a search for a cure for some ailment. Again, we can see many continuities with pagan practice, where religion, travel and health were closely intertwined in visits to various healing shrines. The number of these relics burgeoned alongside the growth in the pilgrim trade. By 570 CE, Antoninus of Piacenza describes seeing the bench on which Jesus had sat as a boy, and his dried blood on the rock where he had been crucified. Pilgrims also sought out holy men so as to marvel at the hardships these ascetics were prepared to undergo in order to prove their faith and move closer to God. The numbers of pilgrims grew so large that they left 'every road resembling a river' (Theodoret, *History of Religion* 26.11). As a result, Basil of Caesarea promoted the idea of setting up hostelries for pilgrims, and Antoninus refers to two such places in Jerusalem, one for men and one for women, with a combined capacity of three thousand. The accommodation was simple and free, albeit in return for an expected donation. These travellers also sought their own kind of souvenirs, such as small models of holy places mentioned in the Bible. And for those who were unable to make the arduous and expensive trip themselves, a new form of travel literature was born, such as *Egeria's Travels*, which enabled the readership to experience a pilgrimage vicariously.

Overseas trade expanded significantly under the empire. *Sailing Around the Red Sea* is a manual of voyages from Red Sea ports, probably written in the first century CE. It offers detailed accounts of the ports along the east African coast, the Persian Gulf and the Indian Ocean, and gives an excellent sense of the quantity of luxury items that were imported and what each side of the trading relationship had a taste for buying. Pepper became something of a staple in Rome, a fact bemoaned by Pliny the Elder (*Natural History* 12.29). It is even mentioned in a document from the Roman garrison at Vindolanda on Hadrian's Wall. Under the emperor Domitian, a large warehouse was built in Rome to store the spice, the Horrea Piperataria, still partially preserved under the Basilica of Constantine. Roman traders paid for their goods partly in coins, a fact reflected in the large quantities of early imperial gold and silver coins found in south India. All luxury items were taxed on their importation to the empire. Tax officials then were as popular as they have ever been, and the list of terms of abuse for them can be found in the second-century CE scholar Pollux's *Dictionary of Terms* (9.30–1).

CHAPTER VII

EGYPT

W E WERE STILL SOME TEN MILES out at
sea when I first caught sight of the lighthouse
at Alexandria. We had reached Egypt, that tourist para-
dise where the exotic landscape is matched only by the
strange customs of the local people, and the great monuments of antiquity stand testament to the end that awaits
any empire that grows weak. The shore of the mainland
forms a bay, since it thrusts two promontories out into
the open sea, and between these is situated the island
of Pharos, lying parallel to the shore and forming two
narrow entrances to the great harbour, and on which
the famous lighthouse stands. King Ptolemy, who had
it built, was so impressed that he allowed the architect,
Sostratus of Cnidus, to inscribe his name on the shim-
mering white marble from which it was constructed.
At night, a beacon burns at the top to indicate the
entrance of the harbour to ships and also to warn them
of the sandbanks that lie nearby. The main problem for
the inexperienced seafarer is that from a distance the

non-stop burning beacon is easily mistaken for a star.

Egypt is full of cities but none is remotely a match for Alexandria, which almost rivals Rome itself in splendour. It is no wonder that so many travellers cross the sea from Italy each year, taking advantage of the many merchant ships that sail from Rome and Puteoli during the sailing season, sent to collect cargoes of linen, carpets, glass, paper, incense and all the other exotic items of which the province acts as both a source and a conduit. The great grain ships are a marvel to behold. We passed close by one and we had to crane our necks to be able to see the sky. It had three masts and must have been 180 feet long and 45 feet across at its widest point. The captain reckoned its tonnage at over 1,500. She was painted, and on each side of her bow had a large picture of the goddess Isis, after whom she had been named. Even this ship was as nothing compared with the floating monsters that were built to transport the obelisks of Egypt to Rome. The emperor Gaius had one constructed to bring an obelisk to adorn the Circus Maximus as well as the stones to make a giant plinth on which it could stand. The ship needed over 800 tonnes of lentils to serve as ballast, and when it docked in Ostia it covered almost the whole of the left side of the harbour. It was so large that his successor, Claudius, had it sunk in the port to serve as foundations for an extension to the harbour mole.

Egypt is another world. Everything is so different from what you are used to in the Latin- and Greek-speaking parts of the empire. It makes even the most ancient antiquities of Greece seem youthful. Time has made no impact on the greatest of these monuments, the pyramids and the graves of the kings. Nor has time changed the locals' peculiar gods and their worship of animals, and their colossal temples are covered with strange hieroglyphs. And Alexandria is itself an oddity within Egypt. It is a Greek city, founded by Alexander in the Greek style, a city thought fit to house his own tomb when he was so cruelly taken by fate in his prime. Among the happy advantages of the city, the greatest is that this is the only place in all Egypt which is well located for commerce both by sea, on account of the good harbours, and by land, because the river easily brings together everything into a single place. It has, as a result, become the greatest emporium in the world.

The city lies in an area the shape of a soldier's cloak. The long sides are those that are washed by the sea and the short sides are the isthmuses. The entire city is criss-crossed by streets that are broad enough for riding horses, or even for driving chariots. It contains the most beautiful public spaces, as well as the royal palaces, which between them constitute perhaps a third of the whole urban area. Every king would add some public amenity and build some new splendid palace. It is in the royal palaces that you will find the Temple of the Body, in which lie the tombs of the kings and of Alexander himself, whose general Ptolemy stole the body from his rival Perdiccas and laid it in a golden sepulchre. It now lies in a glass coffin so that you can see the preserved corpse clearly, although this is now in a delicate state. When the emperor Augustus visited, the body was so fragile that when he touched it a piece of Alexander's nose fell off. You will see the royal palaces on the left as you sail into the harbour.

Next you will see the theatre and you will pass an elbow of land containing a temple to Poseidon. Mark Antony extended this promontory even further, by adding a mole that went out into the harbour and then he built a royal lodge at the end of it where he could go for peace and quiet. It was here that he went after his defeat by Octavian, the future emperor Augustus, at Actium, before killing himself and dying in the arms of his lover, Queen Cleopatra, last of the Ptolemies, who herself died by the bite of an asp.

The first Ptolemy had succeeded Alexander and taken control of Egypt. He was then succeeded by Philadelphius, and he by Euergetes. Then there was Philopator, the son of Agathocleia, and then Epiphanes, and eventually Auletes, the father of Cleopatra. Berenice, Cleopatra's elder sister, who was established on the throne instead of her father, in seeking a husband sent for a certain Seleucus, who claimed to belong to the royal family of Syria. She married him but then found out that he was a charlatan and so had him strangled within a few days, particularly as she could not bear his vulgarity. After her father Auletes had been restored to the throne by Pompey, he killed his eldest daughter but soon died of disease himself. Cleopatra was declared queen alongside her oldest brother, but he quickly conspired to have her banished to Syria. But once Pompey had himself been defeated by Julius Caesar, the boy king was killed. Caesar then summoned back Cleopatra and set her up as queen, and indeed as his mistress, having a boy called

Caesarion by her. After Caesar had been assassinated, Mark Antony left for Egypt and held Cleopatra in such high esteem that he married her and had children by her. They then joined forces against Octavian at Actium.

The Gymnasium is probably the most conspicuous of the public buildings: its colonnades are more than a stade in length. If you climb the spiralling roads up the artificial hill known as the Paneum, you will be rewarded with an excellent view of the whole city. The imperial temple was constructed by Cleopatra for Mark Antony but was later dedicated to Octavian. It is worth spending some time here exploring its many porticoes, halls, libraries and parks, while the whole precinct is full of offerings from worshippers. Only the Capitol in Rome is greater.

The population is almost as innumerable as that of Rome. The city has flourished under Roman rule and this has attracted many new inhabitants, keen to make their fortune in this commercial place. As a whole, they are a most seditious, deceitful and menacing people. But their city is prosperous, rich and fruitful, and the people are certainly hard workers. Everywhere you go you will see them labouring: some are glass-blowers, or paper-makers, or linen weavers, and even the disabled have jobs, whether they are blind or maimed. The only god they really worship is money, and this is the one thing about which all the different religious groups agree.

The Jews live here in great numbers, occupying two of the five districts, but you will see synagogues all over the city. There are Greeks in large numbers, too, and a plethora of others from Ethiopia, Libya, Arabia, Persia and even India, so that Egyptians seem to make up only a small minority. The trade in luxury goods has made the city prosperous. You will find that success has made the Alexandrians arrogant and rude. They are impudent to their Roman governors and there are few public speakers who do not fear their cacophonous hisses, jeers and heckling. Indeed the whole city seems to wear a smirk on its face. Vespasian was a mild-mannered emperor but even he was so incensed by the abuse he received after putting up taxes – they said he smelled like a fish-dealer – that he was almost driven to punish the city. They are two-faced, as well. Hadrian found that, while he was in the city, the people were grateful for all the requests and gifts that he granted, but as soon as he left they mocked his son Verus and his lover Antinous. The people share the Roman plebs' love of entertainments, but the racing and theatre are their favourites, even though they do have an amphitheatre for gladiatorial fights. In fact, their greatest passion is for music and dance and woe betide a musician who hits a wrong note. They play a kind of fusion music that is a blend of the Greek and Egyptian styles and, if you like that sort of thing, you will find it easily in the backstreets of Rome. At least such music serves to calm the rabble and distract them from their complaints. The smallest incidents are always sparking off fights in the circus. It is said that governors walk in fear in Alexandria, always anxious that some mob will hurl stones at them. It is no wonder that the troops are always having to be called out to keep the peace.

Be very careful how you treat animals. A Roman visitor once kicked a cat so hard that it died. It turned out he had killed a sacred animal and nothing could save him from the baying crowd.

I made the mistake at one point of getting involved in a local dispute. Walking down a narrow alleyway, I came across two men who were pushing and shoving and taunting each other with the vilest abuse. Unable to pass easily I intervened and urged them to settle their differences peaceably. Seeing that I was a Roman and, judging by the size of my retinue, important, they immediately sought to persuade me of the rightness of their cause, with our guide acting as translator.

'I am Thouonis, son of Akousilaos, from the Arsinoite nome. I am arguing with this man because he owes me money. He is Bentetis, son of Bentetis, a herdsman of Oxyrhynchus, and he has tried to cheat me out of the pay and allowances which he owes me. He acted insultingly to me and to my wife Tanouris, daughter of Heronas. And he also mercilessly inflicted on my wife many blows on whatever parts of her body he could, even though she was pregnant, with the result that she gave birth to a dead child and she herself is now con-fined to bed and is in danger of her life.'

The other man butted in and rejected everything, saying that he had never even met Thouonis's wife and that he had paid him a fair price for his labour. I had no intention of trying to sort this out: 'You should petition the prefect and ask him to sort this out. That is what he is there for.' And with that I had my slaves push them aside and we were able to continue our tour without further quarrelsome interruptions.

You will find that many travellers come to Alexandria

in search of medical treatments and, should you have an ailment, this is the place to find a good doctor. The place itself promotes well-being: snow never falls in winter, roses bloom all year round, not a day passes without sunshine; and yet the sea winds cool the summer heat. All aspiring young doctors come here to learn their trade. Many other forms of expertise can be found in the city, from philosophy and law to astronomy and geometry. The best places to find these learned men is in the Academy founded by the Ptolemies, and in the Great Library, which is famed throughout the empire. Dedicated to the Muses, the goddesses of the arts, it was founded by the Ptolemies to promote Greek learning. How many tens of thousands of scrolls lie there. It used to be the case that only the finest scholars were granted membership but nowadays it is given as a reward to anyone who has significant achievements to his name, whether in the field of the military, the government or even sport.

Nowhere is more religious than Egypt. Serapis is perhaps the greatest of their gods, and his temple, which sits high on a small plateau overlooking the sea, is the finest of them all. Within the temple precinct you can see a marvellous statue of the god, as well as a branch of the Great Library. Patients flock there in order to receive the god's messages in their dreams.

After a few days I was tired of the city and so decided to make the brief journey up the coast to Canopus, allegedly founded by the Spartans in memory of their helmsman of that name, who was buried there when Menelaus, homeward bound for Greece, was blown across to the African coast. Canopus is a resort made for pleasure. With its refreshing sea breeze, the gentle murmur of the waves, and its sunny skies, it seems a world unto itself. The town is constantly alive with feasts and young men, and the air is full of the sounds of flutes and of wine goblets chinking together. It is always busy and draws in visitors by the thousand who come to enjoy the relaxed atmosphere. Indeed the Canopic life-style is proverbial for its luxury and debauchery. I stayed in one of the many hotels that sit on the banks of the canal that runs between Canopus and Alexandria. It was a very upmarket establishment. There are plenty of party boats, which sail up and down the canal, decked out in flowers. You can see the men and women dining on board, enjoying dancing girls performing to the music of the flute players. Often this descends into lewdness but you can usually tell what class of boat it is before you board.

A short trip inland on a camel or upstream on a Nile boat will transfer you from the hubbub of Alexandria to the awesome tranquillity of the most ancient edifices. We began by visiting the next of the river mouths, the one which is sacred to Hercules, who was, according to the locals, Egyptian-born. There is no good wine grown in this part of the country and most of the people here drink beer, which is easily produced from the bountiful harvest of barley. Next, one comes to the harbour Derrhis, so called because of the black rock that resembles an animal skin, and the neighbouring town of Zephyrium. Then one arrives at another harbour, Leucaspis, and several others, followed by Cynos-Sema and Taposeiris, which is inland and holds a great public festival, but should not be confused with the Taposeiris on the other side of the river. Near here is a rocky place on the sea where crowds of people come to enjoy themselves every summer. And then you will come to Plinthine and to the village of Nicias, and to Cherronesus, a stronghold. Lake Mareotis extends from here as far as Alexandria, being more than one hundred and fifty stades wide and almost three hundred long. It contains eight islands and the wine grown near its shores is good enough to be laid down to age.

The marshes in the lower parts of the Nile Delta region are full of papyrus reeds. These plants grow to about ten feet in height and the stems are bare apart from a tuft at the top. The papyrus reed is very versatile and the stems can be used for making light boats suitable for river navigation while the tougher roots can be used to make furniture or as firewood. The tough outer layer of the stem can be woven into baskets, mats or ropes, or into tough canvas suitable for use as sandals or sails. The central part of the stem can be chewed, either raw or boiled, to provide energy, although the locals swallow only the juice not the fibrous stem itself.

To make paper, the outer skin of the papyrus stem is removed and the inner layers are peeled off. The leaves which are closest to the stem produce the best-quality paper. These strips are laid next to each other in two rows at right angles to each other on a table. Traditionally these are then moistened with Nile water but most now use paper paste. Ordinary paper paste is made from the finest flour mixed with boiling water to which a few drops of vinegar are added. The paper produced from this is quite brittle. The best-quality paste is made from boiling crumbs of leavened bread and then straining off the water. This produces paper with the fewest seams, caused by the paste that lies between the leaves, and is particularly soft. The paper is then thinned out with a mallet, after which a new layer of paste is placed upon it. Then the creases that will have formed are again pressed out with a mallet and the paper is dried in the hot Egyptian sun. Any areas of roughness or imperfections in the paper are smoothed down with a piece of ivory or a shell, although the writing in such places is very likely to fade because this kind of polishing means that the paper does not take the ink so readily.

Paper is judged according to its fineness, its strength, its whiteness and its smoothness. The best paper used to be known as Sacred paper because it was reserved for holy books, but it has been renamed Augusta, in honour of the emperor. This paper is thirteen fingers wide. The second-best paper is named Liviana after Augustus's wife. Sacred paper is now the third-best. There are nine different grades in total with the next being known as Amphitheatrical, because of the area where it is produced in Alexandria, and is ten fingers wide. This kind of paper was improved by using a technique developed by Fannius in Rome, and is called Fanniana after him. Next best is Saitic paper, so called from the city of that name, where it is manufactured in very large quantities from lower-quality leaves. Taeniotic paper, again named after the place of its production, is made from the rougher outer leaves and is sold by weight rather than quality. As for Shop paper, it is completely useless for writing upon but is useful for wrapping things up, hence its name. Finally comes the bark of the papyrus, which is used only for making ropes.

The emperor Claudius brought in a change to the manufacture of Augustan paper because it was almost too good to use. The paper was so fine that it offered no resistance to the pressure of the pen and so thin that the ink would often pass through it to the other side. It was also almost transparent, which made it rather difficult to read. Claudius had a base layer of leaves of the second quality inserted in the middle of the paper in order to solve these problems and Claudian paper has thus become the paper of choice, although Augustan is still often used for important correspondence.

Paper is made in great quantities in this way and is exported all over the empire. The production of the reed is an imperial monopoly because of its importance in governmental record-keeping. Its cost means that you should use both sides of the paper. It is best to start with the side in which the fibres of the reed run in the same direction as the writing, as this is both easier and produces a clearer text, particularly if the document is important or you intend to send it as a letter. Use the other side for more administrative tasks. The paper can be reused by writing over earlier texts, preferably at right angles to the earlier script, either in different ink or when the earlier ink has faded.

As you sail upriver towards Memphis, you encounter many villages, the most pleasant of which are Hermupolis and Gynaeconpolis, the city of women. There are also several canals which empty into Lake Mareotis. Nearby are two nitre beds. The god Serapis is worshipped here and it is the only place in Egypt where people sacrifice sheep. A short distance above the town of Saïs you come to the place where the body of Osiris is said to lie. Many other towns, however, also claim this honour, in particular the inhabitants of Philae in the south. They claim that Isis placed coffins beneath the earth in several places but that only one of them actually contained the body of Osiris because the god was worried that Osiris's brother and killer, Set, would try to dig up the corpse and leave it unburied.

The Nile is Egypt. Without its nourishing waters it would be a barren country. Instead it leaves a rich ribbon of produce in its wake. It begins at the borders of Ethiopia and flows north in a straight line to the region called 'Delta', because it resembles the Greek letter. The Nile makes a triangle, with the sides being formed by the streams that split in either direction and extend to the sea, the one on the right flowing to the sea at Pelusium, the other on the left to the sea at Canopus, but there are, in addition, several smaller outlets in between. Eyewitnesses have perceived that the Nile is flooded by summer rains from Ethiopia, particularly in the region of its farthermost mountains. This fact was particularly clear to those who navigated the Arabian Gulf as far as the cinnamon-bearing country. But what is still unclear to this day is why on earth these rains fall in summer but not in winter.

Timaeus the mathematician has suggested another reason for the flooding. He says that the source of the river is known by the name of Phiala, and that the stream buries itself in channels underground, where it sends forth steam generated by the heat among the hot rocks. But during the flood, because the sun is nearer to the earth in summer and so hotter, the waters are drawn forth by the influence of this heat, and, on being thus exposed to the air, overflow. After this, the stream hides itself again in order to stop from being utterly dried up. He says that this takes place at the rising of the Dog Star, when the sun enters the sign of Leo and stands in a vertical position over the source of the river. Most authors, however, are of the opposite opinion, and argue that the river flows in greater volume when the sun takes its departure for the north, which it does when it enters the signs of Cancer and Leo, because its waters then are not dried up to so great an extent. By contrast, when the sun returns towards the south pole and re-enters Capricorn, the river's waters are absorbed by the heat, and consequently flow in less abundance.

The locals work to support an ancient system of irrigation. The land is divided by dykes into large fields that look like basins, and which contain small canals to allow floodwater to flow both in and out. The exits are then dammed to leave the waters trapped in the basins for more than a month. The soil is saturated and the waters deposit their silt, thereby replacing the fertility that has been drained from them in the growing season. The waters are then allowed to flow back into the river. At this point the growing season starts in earnest, and the peasants spill out into the fields to begin sowing, with the harvest following about four months later. If the flood is small then only the fields closest to the river can be filled with water and a famine is thus certain to result, since not enough food can be grown to feed everyone. Equally, if the flood is excessive then the drainage channels and canals are overwhelmed and the fields do not benefit. But in a normal year, even the upper fields furthest from the river are filled and there ensues a generous harvest, which is enough to feed both the Egyptians and the masses in Rome.

When the river is most swollen, the whole of Egypt resembles a lake, which the cities stick out of like islands, and the waters are filled with small boats criss-crossing from one place to another. It is an ideal river to travel on. The water flows northwards but the wind blows southwards, making travel easy in either direction. The river is almost always calm, apart from when it is swollen in summer. Like many travellers, I had my slaves fill several flasks with Nile water as presents for those back in Rome who worship Isis. The locals drink the water in order to promote fecundity in their womenfolk. I have heard it reported that as many as seven children are sometimes produced at one birth as a result.

Blessed are the people who live on the shores of the Nile, happily sailing through the land in their boats, surrounded by waters in which white lotuses grow thickly, and on which many birds swim, and in which can be seen a hippopotamus lurking in the reeds or a crocodile silently watching for a chance to snap up its prey. On the banks you will spy snakes slithering along the water's edge and ibises preening their feathers with their bent beaks. Palm trees hang over the whole scene and the locals clamber up these by means of ropes in which knots have been tied. I have had a large mosaic made at my villa in Rome that brings all of these Nilotic features into one very satisfying whole.

Heliopolis is worth a small detour. It is said that in ancient times this town was a settlement of priests who studied philosophy and astronomy, although none of the priests there now pursue these subjects, spending their time performing the sacrifices and explaining to tourists what the sacred rites entail. You can see the large houses in which the academic priests used to live, including the houses where Plato and Eudoxus studied. They both spent several years there because of the priests' excellent knowledge of the movements of the heavenly bodies. Eventually, Plato and Eudoxus persuaded some of them to divulge the principles of their doctrines, such as the fractions of the day that should be added to 365 to make a true year. They calculated this by dividing the year into twelve months of thirty days each, and at the end of the twelve months added five days, and then at the end of every fourth year added another day.

From Heliopolis, you come to the Nile above the Delta. For me, this upper Nile is the real Egypt. Sailing upriver, you will soon be able to see the pyramids clearly on the far side of the river at Memphis. The city is both large and populous, and ranks second only to Alexandria. The locals consist of a variety of peoples. But the reason to visit Memphis is that it was the royal residence of the ancient Egyptians. The palaces, which now lie in ruins and are deserted, are located on a hill and extend down to the level of the city below. The place is full of temples, including the famous temple of Apis, the bull god, who is the same as Osiris. It is here that the sacred bull is kept in a kind of sanctuary, and the animal is regarded as being a god. The bull is black, and his forehead is marked with a triangular white spot, and on his back is an image of an eagle. It is by means of these marks that the priests identify the bull suitable for the succession after the current bull has died. In front of the sanctuary you will find a court, in which there is another sanctuary belonging to the bull's mother. Into this court they set Apis loose at a certain hour of the day, primarily so that he can be seen by tourists. It is possible to see him through the window in the sanctuary, but the priests also like him to go out for exercise, and after he has finished a short bout of skipping and bucking in the court they take him back again to his stall inside.

Near to here lies the Hephaesteium, the temple of the Greek god of fire, which is a costly structure in all respects. In front of it stands a square with a colossal statue made of a single piece of stone, and it is here that the locals customarily hold bullfights. Breeders rear bulls specially for this purpose, and the bulls are set loose and fight each other. The one that is regarded as the winner is given a prize. And at Memphis you can see a temple of the Greek goddess Aphrodite, although some say that it is a temple of the moon goddess, Selene. There is also a temple of Serapis at Memphis, in a place that is so sandy that dunes are created by the wind. Even some of the colonnade of sphinxes, which leads up to the temple, lie buried up to the head or are only half-visible.

Not even the sands of Egypt, however, can obliterate

the huge pyramids. You can see them from far off, so huge
are they, lying on a desolate rocky plain. They look like
hills sitting in the middle of sand dunes. As you approach
you can see that each side is smooth with stone right up
to the apex, stone that is covered, as you see as you get
closer still, with hieroglyphs. For a small fee, boys from
the local town of Busiris will climb up these smooth
slopes for your entertainment.

In truth, it must be said that the pyramids rank as one
of the most superfluous and foolish displays of wealth
in history. It is generally recorded that the pharaohs'
motives for building them were twofold: first, to avoid
having so much money that it might encourage their
heirs or potential rivals to plot against them; and second,
just to keep the ordinary people occupied. They are tre-
mendously vain enterprises, and the remains of several
unfinished pyramids are still in existence, where the
pharaoh either died or the money ran out. There is one
in the district of Arsinoe, and there are two in that of
Memphis, not far from the labyrinth, a building that I
will come to later. The completed three pyramids, the
fame of which has reached every part of the world, are
visible to travellers approaching by river from any direction. In front of them sits the Sphinx, that huge lion
with a human head, which really deserves to be more
famous than the pyramids. The inhabitants of the region
regard this monstrous creature as a god and its face is
painted with red ochre as a sign of reverence. They
believe that a pharaoh called Harmais is buried inside it
and that it was carried to the spot where it now stands.
It is in fact carefully fashioned from the native rock. The

circumference of the head when measured across the forehead amounts to 102 feet, the length is 243 feet, and the height from the paunch to the top of the asp on its head is 61 feet.

The largest pyramid is made of stone from the Arabian quarries. It is said that it took 360,000 men twenty years to build it and that the time taken to finish all three was eighty-eight years and four months. Many authors have written about the pyramids, such as Herodotus, Aristagoras, Dionysius and Demetrius, but they do not agree about which kings were responsible for their construction, since chance, with the greatest justice, has caused those who inspired such a mighty display of vanity to be forgotten. Some of these writers record that in feeding the workers, 1,600 talents were spent on radishes, garlic and onions alone. Each of the four sides of the largest pyramid measures 783 feet from corner to corner and is 725 feet in height. High up, approximately in the centre of the northern face, there is a movable stone, and when this is raised up you can enter a steeply sloping passage that leads to the royal vault. As for the second pyramid, this is only a little smaller. The third is markedly smaller but is far more splendid, built as it is with black stone from the Ethiopian mountains. No one has any idea of how the masonry was laid to such a great height. Some think that ramps of soda and salt were piled against the structure as it was raised, and that after its completion these were flooded and dissolved by water from the river. The problem with this theory is that the Nile flows at a much lower level and so could not have flooded the site. Others argue that bridges were built of mud bricks and that, when the work was finished, the bricks were given to individuals for building houses. The Egyptian priests claim that the depth of the pyramids underground is equal to their height but I saw nothing that led me to believe this to be true.

One of the marvellous things I saw at the pyramids should not be omitted: there are heaps of stone chips lying in front of them, and if you search among them you will find chips that are like lentils in both shape and size and others that resemble half-peeled grains. They say that these were what was left of the food of the workmen, which has petrified over time. I do not think this is probable. Indeed, I have visited a plain in Pontus where there is a long hill that is full of lentil-shaped pebbles of porous stone. One other story worth relating is that in the neighbourhood of the nearby quarry where the stone was cut to build the pyramids you can find a rocky mountain called 'Trojan' and a village next to it called Troy. It is believed that this was founded by some of the captured Trojans who came with Menelaus to Egypt but managed to escape and then settled there.

Such are the wonders of the pyramids. Perhaps the last and greatest of these wonders, which makes us realise the stupidity of these rich kings, is that the smallest but most greatly admired of these pyramids was built for Rhodopis, a mere prostitute. She was once the fellow slave and concubine of Aesop, the wise man who composed the Fables. The Egyptians tell the story that, when she was bathing, an eagle snatched one of her sandals and carried it to Memphis, where the king was holding court in the open air. When it flew above his head, the eagle dropped the sandal into his lap, and the king, amazed at both the beautiful shape of the sandal and at the strangeness of the occurrence, sent men in all directions into the country in search of the woman whose sandal it was. When she was found, she was brought up to Memphis, became the wife of the king, and when she died was honoured with this splendid tomb. It is certainly amazing just how many Greek and Roman tourists visit the pyramids and you can see their names carved into the surface of the stone. I saw one carved by the sister of Gaius Terentius Gentianus, who became a consul under the emperors Trajan and Hadrian, where she dedicated her inscription to the memory of her 'sweet brother' who had recently died. There are many other such carvings on the claw of the sphinx.

After Memphis you come to the city of Aphroditopolis, where a sacred white cow is kept. Then you reach the Arsinoite district. This region is the most noteworthy in respect of its appearance, its fertility, and its material development, for it alone is planted with olive trees that are large, full-grown and bear fine fruit, and it would also produce good olive oil if the fruit were carefully gathered. But since it is not, the oil that the trees produce, in large quantities, has a bad smell. The rest of Egypt has no olives trees, apart from the gardens near Alexandria, where they are sufficient for supplying olives, but yield no oil. The district also produces large quantities of wine, as well as grain and all kinds of pulse. It also contains the wonderful lake called Lake Moeris, which is like an open sea in size and has the colour of a sea, too. The lake is large enough that it can bear the floodwaters of the Nile without overflowing into the neighbouring areas. Locks have been added at the mouths of the lake by which the engineers can regulate both the inflow and the outflow of the water.

The famous labyrinth can also be found in this district. It consists of a great palace composed of many smaller palaces and contains numerous courts, surrounded by colonnades, all joined up in a single row along a wall. In front of the entrances are crypts, which are long and numerous and have winding passages communicating with one another, so that no stranger can find his way either into or out of any court without a guide. Doors are set into the walls at frequent intervals to suggest, deceptively, the way ahead, and to force the visitor to retreat along the very same tracks that he has already followed in his wanderings. Each of the courts is supported by twenty-seven monolithic pillars and, at the end of this building, is the tomb, a large square pyramid. Imandes is the name of the man buried there and it is said that the number of courts equates to the number of his provinces, representatives from each of which would assemble there to sacrifice to the gods and meet the king about matters of importance. But the most amazing thing is that the roof of each of the chambers consists of a single stone of huge size. You can go up there and it is like looking out on a plain of stone. The entire structure is made of Aswan granite, great blocks of which have been laid in such a way that even the lapse of centuries cannot destroy them. Their preservation has been aided by the people of Heracleopolis, who have shown remarkable respect for an achievement they detest.

The city of Arsinoe used to be called Crocodilopolis. This was because the people here hold the crocodile in very great honour and there is a sacred tame one, called Suchus, which is kept by itself in a lake and cared for by priests. It is fed on grain, wine and pieces of meat, and you can feed these to the creature if you go and see it, as many foreigners do. We were given a tour by one of the city officials and some of the priests, who brought with them some roast meat and a pitcher of wine mixed with honey. We found the animal lying on the edge of the lake and it clearly recognised the priests' voices and walked towards them. The priests went up to it, then some of them opened its mouth while another put in the cake, and again the meat, and then poured down the honey mixture, before cleaning its teeth with linen cloths. The animal then leapt into the lake and rushed across to the far side.

After the Arsinoite district you will come to the city of Heracles. But whereas the people of Arsinoe hold the crocodile in honour (which, incidentally, explains why Lake Moeris is full of crocodiles, because the people refuse to hunt them), here the people revere the mongoose known as Pharaoh's Cat, which is the deadly enemy of the crocodile. When the crocodiles are basking in the sun with their mouths open the mongooses throw themselves into their open jaws, eat through their entrails and bellies, and emerge from their dead bodies. The animals are also hostile to the asp, for they destroy not only its eggs but also the asp itself, having armed themselves with a breastplate of mud by rolling in it and then drying themselves in the sun. They then seize the asp either by the head or tail, drag it into the river and drown it.

The next city on the tour is Cynonpolis, the city of the dogs. Here Anubis, the god of the underworld with a dog's head, is held in honour, and a form of worship and sacred feeding has been organised for all dogs. On the far side of the river lies the city of Oxyrhynchus, the city of the sharp-nosed fish, which they similarly hold in honour, although this is true of all Egypt. You will find that the bull, the dog and the cat are also worshipped throughout Egypt, as are the hawk and ibis, and the scale fish. Certain animals are held in honour in particular districts, for example the sheep in Thebes, the dog-faced baboon by the citizens of Hermopolis, and the goat by the Mendesians. People do not agree on the reasons for such worship. But what is clear to all, and utterly extraordinary, is how much care and attention even the most distinguished locals lavish on these sacred animals. They feed them with the best food, soak them in warm baths, anoint them with scents, lay them in splendid beds, provide them with mates, and spend vast sums on their funerals.

Inland from here you can still visit the shrine at Ammon and consult the oracle there, although the place is almost abandoned. Among the ancients, both divination and oracles were held in great honour, but now they are being largely neglected, mainly because the Romans are satisfied with the books of Sibyl and with prophecies obtained by means of the entrails of animals, the flight of birds and omens from the sky. It is clear how things have changed when one considers the pains that Alexander the Great took to consult the oracle at Ammon. It is recorded that Alexander conceived a very great ambition to do this, since he had heard that Perseus and Hercules had done so in earlier times. He struggled to reach the place through a sandstorm and was only saved by the guidance of two crows. The priest permitted the king to enter the temple where the oracular responses were given, not in the form of words as at Delphi, but in nods and signs, and Alexander was expressly told that he was the son of Zeus. And immediately a sacred spring that had lain dormant since the Persian Wars began to flow again.

At Abydos they revere Osiris, but in the god's temple no singer, flute player or harp player is permitted to play the rites in his honour, as is the custom with other deities. After Abydos one comes to Little Diospolis, and to the city of Tentyra, where the people, in contrast to other Egyptians, view the crocodile as the most hateful of animals and they hunt it in every way they can. Some say that there is a kind of natural antipathy between the Tentyrites and crocodiles, with the result that the animals never attack them and the people can swim in the river without fear. When crocodiles were brought to Rome for an exhibition, they were accompanied by men from Tentyra, who would get into the water and drag them into a position where they could be seen by the spectators.

You are now entering the territory of Thebes, although that city still lies much further upriver and before it you will come to the city of Hermopolis. This is an important place that serves as the centre of the administrative region that surrounds it. The local official who acted as my guide told me that there are almost seven thousand houses here. Thebes is surrounded by a wall, within which lie two main sectors: the temple precinct in the north, and the residential area to the south, which contains most of its civic amenities as well as several more temples and shrines. The main street runs from just outside the southern limit of the temple precinct, from the Gate of the Moon in the west to the Gate of the Sun in the east, and it is a pleasure to stroll along it and take in the many impressive buildings. There are the temples of Fortuna and of Athene, and also that of Aphrodite, who is associated with the Egyptian god Isis. There is an assembly point from where religious processions set out; temples of Serapis and of the Nile; a marketplace; and a covered market where you can buy all kinds of local delicacies and imported wares. Then there are two further temples, of Hadrian and his ill-fated lover Antinous, who died when travelling along the Nile, perhaps by drowning, perhaps, some say, as a human sacrifice, and whom the devastated emperor made a god, even founding a city in his honour on the far side of the riverbank. All along the course of the main road you will find water basins and fountains to refresh yourself, and there are numerous colonnades where you can find shady relief from the heat of the sun.

The precinct in the northern part of the city is surrounded by a massive wall. Inside stands the great temple of Thoth-Hermes, a most imposing building with a facade that is 150 feet in length. Thoth, I should explain, is the ibis god and you will see him pictured throughout

Egypt. He is the god of writing because when the bird weaves its long, curved bill from side to side through the water in search of food, it looks as if it is writing on the surface. It has to be said that the temple is not in the best state of repair and there are very few priests and temple guards left in service. Centuries of domination by first the Greeks and then the Romans have doubtless left the locals less enthusiastic about the power of their own gods, and they have instead turned to the gods of those who have conquered them, not least the emperor, and you will find numerous monuments dedicated to the imperial cult throughout the city. The priests will, if you pay them, show you the immortal ibis, which is kept there.

Next we sailed until we reached the vast remains of ancient Thebes. Of all the wonderful sites to visit in Egypt, Thebes is undoubtedly the greatest. Homer describes Thebes as the city of the hundred gates, from which sally forth two hundred men with horses and chariots. And the bard speaks of its wealth too. Now everywhere you look there are huge piles of masonry on which many Egyptian letters still remain. We hired one of the senior priests and asked him to interpret the writings and he informed us that 'once the city contained seven hundred thousand men of military age, and with this huge army King Rameses conquered Libya and Ethiopia, the Medes and the Persians, and the lands where the Syrians, Armenians and Cappadocians dwell'. The tribute lists of the subject nations were still legible, and these recorded how much silver and gold, the number of weapons and horses, what quantities of ivory and spices, as well as grain and other basic commodities, were to be paid by each subject nation. The revenues raised in this way were no less than are extracted by the Roman government today. Staring at the decaying magnificence of this once great empire, whose ruins stretch for two miles on each side of the river, it was impossible not to contemplate whether such a fate awaits Rome. Here was a kingdom that had almost equalled ours in might and from which all power has been stripped.

Egypt is now a mere province of our empire. It pays considerable tribute, especially in the form of its bountiful grain supplies. It is governed by a Roman prefect, who is treated by the locals as if he were a king. Second to him are the minister of justice and the idiologus, who arbitrates in property matters. Three legions of soldiers are stationed in Egypt, one of which is in the city of Alexandria, with the others in the country. An additional nine cohorts of auxiliary troops and three cavalry regiments are posted at various strategic points. Various local officials report to their Roman superiors. There is the interpreter, who wears purple and has certain hereditary prerogatives, and represents the interests of the city. Then there is the recorder, the chief judge and the night commander, in addition to many local officials who report to these senior Egyptian administrators. In terms of the revenues that Egypt generates, Cleopatra's father received tribute of 12,500 talents. Given that he was a useless monarch, imagine how much more money is created under Rome's diligent administration, which has seen trade with the East balloon. In the past, only the occasional ship dared to cross the Arabian Gulf and peek out of the straits, but nowadays large fleets sail boldly for India and the farthest reaches of Ethiopia, from which valuable cargoes are brought back and taxed.

The power of ancient Egypt was reflected in its peculiar passion for obelisks, which you can see among the ruins at Thebes but also at Memphis and Alexandria. These huge towers, carved from a single block of stone, were set up by the pharaohs out of rivalry with one another. They were dedicated to the sun god, an obelisk being a representation of the sun's rays, which is what the word means in Egyptian. The first of all the kings to undertake such a task was Mesphres, who ruled at Heliopolis, the city of the sun, and he was commanded to do so in a dream, a fact that is inscribed on the obelisk. Later, other kings also cut obelisks. Sesothes set up four of them in the same city, while Rameses, who ruled at the time of the capture of Troy, erected one of 140 cubits in height. Rameses also erected another of 120 cubits at the exit from the precinct where the palace of Mnevis once stood, and this work is said to have required one hundred and twenty thousand men. When the obelisk was about to be erected, the king feared that the scaffolding would not be strong enough for the weight, and in order to focus the workmen's minds he himself tied his own son to the pinnacle. This obelisk was so greatly admired that when Cambyses was storming the city, and the conflagration had reached the base of the obelisk, he ordered the fires to be put out. There are two other obelisks here, one set up by Zmarres, and the other by Phius. At Alexandria, Ptolemy Philadelphus erected one of 80 cubits. This had been hewn, but left without inscription, by King Necthebis, and it proved to be a greater achievement to carry it down the river and erect it than to have it quarried. According to some authorities, it was carried downstream by the engineer Satyrus on a raft; but according to Callixenus it was conveyed by the engineer Phoenix, who dug a canal right up to the place where the obelisk lay.

I mentioned earlier the great ships that were required for the difficult task of transporting obelisks to Rome by sea. Then there is another problem, that of providing ships that can carry obelisks up the Tiber. The success in doing so has proved that the river has just as deep a channel as the Nile. The obelisk placed by the deified Augustus in the Circus Maximus was cut by King Psemetnepserphreus, who was reigning when Pythagoras was in Egypt, and measures 85 feet and 9 inches, apart from its base, which forms part of the same stone. The obelisk in the Campus Martius, however, which is 9 feet less, was cut by Sesothis. Both have inscriptions comprising an account of natural science according to the theories of the Egyptian sages. The one in the Campus was put to use in a remarkable way by the deified Augustus, as the marker in his great sundial. The third obelisk in Rome stands in the circus that was built by the emperors Gaius and Nero. It was the only one of the three that was broken during its removal.

Thebes is home to the highlight of any tour of Egypt and none would be complete without it. On the west bank of the river lies a great expanse of ancient ruins, all strewn with the remains of walls and columns and statues. Among these lowly fragments tower two colossal stone statues, visible from a great distance, both over 60 feet high. Naked from the waist up, they wear a youthful expression, and sit tall on their thrones with their arms close by their sides and with their hands on their knees. Shortly after the divine Augustus became the first emperor, an earthquake shattered off the top half of one of these great statues, leaving only the knees and hands on the throne. Then suddenly the statue began to talk.

The statue is of the god Memnon, the child of the goddess of dawn who was killed by Achilles after he had founded these palaces, and who had helped to defend Troy against the Greeks. Each day, at dawn, the remains of the god's statue speaks to his shining mother as she appears, greeting her welcome return. You will need to get up early to have time to journey there before sunrise. When I went, there was a small crowd of tourists assembled around the base. For a while there was nothing but silence and the anxious shuffling of the expectant visitors. But then, as the sun's rays were pouring out across the sky and the vast statues were casting their long shadows along the ground, a sharp cracking noise was distinctly audible. It sounded like the string of an instrument breaking or perhaps a bang on a copper vessel, and it was not unlike a human voice. Before, I had been sceptical about whether the noise really came from the colossus, or whether the sound was made on purpose by one of the men who were standing all round. But now that I have heard it for myself, I have no doubt at all.

To commemorate my visit and to thank the god for his communication I cut my name on to one of the legs of the statue. Many others have done this, including some distinguished visitors, to the extent that the writing now covers the statue's legs almost up to the knees. The emperor Hadrian's name is there, as is that of his wife, Sabina. I counted eight prefects of Egypt, and two high-ranking judges, and a priest of Serapis at Alexandria. Obviously, you do not do the cutting yourself but pay one of the local stonemasons, who hang around there in search of such work. Since Memnon was a hero of the Trojan War, I composed a brief verse in Greek in the style of Homer:

O lordly Memnon thou spokest so loud,
when rose-fingered Dawn broke through.

Above the statue of Memnon are caves in which are situated the tombs of the kings. There are about forty of these, all made of stone and marvellously constructed. The valley where they are to be found lies to the west of Thebes and is a desolate place. Not a bush or a blade of grass can survive on the barren rocks or the yellow cliffs, and it is the home of jackals and hyenas. The tombs are vaults and passages dug deep into the rocks. You will need a guide to show you along the lengthy corridors in which the tombs lie. Make sure that your guide pauses at the entrance to these 'pipes', as the Greeks call them, so that you can adjust to the coolness of the air and the darkness, which is alleviated only by the burning torches you bring with you. It is a good opportunity to enjoy the scrawlings of previous visitors. Some are from grand men: 'I Palladius of Hermopolis, a judge, saw and was amazed'; others display genuine awe: 'Those who have not seen this, have seen nothing; happy are they that have'; or, as one gushed, 'Unique! Unique! Unique!'

After Thebes, you will come to the city of Hermonthis, where both Apollo and Zeus are worshipped. A sacred bull is kept here. Then you will arrive at a City of Crocodiles, which holds in honour that animal, followed by a City of Aphrodite, and, after this, to Latopolis, which holds in honour Athene. On the far side of the river you will come to the City of Hawks, which holds the hawk in honour, and then to Apollonospolis, which is a place that hates crocodiles. The final two places I visited were Syene and Elephantine. The first of these is a city on the borders of Ethiopia, the second an island in the Nile, just in front of Syene. This island contains a temple of Cnuphis and a nilometer. The nilometer is a well on the bank of the Nile constructed with close-fitting stones. The water in the well rises and falls in line with the river and there are marks showing the highest, lowest and average levels of the flood. Observers keep an eye on the level of the water each year and let it be known how each year's flood compares with previous years. This is very useful, not only to farmers for the management of the irrigation system, but also to government officials with regard to expected future revenues, since the harvest generally improves in accordance with the size of the flood and so, therefore, does the tax raised. Herodotus often talks a lot of nonsense, embellishing his account with marvellous tales, to give it, as it were, a kind of rhythm or relish. He asserts that the source of the Nile is in the neighbourhood of the islands near Syene and Elephantine (of which there are several), and that at this place its channel has a bottomless depth, when this is clearly not the case.

If you happen to be in Elephantine and Syene at the time of the summer equinox you can see a wonderful natural sight. At midday, there is no shade, and even obelisks, temples and the tallest men cast no shadow but stand in full sunshine. At Syene, there is a sacred well and it is possible to be lowered to the very bottom of this and still be able to see the sun. The Little Cataracts of the Nile above Syene are also much visited. Here, the stream at high water flows over a rocky island in the middle of its bed, and is calm on either side. Whenever tourists come to see the waterfall, the local boatmen will row upstream on rafts beyond the cataract and then let themselves be hurled back over the rapids, without coming to any harm. Some visitors are even brave enough to try it for themselves.

This was as far as my journey took me into Egypt. It is possible to travel further towards Ethiopia but most travellers turn back at this point or even earlier, at Thebes. I can tell you little about Ethiopia. In general, the extremities of the inhabited world, which are intemperate and almost uninhabitable because of heat or cold, make living in them very difficult. This is true of the Ethiopians, who lead for the most part a nomadic and resourceless life, on account of the barrenness of the country and of the unseasonableness of its climate. Their life is hard, and they go about almost naked. Their domestic animals – sheep, goats and cattle – are small, as are their dogs. The Ethiopians live on millet and barley, from which they also make a drink. They use butter and tallow instead of olive oil, and have no fruit trees, except for a few date palms in the royal gardens. Some of them eat grass as well as tender twigs, lotus and reed roots, but they also eat meat, blood, milk and cheese. The Ethiopians use long wooden bows, and they arm their women also, most of whom have a copper ring through the lip. They wear sheepskins, since they have no wool, their sheep having hair like that of goats. As for the dead, some are cast into the river, others are enclosed in glass and kept at home, and others still are buried around their temples in coffins made of clay.

They appoint as kings those who excel in beauty, or in superiority in cattle breeding, or in courage, or in wealth. They believe that their kings are gods, and the greatest royal seat is Meroe, a city on an island said to be like an oblong shield in shape. The island has both numerous mountains and large thickets and is inhabited partly by nomads, partly by hunters, and partly by farmers. It has mines of copper, iron and gold, and of different kinds of precious stones. The following is also an Ethiopian custom: whenever a king is maimed in any part of his body in any way whatsoever, his closest associates suffer the same thing, and they even die with him. The result is that these men guard the king extremely carefully. That is enough about the Ethiopians.

Regarding Egypt, I should just add that the statement of Herodotus is true, that it is an Egyptian custom to knead mud with their hands, but dough for bread with their feet. Kiki is a kind of fruit sown in the fields, from which oil is pressed, and which is used not only in lamps by almost all the people in the country, but also for anointing the body by the poorer classes and those who do the heavier labour, both men and women. So much for Egypt.

·· COMMENTARY ··

 Egypt had always been synonymous with the exotic in the Roman imagination and the defeat of Antony and Cleopatra by Augustus meant that Romans had the opportunity to see the physical reality for themselves. Tacitus recounts how the popular general Germanicus embarked on a sight-seeing tour of the province in 19 CE (*Annals* 2.59–60) and saw all the great monuments that were to become staples of the later grand tour. The Romans seemed to love everything Egyptian, from its animals and plants to its monuments and magic, and this fascination can be seen in the popularity of nilotic scenes in the mosaics and wall paintings of wealthy Romans' villas. An excellent early example of this is the mosaic of Palestrina, near Rome, dating from the first century BCE, which features images of various Nile animals, ancient temples, and Ethiopians in hunting scenes; and several more have also been uncovered from Pompeii. Hadrian even incorporated a mock Canopus into his imperial gardens at Tivoli.

Obelisks were another focus of the Roman interest in ancient Egypt. Augustus brought two obelisks from

Heliopolis: one to use in his giant sundial, the other to stand along the central spine of the Circus Maximus, both symbolising his conquest of the country. But he also did so because the ordinary people of Rome shared something of this fascination with Egypt. A second obelisk was added to the Circus by the emperor Constantius II in the mid fourth century. This huge stone was over 100 feet high and weighed more than 450 tonnes. It is the largest Egyptian obelisk to survive and now stands in front of St John Lateran in Rome. Moving this great block of stone from Karnak across the sea and standing it in the Circus was no mean feat. The historian Ammianus describes the logistical effort it required. It was brought down the Nile by barge, where a specially constructed ship awaited it at Alexandria for the journey to Rome (Ammianus Marcellinus, *Histories* 17.4.13). This ship, larger than any ever built, needed three hundred rowers to move it, and it sailed up the Tiber to within three miles of Rome itself. From there, the obelisk was put on a sledge and was pulled inch by inch to the Circus. It then had to be set upright. So many wooden shafts were placed around it that it was said to look as if it was surrounded by a forest of beams. Bit by bit, the obelisk was hauled up into the air until thousands of men managed to pull it into the correct place in the centre of the Circus. Pliny the Elder contains a description of the history of obelisks (*Natural History* 36.70).

Many Roman accounts of travels in Egypt note that the local temples were in decline and that the number of priests was dwindling. In their eyes, this was a reasonable response to the fact that Egyptian gods had been overpowered by those, first of all, of Greece, when Alexander invaded, and then by those of Rome. When Roman tourists visited these temples it served to reduce local beliefs to a sideshow, turning their ancient religious significance into a mere entertainment for the economically powerful visitor. And yet, back in Rome, interest in new eastern religions grew steadily, as many Romans sought a more personal, internalised experience than that offered by the ritual of traditional Roman religion. Juvenal talks in his sixth satire of people bringing back Nile water to use in Isis worship. For him, this was clearly meant pejoratively, but we can interpret the taking back of such gifts as a physical representation of the absorption of eastern and Egyptian ideas into more mainstream religious practice in the Roman world.

Ancient papyrus is often surprisingly strong even today and the dry conditions of Egypt have meant that many documents have survived that we do not have from elsewhere in the Roman empire. Many of these survived in rubbish dumps, which also means that we get a very different picture of everyday life in the province. One rich source is petitions, which people sent to the governor or his representatives asking for justice in some kind of dispute, often involving what seem very modest amounts of money or possessions. It is striking how often these local disputes became violent. The argument described by Falx is based on a petition from 47 CE between a herdsman and a worker who claimed that he was owed back pay (*P. Mich.* 228). The texts certainly give a clear sense of the competitive world most ordinary Egyptians inhabited. But petitioning the Roman governor was not straightforward. The petition had to be written in Greek, the language of government in Egypt since its conquest by Alexander. For most people this meant paying a scribe. We are not, therefore, hearing the authentic voice of ordinary Egyptians but their reported speech as written by the scribe.

The so-called statue of Memnon was a popular curiosity for tourists, for many the highlight of the trip (see Strabo, *Geography* 17.816; Pausanias, *Description of Greece* 1.42.3). The statue suddenly began to 'talk' in *c*.27 BCE after it broke in an earthquake. Presumably the noise was made by air escaping as it expanded in the heat of the rising sun but the story arose that it was the legendary Memnon greeting his mother, Dawn (the statues were in fact colossi of King Amenhotep III and were finished in 1350 BCE). Many tourists liked to record their visit by having their names and messages carved on the statue. This was not simply destructive graffiti since those who left messages included the emperor Hadrian and provincial governors. Carving a message or name to record a visit became standard tourist behaviour. The nearby Valley of the Kings has more than two thousand pieces of ancient tourist graffiti, most of which was scratched by hand. The message from a sister to her dead brother runs, 'I saw the pyramids without you, dearest brother. Sadly I shed tears here – which was all I could do for you – and mindful of our sorrow do I scribble this lament' (*Carmina Latina Epigraphica* 1.270). Some writers were moved to write poems, sometimes in the epic style of Homer. We can interpret this as another way of expressing Roman ownership of these historical sites but it was the famous sites themselves that had the cultural power to draw the Roman visitors towards them. And as with modern tourists, we find different levels of engagement. Some graffiti inscriptions record a profound, often religious experience, others simply list a name in an act of narcissistic pleasure. It was for the visitor to choose how deeply he or she engaged with the tourist site. Those written by later Christian tourists seem to leave only their names, refusing to be amazed by anything built by pagans. As for the talking Memnon, in a move that was disastrous for the local tourist trade, the emperor Septimius Severus, during his stay in Egypt in 202 CE, had the broken statue restored, a restoration that has lasted to the present day. But it stopped the statue of Memnon talking and the visitors soon stopped coming.

The Romans had a particular fascination with Alexander the Great and artefacts associated with that great conqueror were highly prized. A candelabrum in the shape of a fruit tree, which was taken as booty by Alexander when he captured the Greek city of Thebes, was dedicated by him to Apollo at the Greek city of Cumae, but was later transferred to the Temple of Apollo on the Palatine in Rome. Four statues that supported Alexander's own tent could also be seen in the capital: two in front of the Temple of Mars Ultor, and two in front of the Regia, where the Pontifex Maximus lived. Alexander's tomb could be found in the royal palace in Alexandria, his body lying in a glass sepulchre to permit easy viewing. By the time of the Roman conquest, the three-hundred-year-old mummified corpse was in a delicate state and, as Dio records, when the conquering Augustus touched it part of Alexander's nose fell off (Dio Cassius, *History of Rome* 51.16).

The description of the people of Alexandria is based on a letter attributed to Hadrian (*Augustan History*, Firmus, Saturninus, Proculus and Bonosus 8). The description of the labyrinth is based on Diodorus Siculus (*Library of History* 1.66.3) and Pliny the Elder (*Natural History* 36.19). The account of the sacred crocodile can be found in Strabo (*Geography* 17.811–12). The daredevils who risked riding the rapids at Syene are also recorded by Strabo (17.1.19). Visitors having a go at this extreme water sport included the Greek intellectual, Aelius Aristides (*Oration* 36.47–51).

ꞏ CHAPTER VII ꞏ

FROM AFRICA TO HISPANIA

B ACK AT ALEXANDRIA we made preparations to travel along the coast of Africa towards Hispania. Egyptian ships are widely thought to be the most seaworthy and I was keen to find one for what can be a perilous journey, especially as we were now towards the later part of the sailing season. Several of the monster Egyptian corn ships were lying at anchor waiting to be loaded with the harvest to transport it to Rome. Small crowds of spectators had gathered near the ships at the harbour edge to wonder at their colossal size, and to admire the height of the masts, their scarlet topsails, the huge yard-arms and the lofty sterns with their gradual curve and gilded beaks, balanced at the other end by the long rising sweep of the prow, with the figures of goddesses. People were having guided tours and were gawping at the huge sails, the thickness of the ropes, and the sheer size of the anchors, while watching the tanned sailors clamber fearlessly aloft in the rigging. The very largest of these grain ships can carry a thousand passengers.

I went up the gangplank to discuss obtaining a passage with the captain. The crew was like a small army. I heard some awestruck spectator claim that the ship carried as much corn as would feed every soul in Rome for a year, which is nonsense of course. It is quite extraordinary how such a great hulk can be controlled by one small man with a tiller the size of a broomstick. The captain was pointed out to me. He was called Heron and was a wiry, half-bald fellow, but clearly intelligent. He was headed for Puteoli, via Malta and Sicily, and we agreed a price to take us as far as Malta, from where it would be easy for us to pick up a smaller boat to transport us to Carthage. I asked him how much money the vessel brought in to her owner. Three thousand, he said, in a bad year. You can see this is a very lucrative business to be in. So long as the ships stay afloat, that is.

We set sail with a moderate wind from the direction of the lighthouse. These ships travel at a great clip and can cover as much as 1,200 stades in a single day and night. Puteoli would take only a little over a week if the winds were favourable. Which, thanks be to the gods, they were. We experienced heavy rain on the third night but, since I had been allocated a cabin next to the captain, I was unaffected, although I imagine the slaves on deck were soaked in their flimsy tents. In well under a week we pulled into the harbour at Malta, where a tug took a line from us and guided us to the quayside where the ship was fastened to the huge stone rings set up for this purpose. The captain made a quick sacrifice of a lamb in gratitude for the safe arrival, then the gangplank was lowered and a small swarm of stevedores ascended to unload the goods that were to be left at the port for onward passage. From here we would head south to Africa.

Africa has prospered under Roman rule. Utica, Hadrumetum, Thamugadi, Thagaste, Madauri, Caesarea, Volubilis: at every turn you can see the material benefits in the form of temples, colonnades, baths and aqueducts, and the land's riches are transported to Rome in the form of fine olive oil, figs and corn. I have never seen a lovelier land than my own estates in the region, with their vineyards, orchards and cultivated fields, and their gardens of groves full of songbirds, and fragrant flowers in the meadows by the clear stream that flows down to the blue waters of the Mediterranean Sea. The greatest of the region's cities by far is Carthage. Crushed and destroyed in the wars she fought centuries ago against Rome, the city has been reborn and almost vies with Alexandria in size and cosmopolitanism. If you have the time, you should visit any of the above mentioned places. It is generally sufficient to keep to the coastal areas since the greater part of the interior is desert, and is dotted with settlements that are small, scattered and mostly nomadic. It is also full of dangerous wild beasts. By contrast, the whole of the coast opposite to Italy, from the Nile to the Pillars of Hercules, and particularly the part that used to be subject to the Carthaginians, is settled and prosperous.

The onward journey to Carthage was swift and uneventful. The city is situated on a kind of peninsula, which comprises a walled circuit of 360 stades. The acropolis used to be situated in the centre, which they call Byrsa, and at its top stood a temple of Asclepius. This was where, when the city was finally captured by the Romans, the wife of the Carthaginian general Hasdrubal burned herself to death. Below the acropolis lie the harbours. Carthage was founded by Queen Dido, who brought a multitude of people from the city of Tyre in Phoenicia. The colonisation proved to be highly successful and large parts of these regions are still occupied by those of Phoenician descent. The success meant that the city grew to be a rival of Rome and waged three great wars against us. An indication of Carthaginian power can be gleaned from the last war, in which they were defeated by Scipio Aemilianus and their city was utterly wiped out. When they began that war, the Carthaginians controlled three hundred cities in Libya and seven hundred thousand people lived in Carthage itself. When they were being besieged and forced to surrender, they handed over two hundred thousand full suits of armour and three thousand catapults. When they decided to take up arms again, each day they were able to manufacture one hundred and forty finished shields, three hundred swords, five hundred spears, and one thousand missiles for the catapults. What is more, they built one hundred and twenty decked ships in two months.

For all its resourcefulness, Carthage was still captured and razed to the ground. The territory became a Roman province and for a long time Carthage remained desolate, until it was restored by the deified Caesar, who sent Romans there as colonists, as well as some soldiers, and now the city is more prosperous than any other in the region. I sought out a passable inn not too far from the harbour and found one with a sign outside that read: 'If you're clean and neat, then welcome. But if you're dirty, well, I'm ashamed to say it, but you're welcome too.' The innkeeper was clearly something of a wag and the rooms were indeed acceptable, so I decided to stay.

I was, in any case, to dine that evening with an acquaintance, called Gaius, who was chairman of a local dining club and who, when I had written ahead to him, had organised a dinner in my honour. The dinner was held in a nearby hall, to which we all went after having paid a visit to the local baths, where oil was provided at the expense of the club. My host and I were seated at the centre of the table of honour, with him dressed in white. After he had made the initial offerings of incense and wine to the club's god, Diana, the meal began.

'It is a good club,' he explained to me. 'It costs 100 sesterces and an amphora of fine wine to join, which keeps out the riff-raff. Whenever a member dies, his family gets 300 sesterces towards the cost of his burial and another fifty for the funeral procession. We have lots of dinners and everyone takes it in turn to organise them, when they are expected to provide one amphora of good wine, bread, sardines, hot water, as well as finding a room for the dinner and a waiter to serve. You know how these clubs can easily get out of hand and end up becoming political, well, we try and keep a lid on all that by having rules that are rigorously enforced. So if any member moves about from one seat to another simply to cause a commotion he is fined four sesterces, or if becomes abusive the fine is twelve. If he is rude to me, it goes up to twenty.'

It was a sedate affair and soon after the food was over the men seated at the benches turned to gambling. It is curious how the common people devote their whole lives to gambling. I must confess, though, that the activity does seem to engender firm friendships among the players, as if they have been formed amid the greatest adversities. And if it is not dice that has their attention it is the chariot racing of the Circus Maximus, and they can spend hours discussing which charioteer is the best and which horse has the best pedigree. Personally, I am not remotely interested in gambling and only play for fun when I have to, such as during Saturnalia when I let the slaves win. It costs me a few sesterces but it keeps them happy. And if it helps them buy their freedom eventually then I will get my money back in any case.

The following day we spent walking round the streets of the city. My host was younger than me and I had not realised how his mind was focused on the gods. We all need to keep the gods happy but there are limits, especially when it comes to novelty. I have known several men who are sound of mind in practical matters but who, the moment they see a stone smeared with holy oil or adorned with a wreath, fall on their face and then stand beside it making long vows and craving blessings from it. My host had heard of a renowned prophet who had come to the city and he wanted to seek him out in the forum. When we found him, he was surrounded by quite a crowd and it was clear that even those of high rank were there to see the sage.

The prophet gave a warm greeting to all who approached him and even handed out small gifts to make them think well of him and help spread the news of his arrival. To me it seemed clear that he had devised a simple trick. He asked people to submit their questions in writing and, when he opened and read the scrolls, if he found anything dangerous, he would put them to one side and not reply, as if he had some knowledge of a dreadful fate that awaited the questioner. But to those who asked simple questions, he gave simple, positive answers and they went away happy. My host asked about his son by a former marriage, a young man who was in his prime, and asked who he should appoint as tutor for his studies. The reply came: 'Be it Pythagoras; aye, and the good bard, master of warfare.' I kid you not, but that very day came news of the boy's death. Gaius was at his wit's end, and was determined to see the prophet's reply as somehow predicting this fate. 'Did he not tell me to choose a tutor who was no longer alive, but Pythagoras and Homer who died long ago and are no doubt teaching him in Hades as we speak?'

The loss of his son seemed to send Gaius mad. He sought solace in exotic forms of religion. He told me in great detail of the visions he had received from the goddess Isis:

'It was almost midnight and I woke up suddenly to see a full moon rising above the sea and shining with an unusual brightness and radiance. Now, in the silent secrecy of night, was my opportunity. I realised that this was a visitation of the moon goddess, the Isis of ancient Egypt, who in her guise as mother of all mothers had come to show me that my son was now in her care. I had stared at the radiant image for some minutes but I now

shook myself awake and jumped up happily, and eager to
purify myself I went down to the sea and plunged into
the waves. Seven times I immersed my head, since that
is the number which the godlike Pythagoras has told us
is most appropriate in religious rituals, and then in tears
I uttered my silent prayer to the all-powerful goddess:
"Queen of heaven, nurturing mother of the crops, who
first taught man how to use civilised food, how to love
each other, save me from the wreck of my fortunes, and
grant me peace and respite from the cruel misfortunes I
have endured."

'Such were the prayers that I offered, and accompanied them with pitiful lamentations. I then fell asleep on
the beach and I had scarcely closed my eyes when out of
the sea there emerged the head of the goddess, turning
her face towards me. Her radiant image seemed to take
shape bit by bit until it stood before my eyes. What a
wonderful sight she presented. Human language is too
weak for me to explain adequately.

'First her hair. This was long, rich and curly, and as
it fell it caressed her sacred neck in waves that cascaded
down over her shoulders. Her head was crowned with a
diadem patterned with flowers, and in its centre, a disc
in the shape of the moon gave out a white light. On
either side of this, a snake stood up, and above the whole
scene was a wreath of ears of corn. She wore a multico-
loured dress made of the finest linen, that seemed to shift
from being brilliant white, saffron yellow and flaming
red. But it was her cloak that made me stare the most. It
was jet-black and yet shone with a kind of dark radiance,
and it passed right around her, under her right arm and

up to her left shoulder, where it was bunched together and hung down in folds across her back. The cloak had an embroidered border and all over its surface glistened a pattern of stars, at the centre of which sat a full moon surrounded by flames of fire.

'In her right hand, she held a bronze sistrum, a thin strip of metal curved back on itself and pierced by a number of thin rods, which rattled when she shook it. From her left hand hung a gold pitcher, with a handle in the shape of a rampant asp, its neck all puffed out. On her feet, she wore sandals woven from palm leaves, the sign of victory. And around her wafted beautiful perfumes of Arabia. She then deigned to speak to me: "Gaius, moved by your entreaties, I, mother of the Universe, mistress of all the elements, highest of the gods, who represents all gods and goddesses in a single form, have come to you. My will controls the shining heights of heaven, the healthful winds of the sea, and the mournful silences of hell. The whole world worships me in a thousand different forms and under a thousand different names. But it is the Egyptians, who excel in ancient learning, who worship me in my true name: that of Queen Isis. I am here in pity for your misfortunes. Cease your weeping, stop your lamentation, and banish your grief. By my will the day of your release from suffering is dawning. But first you must follow the orders I give you."'

And Gaius told me how the goddess had told him to take part in one of the ceremonies that was to be held in her honour that coming day. He was to join the procession as it made its way through the streets and approach the priest, who the goddess had forewarned in a dream, and kiss his hand. Gaius had readily agreed but the goddess had added one further condition.

'She told me to remember,' Gaius continued, 'that the rest of life, right up until my last breath, is now solemnly promised to her. "It is only right," she said, "that you should make over the rest of your time on earth to me by whose beneficence you will be relieved from your torment. And you will live happily and gloriously under my protection. And when you finally complete your lifespan and descend to the shades, I shall be there, shining amid the darkness amid the secret depths of the Styx, and you shall dwell in the Elysian Fields and constantly worship me alongside your dead son." This was her awesome statement,' said Gaius, 'one which I have accepted.'

And he announced that from then on his life would be dedicated to worshipping the goddess and that he would seek initiation into her mysteries. I was pleased for him that he seemed to have found relief from his grief, although it was not clear to me that this was a case of divine intervention but of his mind having been turned insane. What was obvious was that it was time to leave. Even if he had no effect on me, my host would doubtless be trying to win over members of my household and I had no desire to lose them to this dubious cult. Without further ado, I therefore wished him the best in his newly devout life and ordered my slaves to pack everything for immediate departure. I myself headed down to the harbour to find a boat that could take us across the sea on the next leg of our tour, to the olive-rich land of Hispania.

My desire to leave promptly meant that I was not as assiduous in my selection as would normally be the case. A local festival also meant that many ships had delayed their departure. But I managed to find a fair-sized ship that was sailing alongside a smaller boat to Hispania. The larger ship had about fifty passengers on board and we set off early at dawn the following morning. It was an inauspicious start that our ship managed to run aground in the bed of the harbour after the skipper had veered off the course of the main channel, but the wind was fresh enough that we were able to be pulled off by the smaller vessel. The sailors on board were a motley crew. The captain, I was told, was close to bankruptcy, and the crew of about fifteen were a mix of Jews and peasants who did not seem to know one end of a rope from another. Every one of them had some kind of physical defect and they remorselessly mocked one another for it: 'Come on, Lamey', 'How's the hernia?', 'Get a move on goggle eyes'. They seemed to find this an endless source of amusement.

The captain had all the sails spread. We were speeding along but alarmingly close to the coast. One of the passengers screamed when he saw some rocks approaching and the captain veered about and turned the ship's head to the open sea, struggling as best he could against the contrary waves. Then a fresh south wind sprang up and carried us along swiftly, and we were soon out of sight of land and on to the main shipping route, where the large merchant ships ply their way. We passengers relaxed and amused ourselves on deck. Most of the men started to gamble, playing dice or knucklebones for small stakes. I took the opportunity to read a travel book about Gaul, to inform me ahead of our visit there. About a third of the passengers were women and in order to separate themselves from the leering sailors they set up a screen by hanging up a piece of torn sail.

One of the old seamen started to tell a tale to amuse those who wanted to listen. It was a story of how he had once set out on a voyage '... where we sailed beyond the Pillars of Hercules, well out into the Atlantic. Why we went, nobody knows, just the captain's passion for novelty and his curiosity about what people might live on the other side of the ocean. We came to an island and proceeded to sail up the mouth of an estuary. We came to fields of huge vines and from each flowed a stream of perfectly clear wine, which all went into the river. The river was full of fish that made us drunk when we caught and ate them. We now crossed the river by a ford, and came to some more vines of a most extraordinary kind. They had a thick stem but the top half had the shape of a woman. They looked like the goddess Daphne turning into a tree. From their fingertips hung great bunches of grapes and their hair consisted of tendrils and leaves. They welcomed us warmly, talking in Greek, and then kissed us on the mouth. And immediately we staggered about like drunken men.

'We hurried back to the ship and set sail on a gentle breeze. But about midday, when we were out of sight of the island, all of a sudden the whole boat was lifted up and began to fly through the air, until we were almost three hundred and fifty miles above the earth. For a whole week we sailed in the air until we spotted a spherical island that had air for sea, and glistened with light. Before we could land, we were captured by horse-vultures, as they are called, which are so large that each feather is thicker than the mast of a large merchant ship. They brought us to their king. "How have you Greeks," he asked, "made it to the moon?"

'We were speechless but he told us not to worry and assured us that he would supply us with all we needed. But that day his enemy, the sun king, chose to attack and we were compelled to take our place in the ranks of the moon king's army. Our force numbered one hundred thousand as well as eighty thousand horse-vultures, and thirty thousand flea-archers, which ride on fleas the size of elephants. I was told that fifty thousand ostrich-sling-ers were on their way from beyond the stars but as they failed to arrive I did not actually see them, and I am not prepared to give you a description of them based upon hearsay, for that might strain your credulity. The enemy constructed a wall across space made of clouds, which cut off the sun's rays from the moon. The result was a total eclipse of the moon, which was plunged into dark-ness. The moon king was forced to negotiate and offered to pay tribute, abstain from hostilities in the future, and give hostages as surety. The following day, peace was concluded on these terms.'

The sailor now began to list all of the strange things he had seen on the moon. 'In the first place,' he claimed, 'babies are not born of women but of men, who marry other men. Every man is a wife until he is twenty-five and then becomes a husband. They carry their children in the calf of the leg instead of the belly. The children are always delivered dead but they bring them to life by putting them in the wind with their mouth open. When a man becomes old, he does not die, but dissolves in smoke into the air. They all eat the same food, which is roast frogs, which fly through the air, but instead of eating them they snuff up the cooking fumes into their nostrils. They think beauty consists of a bald head and a hairless body but they have beards just above the knee and only one toe on each foot. They also have tails in the shape of a large cabbage. Their mucus is a pungent honey and after hard work or exercise they sweat milk all over. Most amazing of all are their eyes, since these organs are removable and often they lose them and have to borrow them from others.'

Then our storyteller finished with a flourish: 'And if you don't believe me you can just go there yourself and you will see that I am telling the truth.'

The hours slip by easily on a boat. On a boat that has a favourable wind, that is. In what seemed like only a few moments, a storm-force wind blew up from nowhere. The ship could not make any headway into the wind and the captain was forced to turn it about, drop the anchor to act as a brake, and let it be blown along by the gale. The timbers started to make great groaning noises, as indeed did most of the passengers. The crew managed to haul in the smaller sails and drag up the small lifeboat that was pulled along behind the ship and they then succeeded in passing ropes under the ship to help hold it together. The sea loomed up round us like mountains and we took a violent battering from the storm for the next few hours. The captain ordered the crew to start throwing the cargo overboard to lighten the load. When the storm still did not abate, they even began to throw the ship's tackle into the sea.

All that night the storm howled about us and nobody managed to sleep even for a moment. After the initial screaming, the passengers seemed to be gripped by a quiet resignation to their fate. All the next day the storm raged and the ship was driven along at the mercy of the sea. Towards dusk, we caught sight of the sister ship we had set sail with, but which had long since been blown off on a different course. The captain tried to steer towards it, hoping that it might rescue us, but, as we approached, it became clear that this smaller vessel was in an even more dire predicament than our own. It was being plunged and tossed upon the waves like a child's toy until, with a great wrenching noise, its keel gave way and the entire boat began to break into pieces. Its skipper ordered those who could swim to jump overboard first and the rest to grab on to planks or other pieces of the ship. Some of them perished almost instantly, their lungs full of salt water, and it seemed to me that such a quick death was a tolerable fate in our situation. A slow death at sea is the worst of all ends. The eye, full of the vast expanse of the waters, prolongs the agony of fear, generating a terror in proportion to the size of the ocean. Some of those in the sea were dashed upon what was left of the hull of the boat or were speared like fish upon the broken pieces of wood, others were swimming about already half-dead, waiting for the next huge wave to overwhelm them.

We cried out at the sight but were powerless to help.

The waves grew worse. 'I think she's going to go down!' wailed the skipper, as our ship let out an almighty groan. We called upon the gods, and thought of our loved ones safe at home on dry land. Then someone shouted that, as is the old sea custom, we should all tie whatever jewellery or gold we had on to string and hang it about our necks so that when our corpses were finally given up by the sea they would carry on them the fee for burial. For nobody who comes across a dead body and profits from it will begrudge sprinkling a little sand on to the corpse.

As night fell again, the ship continued to race ahead, since we had been unable to take down the mainsail. Whenever the crew attempted this, even with all the passengers helping, they were thwarted by the ropes, which would get stuck in the pulleys. Then at about midnight the crew started to panic, having sensed that we were approaching land. They lowered weighted lines and found that the water was 120 feet deep. A short time later they took soundings again and found that it was only 90 feet. Fearing we would be dashed against some rocks or grounded, they dropped four more anchors from the stern and started to pray. I joined in: 'Have pity, Lord Poseidon,' I entreated, 'and make peace with us. If you mean to kill us, do not put off our fate any longer but let one wave overwhelm us.' And I and the rest of the passengers swore that we would offer him our hair if he allowed us to live. I had remembered too late the message from my dream.

It was but a short time after I had uttered this prayer that the wind dropped and the savagery of the waves subsided. The anchors held and the ship steadied itself sufficiently that some were even able to sleep a little. When day broke, I can safely say that I have never beheld the sun with greater joy. We were within sight of land, who knows where, and the winds had softened enough that the crew were able to work the rigging and handle the sails. And within a couple of hours we, who had that night thought ourselves heading for Hades, were disembarking in a small harbour on a remote shore. We all embraced the earth like we would our own mothers. We sent up hymns of gratitude to Poseidon, and we happily submitted our heads and eyebrows to the barber, that he might shave them clean in fulfilment of our vow to the god. We had made it to Hispania.

Hispania, or Iberia as it is also known, is a vast area that stretches from the straits of Gades, where the Atlantic Ocean bursts into our Mediterranean Sea, to the Atlantic coasts of the north and the edge of Gaul. It has been divided into three smaller provinces: Baetica in the south, Lusitania in the west, and Tarraconese Hispania in the east, north and central plain. We had washed up on the eastern seaboard, not far from New Carthage, and I decided to first make a tour of the south before travelling to an estate that I own not far from Tarraco in the north. I also decided that we would winter there, since the travel season was approaching its end and I had no desire to struggle through muddy Gaul or icy Britannia in the winter. We were also exhausted by the combination of the long trip we had already made and the horrors of the sea crossing.

Iberia is like an oxhide, with the long side extending from west to east, and its forelegs towards the east. It is

six thousand stades in length all told, and five thousand
stades at its greatest breadth, although in some places it
is much less than three thousand stades wide, particularly
near the Pyrenees in the north-east. Most of Iberia can
provide its inhabitants only a poor livelihood consisting as it does of mountains, forests and plains whose
soil is thin (and even that not uniformly well-watered).
Northern Iberia, in addition to its ruggedness, is not
only extremely cold in the winter, but lies next to the
Atlantic Ocean, which gives the inhabitants the char-
acteristic of being inhospitable to outsiders. It is, also,
an exceedingly wretched place to live. But almost the
whole of southern Iberia, the province of Baetica, is
fertile and pleasant.

Indeed Baetica, named after the river that divides it
in the middle, surpasses all the other provinces in the
richness of its cultivation and the peculiar fertility and
beauty of its vegetation. It is said to contain 175 cities,
among them Gades, famed for its dancing girls and a city
of almost as great a population as Alexandria or Antioch.
We travelled by the coastal route, hopping from harbour
to harbour, until we reached the city of New Carthage.
This was founded by Hannibal's brother, Hasdrubal, and
is surrounded by handsome walls and secure fortifica-
tions. Large silver mines operate nearby and yield a daily
revenue of 25,000. The fish-salting industry is also large,
and the garum produced there is probably the best I
have ever tasted. Be sure to buy some to take home.

What a far cry the city is now from when it was captured and razed by Scipio in the Punic Wars. Once they
had stormed the walls, the general followed Roman

custom by ordering his troops to attack the citizens inside. They were to kill all they encountered, sparing nobody, whatever their age. The streets were left littered with the corpses of civilians, and even of dogs cut in half and other dismembered animals. Once New Carthage's leader had surrendered, Scipio gave the order for the killing to stop and the ransacking to begin. All the booty they snatched was collected in the marketplace for the general to divide up as he saw fit.

From here, we travelled down into the main body of Baetica. It is a land marvellously blessed by nature. It has timber for building ships, salt quarries, and wool that is spun into fine fabrics. The region has a great abundance of cattle of all kinds, and of game. But there are scarcely any destructive animals, except for the burrowing hares, called 'peelers' by the locals, because they damage both plants and seeds by eating the roots. This pest occurs throughout almost the whole of Iberia, and extends even as far as southern Gaul. They breed faster than you can count and they brought famine to the Balearic Islands by ravaging the crops. It is said that the inhabitants of the Gymnesian Islands once sent an embassy to Rome to ask to be relocated because they were being driven out by these animals. Since then, several ways of hunting them have been developed. The inhabitants breed Libyan ferrets, which they muzzle and send into the holes. The ferrets drag outside all the animals they catch with their claws, or force them to flee into the open, where men catch them as they leave their burrows. The young, when cut out of the mother's womb, are considered a great delicacy and can be eaten without being gutted.

The coast of Baetica is even more productive than the land. Oysters and mussels abound along the entire coast, as do whales, which you can see spouting out a cloud-like pillar of seawater as they breathe. The conger eels are so big they are like monsters, as are the lampreys and other edible fish of this kind. The cuttlefish can be two cubits long. Large numbers of plump tunny-fish congregate along the shore and feed on the acorns of a kind of stunted oak that grows at the bottom of the sea and produces very large fruit.

Where Hispania excels perhaps above all is in the breeding of horses. Its stud farms are home to the purest of pure bloods, who produce offspring of the highest quality. It is well known that in Lusitania, in the area around the river Tagus, the mares become pregnant by turning their faces towards the west wind when it blows. The foals that are conceived in this way are remarkable for their extreme speed, but they never live beyond three years. The regions of Gallicia and Asturia produce a species of horse that has a peculiar gait of its own, with two legs of the same side being moved together.

Horses are the most remarkable beasts, and are the most useful of all animals to the human race. They possess an intelligence that exceeds all description. Those who have to use the javelin in battle are well aware how the horse, by its exertions and the supple movements of its body, aids the rider in any difficulty he may have in throwing his weapon. The horses that pull the chariots in the Circus Maximus show how well the animals respond to the cheers of the crowd and how they seem to possess a desire to win glory. In the Secular Games, which were celebrated in the Circus Maximus under the emperor Claudius, when the charioteer of the white team, called Corax, was thrown from his place at the starting post, his horses took the lead and kept it, blocking the other chariots, overturning them, and doing everything against the other competitors that a most skilful charioteer would have done, and they actually succeeded in winning the race. Some horses are known to live for fifty years, but the mares are not so long-lived. The poet Virgil has very beautifully described the best physical characteristics of the horse: 'He has a long neck, a graceful head, a short belly and solid back, and his spirited chest is muscular.' And, as for the horse's bravery, again that poet cannot be bettered: 'If the distant battle sounds, it cannot stand still, but pricks up its ears and shakes with excitement, snorting in passion from its nostrils.'

We idled in Baetica for some days, enjoying the fine food and riding for pleasure. Slowly, we then made our way up the coast towards Tarraco and our winter quarters. Tarraco is the provincial capital and it contains numerous temples and public buildings that are worth visiting. It is a prosperous city and this is reflected in the fine statues, villas and tombs that you see all around. You could believe that you are back in Italy, so Roman is the place. The amphitheatre is a particularly pleasant spot in which to watch the games, sitting as it does next to the gentle lapping of the sea's waves in a way that reminds me of the circus at Leptis Magna in Africa. The emperor Galba, who reigned for a only a few brief months, lived in Tarraco for eight years. The great emperor Trajan was born in Hispania and served in Tarraco as provincial

governor. Such has been the levelling up of the provinces that emperors themselves can be made outside of
Rome now. Trajan's close companion, Lucius Sura, also
came from Tarraco. When some people were critical of
Trajan's friendship with him, and of the influence he
had over the emperor, the emperor proved Sura's loyalty
by turning up uninvited at his house, and, having dis-
missed his bodyguard, ordering Sura's barber to shave
him.

My estates in Hispania are extensive, with the main
one lying in a small valley about eight miles from Tarraco,
with a distant view down to the sea. I am fortunate to
have an excellent steward who ensures that everything
runs smoothly. For the first couple of days we rested and
then I spent several days inspecting the farm, the slaves
and the books to ensure that all was in order. I then
took a visit from my agent, a freedman who looks after
my commercial interests in the province. He worked his
way up from being a slave in the fields and is completely
loyal to me since he owes me everything. My invest-
ments comprise various rental properties in Tarraco but,
above all, a share in gold mining in the north-west.

Iberia is rich in metals. Not all of the province is rich
in fruit or as fertile as the south, but the north-west is
well-supplied with ores of various kinds. It is rare for a
country to be fortunate in both respects, and it is also
rare for the same country to have within a small area an
abundance of so many kinds of metals. My interest lies
in gold. Gold is mined in three ways. The first is in the
form of dust that is found in rivers, such as the Tagus.
There is no gold found in a more perfect state than this,

since it is thoroughly polished by the continual flow of the water. The second method is to sink shafts down into mountains or to seek it among the surface debris of gold-rich mountains. Mountains with veins of gold within them often contain gold-bearing earth on their surface. By washing this in running waters to leave only the gold residue, it is possible to assess the size of the vein within the mountain. The gold that is extracted from mine shafts is generally found adhering to the gritty crust of marble. The ore that is extracted is first broken up and then washed. It is then heated to a high temperature and the gold is poured off.

The third method of obtaining gold surpasses even the labours of Hercules. Tunnels are driven into mountainsides for long distances, and slaves toil here under torchlight for months on end. Only those at the pit's mouth ever see the light of day. It is dangerous work. Arches are left at frequent intervals for the purpose of supporting the weight of the mountain above but the earth regularly collapses and the workmen are crushed beneath. Few of the slaves live for long and most have been sent there as a punishment. When all of the tunnels have been dug, the supporting wooden pillars are cut away. The workers run out and the mountain is left to collapse in on itself. I have seen this kind of crash once and it generates a noise and density of dust that is impossible for the human imagination to conceive. Even then it is not certain that there will much gold found within the rubble, let alone enough to justify the vast expenditure.

A similarly Herculean task is to divert rivers within

the mountain ranges for the purpose of washing away this debris. Getting the water to the right place takes another thousand labours if it is to work properly. The fall has to be steep enough to make the water run quickly and it needs aqueducts to be built to traverse the valleys and crevasses. Then there are impassable rocks that have to be hewn away. The water has to be free from mud to be in a fit state for washing and the water is run over beds of stones to keep it clean. Reservoirs are hollowed out to store the water, which is then released in one go to create a torrent. This flows into trenches on the lower, more level ground in which the ulex plant has been grown. The ulex is similar to rosemary and is rough and prickly, making it well-adapted for snagging any pieces of gold that may be carried along. Eventually, the water flow reaches the sea and in this way the shattered mountain is washed away. The shoreline of Hispania has been greatly extended by these flows of silt.

You may wonder why anyone would choose to spend so much money on a process like this. The answer is that the gold found this way does not need to be melted, but is already pure. It is also found in lumps, some of which can be larger than ten pounds in weight. The ulex is dried and burnt, after which its ashes are washed upon a bed of grassy turf, in order that the gold may be deposited on it. Asturia, Gallecia and Lusitania between them supply some twenty thousand pounds in weight of gold. Indeed, there is no part of the world that has maintained such a continuous fertility in gold for so long.

Iberia not only supplies a wide variety and great quantity of produce but these are easily transported on the rivers and estuaries that are navigable far inland from the sea, not only by small boats but by large ships too, all the way to the major cities of the interior. In this way, Baetica exports large quantities of grain and wine as well as olive oil, all of which is of a very high quality. Wax, honey and pitch are also exported from there, as are various dyes and ochre. The sheer abundance of the exports is indicated by the size and the number of the ships found in the province's harbours, and merchantmen of the greatest size sail from here to Ostia, the seaport of Rome. Towards the south of Rome sits a huge rubbish heap that is testament to Hispania's fertility. Millions upon millions of amphorae that have been used to import Spanish oil are broken up and carefully piled up into a hill that is starting to rival the Capitoline.

The ease with which it is possible to send and receive all manner of items from all over the empire is one of its great boons. I often send letters with friends and other travellers to Asia and Gaul and likewise regularly receive correspondence from Iberia and Greece. Booksellers will send me parcels of the latest works when I am at my estates in Tarraco or Africa. It seems that anything can be supplied if necessary. One friend of mine even imported live geese from Boulogne into Italy. When hosting games as part of their duties of office, magistrates scour the empire for the finest animals, with most of them coming from the wild regions of north Africa. Spanish horses are to be seen racing in circuses across the empire.

And it is the universal languages of Latin and Greek that enable such great commerce to be effected smoothly.

I have heard it said that in Sebastopolis, on the far side of the Black Sea, as many as three hundred languages are spoken and Roman merchants have to employ one hundred and thirty interpreters to buy and sell their wares. There are no such hindrances within the empire, where even in the furthest reaches you will find traders able to communicate, albeit in rudimentary terms. And all of this trade is facilitated by Roman coinage, the universal language of money, and the silver denarius is accepted in Gaul and Hispania and Syria alike.

Dealers travel from all over the empire looking for opportunities to sell their wares and buy local produce for export in return. In the market at Tarraco, you will find traders from Berytus, Damascus, Tyre and Alexandria, to name but a few. Commerce seems to be the particular genius of the Syrians and compels them to travel the whole world to seek wealth, often in banking. The Egyptians in Tarraco have set up a small shrine to Serapis for their use and in this way their gods travel with them and are taken up by the locals also.

Any goods can be transported to any market. Rome itself has the best, and you can find anything you want there: iron, incense, salted fish, ebony, silk, pepper, wine, you name it. You can even buy snow in summer. Antioch, too, has everything you could ever desire. Indeed all the great cities are supplied with a great surplus of goods. You can buy Alexandrian paper and Gallician tin in almost any city. You can see peasants in Italy wearing amber from the north in necklaces to ward off the evil eye. The potteries of Pergamum and Mutina send their pots and dishes to every corner of the empire, each piece

sporting the unique hallmarks of their makers. Alexandrian glass and Egyptian linen is in demand everywhere. British wheat feeds the legions on the Rhine.
Italy sends out its wine, sausages and hams, and buys in
carpets, garum and spices in return. Back and forth the
merchantmen ply the Mediterranean, which teems with
so many ships that more people seem to live on the sea
than on the land.

Towards the end of the winter, once the hours were
lengthening and the sun had recovered some of its
warmth, I travelled inland to visit my cousin Claudius,
who had retired to his villa on the central plain. He is
filthy rich. He made a killing in the oil business and
then went into gold. It is through him that I myself
have invested in this. His estate is a monument to his
wealth. It has the largest dining room I have ever seen
in a private house and the whole villa is decorated with
mosaics of the most exquisite beauty, with centaurs
and satyrs and dancers and musicians, and the gardens
seem to have more marble statues than plants. He boasts
that he has imported more than thirty different types
of marble from quarries as far off as Egypt. The villa is
located quite off the beaten track so that nobody will
ever find it by chance.

Claudius now devotes his time to pleasure. The villa
is full of artists, whether dancers, sculptors or mosaic-
makers. These people spend most of their lives on the
road, satisfying the desires of their audiences. Actors,
musicians and athletes all make constant tours, either in
small troupes or individually, putting on shows. Often
these performances are at the great festivals, such as those

that are held in Greece each year, or they are for the wealthy in their villas, while others take place in the forum or some small provincial theatre and are aimed at pleasing the masses. If a performance is successful, and arouses the enthusiastic support of the locals, the performers can be rewarded with the freedom of the city.

Claudius is particularly fond of the type of dancing known as pantomime, and, after an extravagant dinner, we were treated to a display by a very skilful troupe of artists. I can only imagine how much they cost. The actors played out in dance the story of the three goddesses and the beauty contest. There appeared on stage a young man representing the Trojan prince, Paris, gorgeously costumed in a cloak of foreign design that flowed down from his shoulders. On his head was a golden tiara. Next there appeared a radiantly fair young boy, whose long blond hair attracted everyone's eyes. He wore little golden wings and represented Mercury. He danced towards Paris and offered him the golden apple. By his gestures he informed him of Jupiter's command and then danced gracefully out of sight.

Then Venus appeared, displaying to all her perfect beauty, naked except for a sheer silk scarf which covered, or rather shaded, her quite remarkable hips, which an inquisitive wind mischievously either blew aside or sometimes pressed clingingly against her. Then two groups of attractive young maidens danced on to the stage, the Graces and the Seasons, who honoured the goddess by scattering flowers around her. They danced with great skill an intricate ballet. The flutes played sweet Lydian melodies that soothed and delighted the spectators.

Venus began to move forward gracefully, rhythmically, slowly, swaying softly from side to side, gently inclining her head. As soon as she came face to face with Paris, the judge, she appeared by her gestures to promise him that if he chose her she would give him a bride who was the most beautiful of mortals. And then the young Trojan prince gladly handed to Venus the golden apple and pronounced her the victor in the beauty contest.

Pantomime is so hard to get right. An actor can easily go too far and what should be great can become monstrous and overdone. I remember seeing this exemplified by a highly regarded pantomime actor. He was acting the madness of Ajax, just after he has been outdone by Odysseus, and he completely lost control of himself so that he really did seem to have gone mad. He tore the clothes from the back of one of the time-beaters, snatched a flute from a musician's hands, and smashed it down hard on the head of the actor playing Odysseus, who had been standing nearby enjoying his triumph, and who, if he had not had a helmet on his head, would have been knocked out by this histrionic frenzy. The whole stage was full of mad leaping, yelling and tearing of clothes. The illiterate plebs in the cheap seats, who cannot tell a good performance from a bad one, thought this was a supreme piece of acting. The more intelligent and discerning spectators could barely conceal their disgust and refused to applaud the actor's folly.

I had thought of travelling on to Lusitania and of staying at its capital Emerita Augusta. This boasts many lovely temples, as well as a fine circus and amphitheatre, an aqueduct, and, above all, a bridge over the valley with

eighty-one beautiful arches. But the weather had clearly
turned for the better and I was keen to press on northwards while the weather was good. If you have time to
travel right across to the Atlantic, you will be rewarded
by seeing the extraordinary tides that happen there. It
is as if the whole ocean is sucked up by some god who
then spits it out to rush up to the upper reaches of the
shore. The locals believe that the soul can only depart the
body during an ebb tide. But I had no time for this. I was
headed for the land of the long-haired Gauls.

·· COMMENTARY ··

As the empire grew and incorporated
many more conquered peoples so, too,
did traditional Roman religion expand
to encompass a far wider range of religious experiences. Isis started life as an
Egyptian deity but began to spread after
the conquest of that country by Alexan-
der. His successor in Egypt, Ptolemy Soter, hit upon a
universal Isis cult as a way of providing a focus of unity
for his mixed Egyptian and Greek subjects. Isis became
the patron goddess of the family, magic, and of sailors,
who helped the cult spread throughout the Hellenistic world. It also moved with migrants westwards and
quickly became popular in Rome, especially among
women and the lower orders, something that provoked
some unease in the senate, as did the cult's associations

with sexual promiscuity (even though it also demanded periods of sexual abstinence from its followers). Augustus distrusted the cult because of its associations with his opponents Cleopatra and Antony in Egypt, and his successor Tiberius had images of the goddess thrown into the Tiber. But the imperial attitude softened over time, with Vespasian seeming to have become familiar with the cult during his campaigns in the east. Part of the attraction of Isis was no doubt that its Hellenisation had left it safely exotic, an appealing combination of Greek familiarity and Egyptian mysticism. Initiates were often called to the goddess by dreams and visions, and the account by Falx of his friend is based on Book 11 of the ancient novel, *The Golden Ass* (as Apuleius's *Metamorphoses* is traditionally known). This goes on to include a detailed account of an Isis procession held to bless the boats at the start of the sailing season. The cult included rituals of purification and rebirth, as well as offering hope of a happy afterlife, something that was missing from traditional Roman religion. The account of the charlatan is based on the satirical work by Lucian (*Alexander* 30) and shows that all kinds of religious quackery could be found in the religious supermarket that the Roman empire became.

The details of the huge transport ships come from Lucian's *The Ship* and the old seadog's tale of the trip to the moon from the same author's *True History*, which is a parody of the gushing tales told by tourists of their travels. The account of the storm and shipwreck is based on three sources: a letter by the fourth-century Christian bishop of Cyrene, Synesius, who wrote a quite comical account for his brother of a disastrous journey along the coast from Alexandria; a fictional account from the ancient novel *Leucippe and Clitophon*, written in the second century CE by Achilles Tatius (3.3–4); and from St Paul's description of his shipwreck on the island of Malta while being taken as a prisoner to Rome (Acts 27). All three give a powerful sense of the terror that a storm could evoke in the passengers and crew of a vessel. Those on board were powerless to do anything except pray to the gods for deliverance and promise their hair as an offering in return for safety.

Strabo's description of Roman Spain gives a good sense of the scale of trade in various commodities. Agriculture was always paramount in the Roman economy but trade was clearly encouraged by the relative security of travel and by the use of standard coinage within the empire. Barter continued but most transactions became monetary. And, as we saw earlier, trade in luxuries from outside the empire also increased considerably. The number of shipwrecks found in the Mediterranean from the early empire suggests a level of trade that was not reached again for a thousand years. It also, of course, highlights the perils of ancient sea travel. The rubbish heap of amphorae in Rome that Falx alludes to is the Monte Testaccio, which is estimated to consist of over fifty million containers used to import oil, primarily from Spain. Oil was used both for cooking and for lighting, and it took huge quantities to supply Rome's million-strong inhabitants. The mound is enormous, and even today stands about 35 metres high and almost a kilometre in circumference. But the amphorae were never simply dumped there. Instead, the waste was carefully managed, with layers of terracing and retaining walls being used to prevent collapse. The amphorae seem to have been broken up and the pieces laid down to form a stable base. There is evidence that lime was even sprinkled over the shards to neutralise the odour of rancid oil.

The rich cousin's extravagant villa is based on the recent and ongoing excavations at the fourth-century Villa de Noheda, in central Spain, which looks set to become the finest surviving villa from the Roman world. The dining room alone is almost 300 square metres in size and contains enormous mosaics of the highest quality. One mosaic portrays a pantomime artist giving a performance. Pantomime is not to be confused with the farcical British Christmas plays, but was a sophisticated art form that told mythical stories in music and dance, without words. Consisting of a graceful performance in the style of modern ballet, the principal dancer relied on his or her vigorous physical training to be able to express a wide range of action and emotions. Pantomime was extremely popular and Seneca refers to the clamour and applause of the common people for the pantomime (*Moral Letters* 29.12). The account of the artist is based on Lucian's *On Dancing* (82–3). The dancer needed to have a body like that of a professional gymnast, whose legs, Galen tells us, could assume positions that ordinary people could not hope to imitate, even if they tried to force them with their hands (K4:451). Often the panto-mimes used well-known myths for their storylines and Apuleius describes a performance that dealt with the beauty contest between the gods that Paris adjudicated in and which led ultimately to the Trojan War (*The Golden Ass* 10.29).

The account of gold mining comes from Pliny the Elder and shows the lengths to which Romans went in the pursuit of the precious metal (*Natural History* 33.36–61). The rules of the dining club come from Lanuvium, near Rome (*CIL* 14.2112). The description of the plebs' passion for gambling comes from the fourth-century historian Ammianus Marcellinus's account of the people of Rome (*Histories* 28.4.21). Polybius describes what happened when Roman forces took the city of New Carthage in Spain in 209 BCE (*Histories* 10.15). Pliny the Elder describes the ravages of the rabbits in Spain (*Natural History* 8.217), and Virgil's account of the horse is from the third book of his *Georgics*. The story of Trajan and Sura's barber comes from Dio Cassius (*History of Rome* 68.15), while the inn sign welcoming even the dirty is from Tarragona in Spain (*ILS* 6039).

· CHAPTER VIII ·

WILD PLACES OF GAUL

G AUL IS DIVIDED into three parts. One of these
is inhabited by the Belgae, another by the Aqui-
tani, and a third by a people called in their own tongue
Celtae, or in Latin, Galli. All three differ from one
another in terms of language, institutions and laws. At
least, that used to be the case. Since Gaul was long ago
united by Roman conquest it is now divided into three
provinces, that of Gallia Aquitania, Gallia Belgica and
Gallia Lugdunensis. But these administrative divisions
cannot counteract the impression that this is a most
harmonious country. The rivers and the seas mean that
the necessities of life are easily exchanged among the
different regions and everyone therefore has a share in
the best that the land is able to offer. This is especially
so nowadays, when the whole country is freed from
the need to bear arms because it is protected by our
legions. Contrast this with their former state, when the
tribes bordering Germany were involved in constant
fighting with the barbarians. Instead, the people now

till the land diligently and devote themselves to the civilised life.

Gaul has flourished under Roman rule. I have read that it contains more than one thousand towns and cities. Of these, the largest are all worth visiting, depending on your route: Vasio, Avenio, Arausio are all grand places, as is Narbo, the home of the proconsul. Two splendid amphitheatres can be visited at Nemausus and Arelate, while Vienna contains a temple to the emperor, a theatre, an amphitheatre and large baths. Lugdunum is the capital of Gallia Lugdunensis and, sitting at the confluence of two of the largest rivers and two of the main roads, has become a prosperous city that is full of impressive architecture. In Aquitania, the principal towns are Eliumberum and Burdigala. Remi is the main city in Belgica.

It has to be said that touring southern Gaul's cities is not so different from travelling in Italy, they are all so comfortably Roman in the facilities they offer: amphitheatre, baths, forum. They also lack much by way of history to interest us. Did anything of note happen in Gaul before the Romans arrived? Whereas Egypt and Greece overawe us with their monuments from antiquity, with their myths and legends, with their literary associations, their great works of art, and their remarkable sights, what can Gaul – or Britannia, indeed – offer us of a similar ilk?

It is the countryside of Gaul that makes the deepest impression on the traveller. The harmony of the various regions actually makes me believe in the workings of fate, since they are laid out, not in any random way, but as though in accordance with some calculated plan. To begin with, the Rhodanus river allows for travel deep inland, even for very large vessels, and is joined by other rivers that are themselves navigable, so that getting to many different areas is straightforward. These rivers can be used to journey in either direction. It is obvious that floating downstream is a fast and effective form of travel, since the boatmen's oars work alongside the rushing waters of the river. But it is simple to go upstream, too, by using a tow rope to pull the boat along the banks, and you see the sailors heaving on the ropes as the knots strain on the neck of the mast. It is actually surprising how fast travel in this manner can be, and it often seems that the boats are moving upstream far more quickly than the water flows towards the sea. It is possible to go all the way to the coast facing Britannia with only a short stretch of overland travel. And even where the Rhodanus flows swiftly and is difficult to navigate, the road to the west is level and short enough to make it an easy journey by land.

The land is rich and fertile but that does not prevent the Gauls from trying to make it more fertile still. As in Britannia, they use marl to enrich the earth. Marl is a kind of lime-rich mud and contains a great amount of goodness. It is the equivalent of fat in the body, a place where excess is stored. There used to be only two varieties known, but more recently, with the progress of agricultural knowledge, several others have begun to be employed. The substance is rough and greasy to the touch and when added to arable land or pasture, it can fertilise it for up to fifty years. The marl should always be laid on the land immediately after ploughing so that the soil can start to imbibe its properties at once. It also needs a little manure or else it can be too acidic. It takes a year or two to work but after that the yields of both hay and corn are substantially increased.

The Gauls also employ a very sophisticated machine to help bring in the abundant harvest. A large hollow frame, armed with sharp teeth at the front and supported on two wheels, is driven through the standing corn by oxen that are yoked behind. The result is that the ears of corn are torn off and fall within the frame.

Certain delicacies are the speciality of Gaul, not least of which are snails and dormice. Breeding snails is not as simple as you might think. First you must find a suitable place out in the open and surround it with water to stop them from wandering off. The ideal place is somewhere shady and where the dew falls to keep it moist. In some places they use land at the foot of a cliff where there is a pool or a stream. Dew is even faked by spraying out water in a mist from a pipe with small holes. Snails do not need much feeding. They find their own food while moving about and even when at the dealer's shop they can stay alive for a long time by nibbling on a few laurel leaves sprinkled with a little bran. The farmers are able to earn a great deal of money from snail rearing. The snails can also be fattened up to increase their weight, and therefore price, by placing them in a jar containing holes, in which must and spelt is placed.

Dormice are farmed in a walled area that is covered on the inside with smooth stone or plaster so that they cannot escape. The animals should be fed with acorns and chestnuts and be allowed to eat as much as they want, but only with a little water since they prefer dry conditions. They are then fattened up in jars, which you will see outside many houses. Potters make these jars in a very particular way, as they run channels along the sides and make a hollow in which food is placed. A cover is then added and the mice grow fat in the dark.

The Gauls are also most inventive when it come to the use of water. A few miles north of Arelate I happened to pass by a colossal watermill. It is supplied by an off-shoot from the aqueduct that supplies the city. This water flow cuts through a steep hill before running down the other side to turn as many as sixteen waterwheels, arranged on either side of the flow in two rows of eight. The water cascades from one to the next, before running off into a nearby marsh. The purpose of the mill is to grind flour, which it does on a vast scale. The manager told me that it ground enough grain to feed the entire city, with the grain and flour coming and going via a purpose-built road. Despite this size it is striking how compact it seems, with everything being covered by a single roof. I believe this great feat of engineering was carried out by a certain Quintus Candidus Benignus, whose monument rightly describes him as 'cleverer than anyone when it came to building water channels and machines'. The only similar complex I have ever seen is on the far side of the Janiculum hill in Rome. Whether it is worth the effort, when you could just use slaves, I am not sure.

What Gaul has above all is nature, and it is perhaps the most naturally beautiful of our provinces. Nature refreshes the spirit in a way that nothing man-made ever can. It can also inspire the traveller and fill him with awe. When you pass through a wooded glade in the Gallic countryside and come to a special spot, it is as if all the shapeless spirits of the area have come together to form a mysterious presence, an unknowable yet palpable genius of the place. Whenever a place of such beauty is found, be it somewhere that provokes pleasant memories or a fine view that stirs the soul, or the spot where hot springs bubble up from the earth, or a misty lake, the locals are driven by this sense of awe to set up a small shrine in gratitude for the divine gift that has been bestowed upon them. For all the new gods that have traversed the empire, this simple reverence for nature will always keep its hold on the human spirit.

Near Lugdunum, I remember seeing a grove not far from the road. Stopping to explore, I could see that the ancient trees were thickly clustered together and their height and their dense foliage shut out the sky, creating a huge darkness in the open fields. I was at once seized by a sense of bewilderment and knew I was in the presence of a god. Some miles further on I visited a grotto, where a deep cave had been hollowed out by nature into the solid rock. Creeping inside, the wonderful formations in the stone, the water dripping down from the ceiling, and the shafts of sunlight streaming in from outside, I could almost hear the nymphs playing in the gloom. Again, my soul immediately felt lifted by some great spirit and I was moved to offer a simple offering in worship.

And then, not far beyond, I came to a spring, where

living water emerged out into the light, and it was impossible not to thank the god of that place for his bounteous gifts. Some throw coins and others set up small shrines, or even large temples, as indeed I saw at the source of the river Sequana. This reminded me of the large semicircular shrine built on top of a sheer cliff overlooking the source of the crystal-pure water for the aqueducts that run into Carthage, which has the loveliest of views. Or the well head of the Clitumnus in Umbria, where the icy waters flow forth from a cypress-crowned hill and where an ancient temple stands. In this way, we can see that beauty and holiness are one and the same.

What is more wondrous than water? In the foothills of Gaul's central mountainous region, I came across a shell-shaped sea lake whose waters lapped on to its shores surrounded by olive-covered slopes, and I traced the vineyards that come down from the hills towards the water's edge. Snowy waters still trickled down into the lake and by the shores grew chestnuts, laurel and myrtle. It is the waters supplied by nature that bring life to all else. It is the flow of water that keeps a place tolerably cool in the summer. Even the dullest river supplies endless interest: the torrential flow of the winter rains, the thickets of reeds where the songbirds nest, the oak woods on the banks. And if you are lucky enough to happen upon a waterfall, what hours can you spend glorying in the crash and dance of the foaming waters.

I am never happier than when in the lush countryside of Gaul. To be in Rome is a necessity but who cannot yearn to leave the heat, the crowds, the dirt, the smell and the noise? By contrast, rural Gaul offers peace and solitude and the refreshing sight of Mother Earth. Next to the splendour of her gargantuan achievements, how small and pathetic seem those of mankind. The greatness of paintings by the Greek old masters cannot approach the simple beauty of an ancient glade; the grandest amphitheatre is but a pale imitation of the great bowl of a valley; and the most sophisticated food of an urban dinner party can never satisfy in the way that a few ripe home-grown figs can.

The town is made by man, the country is given by the gods. Who could not be content to lie by a brook on the grass beneath a verdant bough, when the sun is smiling on the flowers that dance in the wind? Others may have luxuries of banquets and the lamplight of towns. I can never satisfy my eyes with views of Gallic pastures, while the marbles and mosaics of villas I have learned to despise. I can scarcely believe that people who have frescoes painted in their houses of woods and seas and rivers have ever seen in real life a broad green stretch by a quiet stream, or the sea in a winter storm, for who, after seeing such natural beauty, would ever wish to gaze on a poor copy? A villa succeeds only to the extent that it lets you see the natural world which surrounds it. A view of the sea, a glimpse of the hill and its vineyards behind, a window to let the soft breeze flow through. This is the best kind of picture.

Happy is the rustic who is ignorant of the city. Theirs is the calm, pure life of the country, the joys of valleys and fresh, cool streams. Their music is the gentle lowing of oxen, the twittering of birds, and the rustle of the wind in the leaves. Their luxury is the bed of soft grass and the fruits of the trees. How much more impressive is the splendour of a lonely ravine or some pebble-strewn seashore when compared with the fake neatness of a town garden, trimmed to within an inch of its life. Free from the bonds of urban life, it is possible to think.

Travelling north-westwards in Gaul brings you to ever more wild places. Leaving Cenabum, which was crowded with boatmen and greedy innkeepers, we sailed to Caesarodunum. Here an overly eager inn-keeper almost burned down the whole place while roasting some scrawny thrushes on a spit. Some sparks from the fireplace fell on the floor and the flames spread quickly through the ancient kitchen and raced upwards and were soon licking the roof. Everywhere there were hungry guests and frightened slaves grabbing the food and trying to put out the fire. At the next place we stayed, The Wheel and Mercury, the inn was filled with eye-stinging smoke because there were damp branches and leaves burning in the fireplace. The bread was so gritty it was barely fit for the slaves. The area was full of cursed gnats and croaking frogs that between them made sleep impossible. The area can be wet at any time of the year because of its proximity to the great waters of the Atlantic Ocean and so it proved. We were in no hurry and so rested for a few days until the weather improved, in as far as rest was truly possible in such a place.

Here the river turns almost to the south, but we headed north and so looked to the roads to take us on the final leg of our Gallic journey, which would take us

up the coast from where Britannia is but a short voyage
away. It is extraordinary that even in this sleepy backwater we were able to find a well-kept, well-surfaced
road. What better proof could there be of the advantages of Roman rule than a highway such as this? The
roads are the arteries of the empire and, wherever the
wayfarer travels, they remind him constantly of Rome's
greatness.

The first road is the Via Appia, the queen of roads.
It is broad enough for two carriages to pass side by side,
is built of a specially imported stone of great tough-
ness, and the smooth blocks fit together with almost
no gaps. But the Romans have expanded their road
network wherever they have conquered. Gaius Gracchus did much good work in this regard when he busied
himself most earnestly with the construction of roads,
laying stress upon their practicality, as well as upon their
appearance. His roads were straight and passed through
the country without deviation. They had pavements
of quarried stone, and substructures of tightly packed
sand. Any holes or depressions in the ground were filled
up, all rivers and ravines were bridged, and both sides
of the road were made of equal height. The result was
a beautiful uniformity. He also had milestones set up
so that travellers knew how far they had to travel, as
well as other stones so that horsemen would be able to
mount their horses from them without any assistance.
In Italy each milestone is inscribed with a figure giving
the distance from Rome or from the city where the
road originated. And in the forum in Rome stands the
golden milestone, so called because it is embossed with

gilt borders, and on which is written the mileage from Rome to various key points in the empire.

Gracchus's techniques have not changed greatly over time. The main point of the road is to allow swift travel all-year round, whatever the weather. Roads need a firm foundation, must be properly drained of surface water, and must be topped with durable paving in areas where the traffic is heavy.

It is best to avoid building roads in valleys so as to avoid the marshy deep soil and the floods that rivers bring. By contrast, some land is so firm that no bed is required at all and the stones can be laid straight on to the ground. For roads that are expected to have light traffic, a trench is filled with stones that have been natu-rally rounded by the pounding of the sea. These are then packed in clay and a gravel surface is laid on top. For heavier traffic, the road is paved with a durable rock such as basalt or granite, which has been hewn into pieces about two feet across and eight inches deep. The road builders then fit these together as best they can to leave only minimal gaps. Sometimes, passing through a marshy or sandy area cannot be avoided, and in these instances a proper bed must be laid. A deep trench is then dug, which is filled with rock, or else wooden piles are driven into the ground, on to which a wooden grill is laid, with the gravel laid on top of that.

The road is shaped in such a way that it has a crown in order for rainwater to run off easily. Busy roads will be finished with a raised stone border and also an unpaved track to the side for the use of pedestrians and pack animals. Channels on either side carry away the rainwater. If there is a risk of skidding, artificial ruts are sometimes added to keep vehicles on the road. The width of the road will vary according to the quantity of traffic. There are a few particularly busy sections of the Via Appia, for example, where it is as wide as twenty feet, making a three-lane carriageway. Most of the roads entering Rome itself widen to thirty feet or more just before they reach the city gates. On smaller, rural roads, people generally travel on horseback or in a two-horse carriage meaning that a much more narrow track is sufficient.

Occasionally, the route encounters some significant natural obstacle, such as a mountain or river. Bridges are used to cross large rivers and can be made of either wood or concrete faced with stone. The largest tunnels are like those we passed through at Cumae. If it is impossible to tunnel or to cut through the hill, the engineers will try to pin a wooden scaffolding to a cliff. This framework can then be used to support a wooden road and thereby bypass the obstruction. Each road in Italy has its own curator to keep it in good repair. In the provinces it is one of the primary duties of the governor to ensure that the locals fulfil their obligations with regard to the upkeep of the roads.

The great system of roads starts by radiating out from Rome. There are five main routes. The first is the Via Appia, which we took earlier on our journey to Baiae. It is possible to keep travelling south to Messana and from there along the north coast of Sicily to Lilybaeum, from where the boats make the crossing to Carthage in no more than a day if conditions are favourable. Carthage is linked by the coastal road to the other cities in Africa and, as we found, it is possible to cross from here to Hispania. The road to the east runs to Alexandria, before continuing all the way to Antioch. It is also possible to head inland from Alexandria on two roads that run on either bank of the Nile down to the border with Ethiopia. A branch road on the right bank leads off to the Red Sea port of Berenice.

The second route from Rome keeps on the Via Appia all the way to Brindisium from where the boats cross regularly to Dyrrhachium in Greece. From here, the great Via Egnatia passes through Macedonia and Thrace towards the Hellespont. Two roads branch off and head down to Athens. Having crossed the Hellespont to Lampsacus, you can follow the road through Asia Minor to Antioch.

Three routes head northwards from Rome. The first is the Via Flaminia, which heads out to the centre of Italy where it joins the Via Aemilia and runs to Mediolanum. One route heads east from here towards Aquileia, which is the centre for trade coming into Italy from the river Danube. From here, one road heads through Dalmatia to Dyrrhachium while the other passes along the Danube down towards the Hellespont. The second main road to head north from the capital is the Via Aurelia, which runs up the west coast towards the Alps, before the road turns off towards the coastal cities of Gaul, ending up in Narbo. From here the road runs down to Tarraco. Finally, there is the Via Cassia, which runs up through the centre of Italy before it joins the Via Claudia Augusta and heads towards the northern borders. Every province has its principal routes and branch roads that lead off in all directions.

This elaborate network of roads keeps the empire safe. If ever there is any incursion by barbarian tribes or a local uprising, it is possible for legionary forces to be dispatched there with the utmost speed. Such an increase in security means that agriculture and commerce have flourished and farmers and merchants alike use the roads to transport their produce and goods to market. Workers and craftsmen can travel where they wish to and try to earn their livelihood wherever they think it likely to be most profitable. The empire has become a great mixing pot of different peoples, bringing with them their own local customs wherever they go. The Greeks work as schoolmasters and physicians all over the empire, or as artists and painters and sculptors, since demand for such works seems insatiable. Jews and Syrians have settled everywhere. There is no town without its foreigners. I have heard it said that even barren, savage Corsica has more foreign residents than locals.

The roads also deliver the good government for which the Romans are justly famous. They are the oil of the administration so that if a governor is in the least doubt concerning the justice of a case, he can send to the emperor for advice and await his instructions. It also means that the emperor need not exhaust himself by travelling everywhere to settle matters in person. Instead, he can stay in his palace and manage the world through letters. These arrive almost as soon as they are written, borne on the roads as if by wings. And the road network allows all manner of imperial officials in the provinces to travel in the conduct of their business, holding regular assizes to deliver justice to the locals.

It is not only officials who need to travel. High-status provincials, such as town councillors, who have been accused of a capital offence in the provinces and are not subject to the jurisdiction of the governors, are sent to Rome for trial. Many others head to the capital in order to promote their claims. Towns will send embassies to beseech the emperor to support their particular cause. These ambassadors are local worthies who carry out the onerous task out of their love of, and sense of duty towards, their home city. Sometimes these go too far. Every year, Byzantium used to send a deputy to Rome to congratulate the emperor Trajan and donate to him some 12,000 sesterces until the emperor himself suggested that this exchange of greetings should be done by letter. Vespasian limited the number of such ambassadors to three, partly to reduce the cost for these cities but also so that he did not have to meet them all. If the emperor is on campaign, these embassies can become especially difficult. Augustus spent two years in Tarraco yet embassies still reached him from the Greek isles of Lesbos and Samos.

When the emperor travels it is a sight to behold. As he approaches a city, all its dignitaries will line up outside the walls to greet him, along with crowds of the citizens arranged by age and social status, and there will be speeches and acclamations. Then the city gate is opened and the emperor and his retinue are welcomed within by further acclamations and festivities, with women dressed as bacchants, and men and boys as satyrs, who lead the way into the city to the accompaniment of flutes and pipes. The city becomes a temporary capital and is lavishly decorated for the occasion. A procession bearing laurel branches and palm leaves, as well as statues of the local gods, accompanies his majesty as he passes along the main street, and he will respond by making gestures of warm acknowledgement. It is as if a god has deigned to visit.

Trundling along a minor road in northern Gaul, to the accompaniment of the bumps of the carts and the twittering of the birds, we headed ever closer towards the sea. Whenever we stopped to rest, we would look at the many shrines and tombstones that sit by the roadside. These are not the monumental sepulchres that line the Via Appia as you leave Rome, but simple shrines to Mercury, the god of travel and business, often in the form of a heap of stones, to which passers-by add their own pebble as an offering. As we left one large town, we passed by an infant that had been abandoned by its parents, who by dint of poverty or some other inclination, had decided not to rear their offspring. The slave dealers or dogs would soon pick it up.

We came to some small tombs bearing inscriptions that called out to us, the traveller, to read them, and, as we were in no hurry, we stopped since they can often be amusing. One said, 'if you want to know who I am, the answer is ash and burnt embers'. Another urged the reader to seize the day and enjoy himself: 'Friends who read this, heed what I say: mix the wine, bind the garland round your forehead, and drink. And do not hold back from the pleasure of love with beautiful women.' Wise words. Most people believe that a person's soul hangs around its place of burial and so they see it is as a kind of home: 'Here is my home forever', as another tomb was inscribed. I cannot say that sounds very enticing. I also cannot say whether I think these souls are still living in some way. Perhaps they simply sleep: 'Life was a pain, death prepared me rest', as one grave said. Let us hope that such souls are awake for the banquets that family members often hold for them on their birthdays, when they travel out to the deceased's tomb and feast together. Nearby, we saw a lone figure pouring an offering of wine down a pipe that led to the remains of her dead loved one. That should cheer the spirit up, whatever condition they are in! Wherever there are roads, there are tombs, and the voices of the dead will call out to you as you make your way, urging you to stop and read what they have to say, to give the lonely shade within a few moments company and perhaps a small offering, and to give a moment's thought about the end to which your own life's journey must ultimately come.

I dallied to read a few more of the graves that we had encountered, telling the rest of the party to continue on their way and that I would catch them up. I must have spent longer than I realised and on moving on I rode for almost an hour without sight of them ahead. When I approached a spinney of oaks, several armed men ran out towards me, and, before I could race ahead, they had grabbed my horse's reins and pulled me to the ground. They bound my hands, took away my knife and pushed and shoved me into the cover of the woods that lay beyond. I had been captured by bandits.

Bandits are a perennial problem for the traveller. Every region has them to some degree but the north-west of Gaul seems to be riddled with them. Many bandits are runaway slaves or deserters from the army and any kind of conflict increases this latter group significantly. That is why I travel with a retinue, of course, and I make sure that a couple of the slaves are big men who are handy with a blade. If you cannot afford to have a retinue, I recommend that you try to attach yourself to a group of wealthy travellers, particularly if you have heard that the road ahead is infested with bandits. Or wait until an ambassador, a governor's assistant, or the governor himself is heading that way and hang on to his party. Even then, it is not always safe. One of my friends, an equestrian called Robustus, vanished without trace, and the same thing happened to my fellow townsman, Metilius Crispus. Whether he was killed by his slaves or along with them by bandits no one knows. And another friend of mine was wounded in an attack at the roadside, meaning that the various letters he was carrying for me failed to arrive. All you can do is report it to the commander of the local forces and hope that he does something about it.

The problem is worse in the frontier regions and in the most rural areas. These wild places have plenty of woods and marshes or other inhospitable areas where the thieves can make camp and hide. You should be particularly careful in sites such as the swamps near Damietta in Egypt, where some savage thugs known as 'the Shepherds' lurk. Mountains are also consistently dangerous places. The Mysian Olympus in Pamphylia has huge oak forests and is full of bandit strongholds. I heard of one robber there who used to cut off his victims' legs. I suspect that most of the mountain dwellers of Sardinia and Corsica live off the loot they have robbed from honest travellers. But even civilised parts of the empire suffer from this curse from time to time and outlaws terrorise the locality by burning villages and farmsteads, even raiding great cities, until they are inevitably hunted down by imperial forces and destroyed, either by being tortured to death or by being thrown to the wild beasts in the games. Their corpses are then hung up as a warning to all and as a consolation to their victims' families. In mountainous areas their bodies are often simply left unburied by the roadside. I remember coming across one of these once while travelling with a physician. So much flesh had been torn away by the carrion birds that the doctor found it very instructive to examine the inner workings of the body.

My captors took me for miles off the road until we came to a cave in the side of a hill. The area was shaded by leafy forests and the steep slopes were covered with thorny bushes, forming a kind of natural fortress. A nearby spring produced a stream of clear water that supplied their needs. Above the cave, they had built a small lookout post, where one of them stood guard, and strong fencing had been erected near the front where they could pen any sheep or cattle that they had raided from farms.

At the entrance to the cave an old woman, almost bent double with age, was busy cooking on an open hearth, making what looked like a pot of stew for the communal supper. 'Well done, boys,' she cried in a high-pitched, shaky voice when she saw me, 'There's plenty of tasty stew for you, my brave and loyal young warriors.' And she began to hand round the meal in bowls, along with coarse bread and cups full to the brim with wine. In the cave I could see items of silver and some fine clothes, which had obviously been stripped from other poor travellers.

'Why do you live like this?' I asked them, 'Why do you harm the honest people of the empire?'

'I was too poor to feed my family. What else could I do?' answered one, defensively. But another was more upbeat: 'Why should I live in the city as a slave when we can live as we like here? There is no deception here – we all look out for each other.'

Another, who had already drunk several cups of wine, looked at me aggressively. 'Let me tell you why we live here. Why should we put up with corrupt magistrates, or the way the government seizes everything we have in taxes? They are the real robbers!'

This produced a general murmur of agreement and I could see no point in discussing it with him. But he had warmed to his task and went on. 'The dreadful injuries that poor men like us suffer force us to become outlaws. The Druid prophetess has foretold what will happen to you Romans on the day the Gauls finally pluck up the courage to throw off our hated yoke!'

Such were the empty prophecies of the Druids. The bandits ate and drank with abandon, downing piles of meat, great chunks of bread and swilling down the wine as if it were water. As they grew drunk they began to tell jokes and roared with laughter, sang deafeningly, and hurled abuse at each other. It was a feast of thieves.

That night, I was tied to a post within the cave where I managed to sleep only fitfully for a little as the robbers slept off their celebration. The sun rose early but it had little effect on them. My captors, once they realised that I had no wealth on me but that I was an important person, had already made it clear that they planned to demand a ransom. I could have been stuck for months in this dreadful den. I then realised that because of their celebration no guard had been placed that evening. I decided that I would have to make the most of this opportunity.

I always carry a small, curved knife concealed in the hem of my cloak for emergency use. The robbers thought that they had disarmed me but I managed to pull out the weapon by unpicking the hem and then used it to cut my ropes. It took time, and I was constantly fretting that one of them would wake up at any moment, but eventually I succeeded. I sneaked past the empty pens and in a few minutes was moving through the forest as quickly as the thick undergrowth would allow.

Hour after hour I crashed through the woods. I used the sun to ensure that I kept travelling in a westerly direction, which I knew would eventually bring me back to the road. My party would no doubt be scouring the area. I hoped that the bandits would not try to chase after me. I had tried to conceal my tracks and they did not seem to have dogs that might be used to pursue me. Eventually the forest began to thin out and I came to some grazing land. I was tired and famished, and the light was beginning to fail, so I prayed to Mercury to send me help. Almost immediately I came to a small house, roofed with reeds and stems from the marshes. The elderly couple within were shocked when I called to them and rattled the door but they took me in. Stooping down, I passed through the low doorway, and the old man pulled out a bench, and invited me to rest, while his wife covered it with a rough blanket. Then she raked over the warm ashes in the hearth and brought the fire back to life, feeding it with dried leaves and bark and puffing on it with as much force as she could muster. Once it was going nicely, she stripped the leaves from some vegetables that her husband had gathered from a store outside. He used a two-pronged stick to lift down a wretched-looking piece of dried meat that was hanging from a smoke-blackened beam. He cut some small chunks from it and put them in a pot of water to boil.

While we waited for the food, the old couple made conversation with me to pass the time. There was a tub made of beech wood, and this was filled with some of the water as it warmed and offered to me so that I might refresh my limbs. In the middle of the floor lay a mattress of soft sedges, which was placed on a wooden frame to make a couch. They covered it with cloths, that they clearly only brought out during sacred festivals, though even these were old and worn. They invited me to sit down. The old woman, her skirts tucked up, her hands trembling, placed a table in front of me and wiped it clean with fresh mint. On it she put some black and green olives, cherries preserved in wine lees, radishes and endives, then a lump of cheese and some lightly roasted eggs, all in clay dishes. After this she set out a carved mixing bowl for wine, with cups made of wood and lined with yellow beeswax. The fire quickly produced the hot food and the wine was poured. It was a simple, local vintage, of no age. For the second course came nuts, and a mix of dried figs and plums, as well as sweet-smelling apples in open wicker baskets. In the centre sat a gleaming honeycomb.

What a feast was this. Never have I dined so well, not even at the emperor's table on the Palatine. This old couple made light of their poverty by acknowledging it, and bore it without any discontent. They told me they had married in this cottage when young and had grown old together. They had no slaves but gave orders to each other, which they willingly carried out together. Poor they might have been, poor in spirit they were not.

The next morning they directed me to the road where, as I had suspected, I soon came across some of my slaves, who were overjoyed to see me alive and well. I sent one of them back to the old couple's cottage with a few gold coins. I sent another with a letter to the local centurion, telling him to hunt down the outlaws who had captured me and to inform me when he had crucified them. This he did a few days later.

·· COMMENTARY ··

The ancients' sense of natural beauty was in some ways similar to the modern, post-romantic notion, in that it saw something authentic and unconstrained about the simple life of the country, however far from the reality this was for most peasants and agricultural slaves. But it was also very different since it was closely linked to the perceived sanctity of nature. Seneca's account of his feeling close to the divine in a shaded glade gives a good example of this (*Moral Letters* 41). Elite writers often claim to hold the city in deep distrust, by contrast, and say that it is in their country estates that they find true happiness (the examples given by Falx come from Varro, Lucretius and Seneca the Elder, among others). Much of this is, of course, a literary pose, but it certainly seems to be the case that the wealthy took great pains to make their villas as natural as they could contrive them to be.

The Roman road network was an extraordinary achievement, with the major roads managed by the state, the viae publicae, amounting to some 67,000 miles, and was primarily built to enable a quick military response to any threat, whether internal or external. The quality and consistency of the construction was established early on, as is seen in the passage about the second-century BCE Gaius Gracchus (Plutarch, *Life of Gaius Gracchus* 7). Stones had to be set up at intervals to help travellers mount their horses for the simple reason that the Romans did not have stirrups. But whatever the military benefits of the road network, travel for most ordinary people, and traders with heavy goods to transport in particular, was almost always faster, cheaper and more comfortable by water. The description of boats being towed upstream comes from the poem about the Moselle river by the fourth-century writer Ausonius (*Mosella* 39–44). The account of an emperor's arrival in a city is based on that of the general Mark Antony in Ephesus in 41 BCE (Plutarch, *Life of Antony* 24).

Tombstones survive in great numbers and their epitaphs can offer us a glimpse into various Roman beliefs about death and the afterlife, although there is very little uniformity (Falx's examples can be found in *CIL* 9.1837, 6.17985a and in the *Carmina Latina Epigraphica* 587). Some epitaphs were resolutely nihilist and the sentiment *non fui, fui, non sum, non curo* (I was not, I was, I am not, I don't care) was so common that it was often abbreviated to simply *nffnsnc*. Many epitaphs do, however, imply or suggest a belief in life after death, although it is rare to find positive statements of the exact form that took. There seems to have been a widespread sense that an individual's spirit inhabited the area in the immediate vicinity of the burial. Cremation was usual in the early empire and the location of an individual's ashes would be marked with a small monument if his or her family could afford to do so. Some of these took the form of round head shapes, which seem to have been painted, and which may have represented the spirit of the deceased, referred to as the *genius* for male dead and *iuno* for female. The association of spirits with the place of burial meant that the tomb was often perceived as their eternal home. Graves sometimes contained suitable goods for the spirit contained within: toys for dead children, mirrors for women, dice and drinking cups for men. Such artefacts implicitly understood the afterlife as maintaining all the social hierarchies of earthly society. It is possible that these goods were conceived of in purely metaphorical terms, in that they represented an earthly image of the spirit's unknown and unknowable future requirements, something that was not meant to be understood literally. Most bodies were cremated, after all, which would seem to contradict a literal belief in the continuing physical needs of the spirits of the dead.

Many epitaphs are unclear about whether the spirit of the dead person is alive or conscious. Rest is a common theme and many refer to the deceased being asleep. One husband commends his 'incomparable wife' to 'eternal sleep'. To be asleep is to be alive, albeit unconscious, but this text makes it clear that the husband understands this metaphorically: 'no one is immortal', and 'though dead, yet she will live with me', 'she will always be golden in my eyes' (*CIL* 6.11082). Other epitaphs, however, express the belief that the spirits of the dead both maintain an active life and keep in contact with the living. Banquets were held regularly at the tombs of the dead: after the funeral itself; nine days later; annually on the deceased's birthday; and also on certain other festivals. Pipe burials contained pipes that led down to the remains of the dead so that food and wine could be poured in to feed them. What all these varied beliefs emphasise is that the dead were understood to continue to play a part in family life. Death was not generally seen as a final, purely biological event but more as a process whereby the dead gradually faded from immediate memory into a broader, hazier familial remembrance of their ancestors.

Bandits seem to have been a common problem for travellers although it is impossible to quantify the issue. Epictetus advises safety-conscious travellers not to venture out alone along a road, but to travel in company with officials (*Discourses* 4.1.91). The empire had no police force, as such, but local governors were expected to hunt out bandits and those who were caught suffered the most brutal punishments. Again, it is impossible to know how many criminals were caught and whether it was fear of crime rather than actual banditry that is reflected in the sources. Certain semi-habitable areas, however, were clearly more dangerous than others, and any civil war would lead to an upsurge in soldiers who had either deserted or been defeated and who had turned to banditry to survive. And some travellers did go missing. The stories of how Metilius Crispus and the equestrian Robustus vanished without trace are from Pliny the Younger (*Letters* 6.25) and from Cicero, who complains in a letter to his friend Atticus that he failed to receive one of his letters because his friend, Lucius Quinctus, was robbed on the journey (*Letters to Atticus* 7.9.1). The description of the robbers' cave comes from Book 4 of Apuleius's *Golden Ass*, while the complaints of the outlaws are based on various sources from the later empire when central governmental weakness seems to have led to an increase in brigandage in northwestern Gaul, with the appearance of a group known as the *bagaudae* (see Anonymous, *The Complainer* 4.2;

Anonymous, *On Military Matters* 4.1; Salvian, *On the Government of God* 5.22). Stories of doom predicted by Druids can be found in *Augustan History*, Alexander Severus 60.6, and Tacitus, *Histories* 4.54. The scene of contented rural simplicity in the elderly couple's cottage is from Ovid's *Metamorphoses*.

Julius Caesar and Strabo supply the basis for the descriptions of the geography of Gaul (*Gallic Wars*; *Geography* 4.1.14). The account of marling comes from Pliny the Elder, as does the description of a primitive harvester (*Natural History* 17.42 and 18.72). Varro is the source of the information on how to rear snails and dormice (*On Agriculture* 3.14–15).

CHAPTER IX

IN BRITANNIA

THE BRITONS ARE UTTERLY SEPARATED from the whole world. We had travelled to Portus Gesoracum to make the crossing, which took some eight or nine hours and passed off without incident. As you sail towards the harbour at Rutupiae, the gleaming granite of its triumphal arch is visible from some distance and makes a powerful statement that Britannia has been conquered by Rome.

Britannia used to be called Albion, said to have been because of the whiteness of its cliffs opposite the coast of Gaul. It is the largest of all the islands in the Roman empire and lies with Germany to its east, Gaul within sight to the south, and Hispania further south still, to the west. Its northern extremities, which have no shores opposite to them, are beaten by the waves of a vast open sea. The form of the entire country is similar to an oblong shield or battleaxe. There is, however, a large and irregular tract of land that juts out from its furthest shores to the west, tapering off in a wedge-like form. The Roman fleet first sailed around the shores of this remote island at the time of the conquest and in doing so ascertained that Britannia is indeed an island. The sailors described the northern waters as sluggish, only yielding with difficulty to the oar and not even raised by the wind in the way that other seas are. The reason, I suppose, is that mountains, which are the cause of storms, are comparatively rare in Britannia, and also that the ocean surrounding the island is so deep that it is harder for the wind to move the water. It is an extraordinary sea, with currents running in every direction, and it does not merely ebb and flow along the shore but penetrates far inland.

In ancient times the island remained unvisited by foreign armies, and neither Dionysus, tradition tells us, nor Hercules nor any other hero campaigned against it. In more recent times, Julius Caesar, who has been made a god because of his deeds, was the first man to conquer the island, and after subduing the Britons he forced them to pay tribute to Rome. Who the original inhabitants of Britannia were, whether they were indigenous or foreign, is, as usual among barbarians, not known. Their physical characteristics are various and from these some conclusions may be drawn. The red hair and large limbs of the inhabitants of Caledonia point clearly to a German origin. The dark complexion of the Silures, who live in the west, their curly hair, and the fact that Hispania is on the opposite shore, suggest that Iberians long ago crossed over and occupied these parts. Those who live nearest to the Gauls are also like them, either because they are descended from them or because the similar climate has produced similar physical qualities. It seems to me that the first is the most likely because their language is very similar, they are both quick to stand up to threat of danger, and then are equally cowardly when it actually arrives. The Britons, however, are more spirited, no doubt because they have not been softened by such a long period of peace as the Gauls have enjoyed. Even the Gauls were once renowned as warriors but sloth has long since crept over them and they lost their courage along with their independence. This is clearly now starting to happen to the tribes in Britannia.

The Britons' military strength lies primarily in their infantry, although they also fight with chariots. They are divided into tribes led by chieftains and the inability of these powerful groups to work together in concert has been to the greatest advantage of the Romans, as we have been able to dominate them one by one.

The sky is obscured by continual rain and cloud. But it is never very cold. The days are much longer than in the Mediterranean and the nights are bright. In the extreme north the nights are so short that it is almost impossible to tell the difference from the day. It is said that if there are no clouds in the way, the splendour of the sun can be seen throughout the night, and that it does not rise and set, but only crosses the heavens. The climate is warm enough to grow all the normal crops produced by other provinces of the empire, with the exception of the olive and the vine. The excessive dampness in the soil and atmosphere do mean, however, that all crops take a long time to ripen. Large deposits of gold and silver are found in Britannia and are one of the main benefits to accrue to us from conquering the island. The ocean also yields up pearls with a dusky, bluish hue.

Their houses are humble, being built for the most part of reeds or logs. The method they employ of harvesting their grain crops is to cut off no more than the heads and store them away in roofed barns, and then each day they pick out the ripened heads and grind them into flour. They live modestly since they have little wealth and the island is thickly populated. The inhabitants of Britannia who dwell on the promontory known as Belerium are especially hospitable to strangers and live in a civilised manner as a result of the frequent contact with foreigners who come to buy the tin produced there. The miners quarry the rock containing the metal and then melt it down to cleanse it of impurities. They then work the tin into pieces the size of knucklebones and transport it to an island that lies off Britannia and is called Ictis. A peculiar thing happens in the case of the islands such as this that lie off Britannia. The sea swells up and the passages between them and the mainland run full of water and they seem to be islands, but the sea then recedes and leaves the passage dry, so that the island looks more like a peninsula. The merchants and miners meet on this island and then transport the tin back to Gaul.

The island of Hibernia lies beyond Britannia and is almost as large. During the conquest of Britannia, the general Agricola posted some troops in the area facing Hibernia and considered invading it. He thought that Hibernia, lying as it does between Britannia and Hispania and being conveniently situated for the seas round

Gaul, might have been the means of connecting these powerful parts of the empire, which would bring great benefits to all. It differs little from Britannia in terms of soil and climate, or in the disposition, temper and habits of its population. Agricola believed that a single legion plus a few auxiliaries would be enough to conquer and occupy the island, and that it would have a salutary effect on the Britons to see Roman forces all around them and thus, in this way, for freedom to be banished from their sight.

There are a great many other small islands off the coast but none have a circumference greater than 125 miles. Demetrius of Tarsus once made a voyage of inquiry on the emperor's order to some of these. He observed that they had few inhabitants, most of whom were holy men held in great reverence by the Britons. They are a superstitious lot. Shortly after Demetrius's arrival a great storm erupted, with violent winds and lightning flashes darting to the ground. When the storm abated, the locals claimed that a mighty soul must have died and infected the air with great pestilence.

Even Britannia has its cities. Londinium is a busy commercial centre with much wealth on display in its architecture. The city was badly damaged by fire some years ago but it has largely recovered. It has a forum and amphitheatre, a temple to Jupiter as well as various Roman deities who have taken on a British guise, some baths, and perhaps fifty thousand people live there, all told. One building worth visiting is the basilica in the forum, which is enormous and, to me, seems out of all proportion to the size of the city. I assume it was built to impress the locals and emphasise that London was the capital of a province that would remain Roman forever, but when you enter its huge hall you are actually struck by the lack of business going on. Normally you would expect such a place to be buzzing with legal proceedings and other civic business. Here, you are struck more by the quiet.

It is almost impossible to travel anywhere in Britannia without passing through Londinium, since nearly all the main roads start from the capital. There are fords and ferries further upriver but London's bridge offers the easiest and quickest means of crossing and it connects with the other parts of the road network. The city itself is laid out in the familiar grid and you will find the best shopping on the decumanus and cardo, which are broad streets. There is a busy port just upstream of the bridge over the river and you can watch the stevedores unloading the boats of their cargoes of pottery and amphorae of oil and wine. There is little by way of warehousing and most of the imported stock goes straight to market. Some areas of the city consist of town housing but wherever you go you cannot escape from the dominant view of that basilica.

Heading north or east, you will come to the two other main cities in the south, Verulamium and Camulodunum. Verulamium has a forum and a theatre. Camulodunum used to have a theatre and a temple to Claudius, before they were burned in a revolt. But, in truth, travellers do not come to Britannia to experience its cities. Indeed, it has to be said that very few tour Britannia at all. I have to admit that my reasons for making the effort were twofold. First, as I have mentioned, I came to see my son, who is stationed on the wall built by Hadrian to control the Caledonians; and second, I came to visit my old friend Septimius, who is currently developing his estate in the west of the country. I did not linger in London, therefore, but headed westwards to Aquae Sulis, which is the nearest town to the estate, where I planned to take the waters of the spring.

As one travels through the verdant countryside, Britannia seems a happy and prosperous province, and the Britons seem content with their lot, cheerfully bearing the conscription, the taxes, and the other burdens imposed on them by the empire. It was not always so. Not long after the conquest by the emperor Claudius, the Britons constantly complained about the supposed miseries of subjection and, by endlessly talking about them, exaggerated them all the more. 'All we get by patience,' they said, 'is that heavier demands are exacted from us, as from men who will readily submit. We used to rule ourselves, now we are tyrannised by imperial legates and their centurions, who combine violence with insult. Nothing is safe from their avarice, nothing from their lust. Our homes are ransacked, our children torn from us, our men forced to serve in the army.'

'Look at the Germans,' they said, 'they managed to drive the Romans out. The Romans' motivation is just greed, whereas ours is the safety of our families and freedom. Surely they will go back to Gaul like Julius Caesar did? We have already taken the hardest step by daring to talk about rebelling. Now it is time to dare to act.'

Rousing each other in this way, and under the leadership of Boudicca, a woman of royal descent, they rose in arms. 'As your Queen,' she cried in rallying her troops,

I pray to you to ask you for victory, security, and freedom against men who are arrogant, unjust, and godless, if I must call 'men' these Romans who bathe in warm water, eat fancy delicacies, drink unmixed wine, smear themselves with myrrh, take boys who are nearly adults to their soft beds, and act like slaves to a bad lyre-player.

The Britons fell upon our troops, which were scattered on garrison duty, stormed the forts, and burst into the colony of Camulodunum. With a barbarian cruelty, they spared no one. Londinium and Verulamium were also sacked. The ninth legion under Quintus Cerialis was ambushed and annihilated. Gaius Paulinus had been campaigning in the west, and, hearing of the uprising, he moved quickly with his cavalry to Londinium but hesitated whether to stand and fight there. Eventually he decided that he lacked sufficient troops to hold the city and chose to sacrifice this single site in order to save the province as a whole. Unmoved by lamentations and appeals, he departed, allowing any inhabitants who wished to do so to join him. Those who stayed, because they were old or simply attached to the place, were slaughtered by the enemy. Paulinus then quickly brought reinforcements in the form of his infantry, and, confronting the Britons, he killed as many as seventy thousand. In one single battle, he brought the province back to obedience.

In the aftermath, the Romans sought to assuage the British rage. Agricola aimed to distract the barbarous people from thinking about warfare by getting them accustomed to the charms of luxury and he therefore encouraged and subsidised the building of temples, courts of justice and houses, praising the natives who energetically supported this policy and reproving those who did not. In this way a kind of honourable rivalry grew up among the local leaders. He also provided a liberal education for the sons of the chieftains so that they would realise the benefits of Greek and Roman culture. Many people now wanted to speak Latin to improve their eloquence. It became fashionable to adopt a Roman style of dress, and the toga could be seen everywhere. Little by little, they developed a liking for the couch, the bath, the elegant banquet – all those things that generate softness and decrease the military spirit. In their ignorance, the Britons thought they were becoming civilised, when in reality it was all part of their enslavement.

Septimius lives in a large villa south of Aquae Sulis. I knew him well from my days in the army. He comes from Africa but has always had a keen sense for a good deal and has made a great deal of money from importing luxury goods from the East and from investing the profits into land all over the empire. He has considerable estates in Italy, Hispania and Dacia, as well as in his native province. His most recent acquisition has been the Villa Ventorum estate in Britannia and he is currently spending a considerable amount of time and money in reinvigorating what had become a rather run-down place. It is a quiet part of the world and we passed few travellers on the road, mostly simple wayfarers walking alone with their mantle pinned up over their shoulder and what little baggage they had packed on to a mule.

The villa stands on the top of a hill and is exposed to the mild winds from the south-west. It is modest by the standards of his other villas but contains several well-appointed reception rooms, complete with new frescoes and mosaics. The work was carried out by specially imported Gallic craftsmen and so is well above the usual standard that you find in Britannia. There is a small bath complex at one end of the range, and the hypocaust works sufficiently well that it is able to generate a more than decent heat.

I had a delightful time during my visit there. Septimius is hard-working but always finds time to entertain his guests in the evening. During the day, you are at liberty to enjoy the gardens, which have been laid out in the formal manner, or the estate itself, which contains much longer routes for a more vigorous expedition on horseback. At dinner, Septimius is a learned and charming host, and he entertains his visitors with anecdotes about his various escapades. After food, we relaxed and I would discuss his business interests with him, keen as I am to learn from some of his ideas. He, in turn, was keen to find out what was going on in the world of high politics in Rome.

The upgrading of the villa is almost complete, with only some of the orchards needing to be replanted. Septimius has also invested in property in nearby Lindinis and plans to rent this out. His other mercantile enterprises include a significant percentage of the concession in the imperial salt works in the low-lying estuaries by the ocean to the west, and a large pottery that supplies black burnished ware to the military in the north and to the markets in Londinium. He is concerned about the salt works because work is needed on the sea defences and he fears that they might fail if there is a big storm, allowing the sea to inundate huge swathes of farmland in the low-lying coastal areas, not to mention destroying his own salt works in the coastal marshes. His latest project is to acquire the imperial franchise to operate the lead mines at Vebriacum. 'I know the man who runs it at the moment,' he said, 'and he couldn't run a bath. The whole mine is going to collapse if he's not careful and I know I can improve production considerably.'

Septimius is dynamic and full of ideas of this kind. He is an educated man but not bookish and keeps a library of about sixty scrolls in the house in specially built cupboards, partly for the benefit of his guests but also because his wife and daughter love to read. He has a passion for oysters and spends liberally on having them supplied fresh from the nearby coast. He is also passionate about hunting and has established a deer park close to the villa. He keeps a number of fine horses and hunting dogs, for which Britannia is a noted source. He is popular in the area because, as a wealthy landowner, he has recently served as a magistrate and paid for various entertainments at the religious festivals. The previous owner of the estate lived in London and relied on a steward to oversee the running of the property. As is so often the case, the steward failed to carry out his job diligently and the lack of interest shown by the owner was reflected in a decline in yields.

His wife, Claudia, is from a wealthy family in Gaul but comes from Roman ancestry. She is an educated woman who loves to read in both Latin and Greek. She was delighted with the gift I brought her of a copy of Horace's poems. She broke her ankle as a child, and, even though her parents were able to bring in the aid of an expensive Greek physician, who set the bone with great care, she still walks with a slight limp. She has read many medical treatises and keeps a small herb garden to help make various medicinal potions. She also has a flower garden and makes perfumed oils to sweeten rooms and to be used in the baths to massage and perfume the body.

Septimius showed me round the villa. He has three children, two boys and a girl. His wife makes most of the decisions about the decoration and management of the household, and she gives the domestic slaves their daily orders and oversees the education of the two younger children. She taught them herself to read, write, sing, dance and play music, but now that they are older she has hired a Greek tutor. The older boy seems bent on joining the army despite his father's attempts to get him to follow him into business and land. Claudia worships daily at the household shrine, in which Mercury has pride of place. As the god of trade, travel and money, he is Septimius's favoured deity. One interesting aspect to Septimius's character is that he has been influenced by various stoic texts he has read and this makes him far more indulgent to his household than I am to mine. 'We all have souls,' he claims, 'even the slaves. Indeed, no man is free unless he is master of himself.' He addresses his slaves and freedmen almost as equals and even tells me about them. He has been trying to learn some of the local Brittonic language and laughs as he tries to twist his mouth round the strange guttural sounds.

He had his steward, Sextus, give us a guided tour of the estate. Sextus, he tells me, came to the estate as a sixteen-year-old slave, and, after twenty years' good service, has been rewarded with both his freedom and with promotion. Sextus was born in north Africa, near Sabratha, but was captured by pirate raiders in his early teens, who sold him to slave dealers in south-west Britannia. His mother tongue is Berber and he speaks Latin with a heavy accent. He is recently married to a woman called Julia whom he bought from her owners at the time of his own manumission. Septimius had been generous enough to lend him much of the money for this, arguing that it will ensure that the estate will be well managed when he comes to leave and return to his principal residence in Italy. Julia had been sold into slavery at about five or six, after her parents both died of disease and no relatives could be found to take her in. She thinks that she came from near Antioch but remembers little about how she came to be in Britannia. It is part of what attracted the pair, that they had both been washed up on a foreign shore after having started life so far away. Julia is a skilled hairdresser and Claudia has had her instructed in the complicated hairstyles that are all the rage in more fashionable parts of the empire.

The tutor is called Antonius and comes from Greece.

As a Roman citizen, he expects to be treated with respect, although I have little time for these jobbing educational mercenaries. They expect to be paid handsomely just because they can speak their own mother tongue. This one does at least seem to know something about geometry and rhetoric but he also seems to have had about a dozen posts in different parts of the empire over the past few years. I suspect he is using the work to fund his own miniature grand tour. He has certainly travelled widely and he confides to me that he find the Britons surly and unsophisticated. 'They are always drunk,' he complains, and adds, 'Everyone in the empire knows that they are treacherous and unreliable. And their women are loose.' I am not surprised when Claudia tells me later in confidence that she is looking for a replacement but that they are hard to come by in this far-flung place.

The cook is a slave called Britivenda. She is in her twenties and a Briton, from the nearby Durotriges tribe, but was sold into slavery by her parents when she was around the age of eight as they could not afford to keep her. She has red hair and pale, freckled skin. She is a passable provincial cook but there is something wild and furious about this woman. No doubt it is her freeborn status that means the yoke of slavery rankles with her so much: slaves who are born slaves, preferably in the household itself, are so much easier to manage. The meals consist mainly of food grown on the estate, although certain items, such as olive oil, spices and garum, are imported from other regions of the empire and, while expensive, are easily available in the local town. The cook's speciality is savillum, a local cake that contains cheese and has a honey and roasted seed topping. Interesting, to be sure.

There is a motley group of lesser slaves who have specific tasks, in addition to the undifferentiated slaves who work in the fields and apple orchards. Felix, the latrine cleaner, is from a tribe near the large estuary west of here, the Dubonni, but he smells so bad that he is kept at a distance. A large, fat slave called Ebrius brews the beer and clearly enjoys tasting it as he does so. His accent was so heavy that I could barely understand what he said. He is foreign but nobody knows where he comes from, not least himself since he was transported to Britannia as a child. Finally, I am shown Onesimus, the slave whose job it is to feed the furnace that heats up the hypocaust. He is a young man but was branded on the forehead with the mark of a runaway when he fled from a previous master. Septimius picked him up cheap as a result. 'He looked terrifying enough that I thought he would help scare off robbers,' he explains. The slave has an iron collar riveted around his neck and is kept chained to the wall at night. He is not allowed into the house. I congratulate him on the heat of the baths and he grunts a reply once my comment has been slowly explained to him. I am told he is from Caledonia. He has an unsettling habit of muttering under his breath and spitting frequently.

'You can see,' explains Septimius, 'that I have taken your advice and brought together a mix of slaves from different backgrounds. It certainly makes it less likely that they will plot together against me. Some of their Latin is so bad they can barely understand basic orders.'

The days pass easily in this corner of the empire.

The weather is mild, the cares of Rome seem a lifetime away, and the people are friendly and somewhat in awe of anyone from the imperial capital. I felt some regret when it came time to move on, but I faced a long trip up north. It began with a short journey to Aquae Sulis to enjoy the baths. This is a pleasant resort and contains a number of fine buildings, such as the temple of the goddess Sulis Minerva. Taking advantage of the decent range of shopping, I bought some new shoes here and a pair of slippers for use in the bath complex. I also had my cloaks cleaned at a fullers.

The baths here are very popular and people travel from considerable distances to enjoy them. It is funny to think that dreaming of baths used to be considered unlucky, since men did not wash regularly, whereas now some people do not eat unless they have taken a bath beforehand. The entranceway is lofty and has a wide flight of steps that are low rather than steep so that they are easy to walk up. You enter into a spacious area next to the temple, which provides a large waiting area for slaves and attendants. Off this hall are rooms designed for relaxation and therefore particularly well-suited to a bath building – elegant and well-lit. Beyond this room is a spacious locker room and between them a lofty and brightly lit hall that contains the main swimming pool. It is decorated with several white marble statues. The water that wells up from the sacred spring is hot but there is a cold plunge pool as well. There is an area arranged for rub-downs with oil where it is possible to stand about and while away the time, and this is also very elegantly decorated.

We quickly undressed, went into the hot baths, and, after working up a sweat, passed on to the cold pool. A rub-down from the masseur left our skin glistening all over with perfumed oil. I could not help but ruminate on the difference between these baths and the ancient baths of Scipio that I once visited, where the tiny bath area was narrow and dingy. Our ancestors thought a bath should not be hot unless it was taken in the dark. Scipio kept himself busy with hard labour and washed a body exhausted by farm work. He took his bath beneath a shabby roof and on a wretched floor. Who nowadays could bear to bathe in such a place? Everyone thinks himself impoverished and distressed unless the walls of his bathing area sparkle with marble, paintings and glass, and the water pours out of silver taps. And Scipio didn't bathe every day. Our ancestors only washed their arms and legs if they were dirty from farm work. The rest of the body was only washed once a week. Of course, someone will say, 'Sure, but they were very smelly men'. And what do you think they smelled of? Of the army, of farm work, and of manliness! After all, what is bathing when you think about it – oil, sweat, filth and greasy water. It is best not to dwell on these thoughts. It makes you fear for the future of the empire when its men are softening themselves in so many hot steam rooms.

Returning to the changing area I was annoyed to see my slave chatting to some young girl. I shooed her away and then we realised that she had been a distraction in every sense, for while she was talking to him her accomplice had stolen my cloak. This made me furious, not because of the money, but the insult. Leaving the building I noticed a hawker shouting out that he was a curse writer. This seemed an excellent way to get my revenge. Taking out a lead tablet he scratched on to its cold dark surface the following words: 'Whether man or woman, whether boy or girl, whether slave or free, whoever has stolen from me, Marcus Sidonius Falx, my fine cloak, you, Lady Goddess, are to exact from him a price. Let the thief responsible lose their mind and eyes in the goddess's temple.' He then rolled it up, uttered an invocation over it, and gave it to me to throw into the sacred spring so that the goddess might act upon it.

The journey up north is long and tedious. We followed the road via the military camp at Venonis as far as Lindum Colonia. This was originally built as a legionary fortress but was upgraded to a colony some decades ago and is now home to about five thousand souls. It is full of retired soldiers and everywhere you go you find yourself being regaled by tales of fighting the Brigantes or the like. Most soldiers retire near their final posting, often in colonies like Lindum that have been set up to house veteran soldiers in a recognisably Roman town where they will feel safe and at home. Of course, these veterans also serve to keep an eye on the local population and can act as reserves in the event of a crisis. More recently, colonies have been established to relieve the population pressure in Italy. The result is that there is a steady movement of loyal peoples around the empire, which serves to unify it with a common Roman culture.

Lindum is divided into two areas on account of the steep hill, and you will find everything you would expect of a city in the upper part: a forum with statues, basilica, baths, temples and shops, all laid out in a grid, with fresh water supplied by an aqueduct. The presence of well-paid soldiers has attracted a whole host of hangers-on and, in Lindum, these live on the slopes of the hill running down to the lower area by the river. Here among their huts and hovels you will find traders selling all manner of goods, both local and imported, artisans making everything from shoes to silverware, hawkers of food and drink, and plenty of prostitutes. You will also find all the unofficial wives of the serving legionaries living here, waiting for their menfolk to be free to call on them. Soldiers are legally prohibited from marrying in order to discourage them from deserting if they are posted to a far-off province, but now that most legions serve for extended periods in the same areas the practice of taking on a family is tolerated. Legionaries must be Roman citizens but their children are not, since they are illegitimate. However, should their sons decide to join the army when they are older, as many do, a blind eye is turned to this fact and they are often granted citizenship when they enlist, particularly in a province like Britannia where there are few Roman citizens.

Non-citizens join the army as auxiliaries and about twenty thousand a year join up for a twenty-five-year period of service. Many auxiliary units were originally recruited from local tribes that were then posted away from their home provinces and some of these have retained their name even though they now recruit locally. Others continue to bring in troops from their home area, such as the Batavians who are stationed here in Britannia. And the Danubian provinces of Raetia,

Pannonia, Moesia and Dacia supply plenty of recruits for units stationed all over the empire.

From Lindum we continued up to Eboracum. Travelling through the north of Britannia is like passing through one extended military camp. The signs of civilisation become rarer and rarer. Eboracum itself sits on the east bank of a river, a fort originally built for the Legio IX *Hispana*. Now it is home to the Legio VI *Victrix*, and is the headquarters of the northern command. The fortress contains barracks, granaries, headquarters and military baths. It is no different from any other legionary base you could see elsewhere in the empire.

I had intended to travel straight to Cataractonium, from where it is only a short journey to where my son is based, but my friend Septimius had given me a letter of introduction to a friend of his who maintains a villa over towards the coast, east of Eboracum. Feeling in need of some civilised comforts, I decided to make a detour to call on him and sent a slave ahead to warn him of our imminent arrival.

The journey turned out to be more difficult than I had imagined. There had been heavy rains and the last leg was on tracks that had become muddy and slippery. At length we approached the range of buildings. A large, ruddy-faced man emerged almost immediately, clearly the owner, and almost ran up to us. 'Groatings!' he cried, 'Long live the umperor!' It was going to be a long couple of days …

I shall put a curse on Septimius for setting me up like this. I have no idea how he knew the man but he obviously thought it would be hilarious to inflict him upon me. For two days I had to put up with this bumpkin's desperate attempts to impress me with his sophistication. On the first evening, when I was still tired from the journey, he insisted I join him for dinner. On entering the dining room, I stopped in my tracks. On the floor was a fearful mosaic of some hideous harpy. 'Your craftsmen have certainly captured the very likeness of the monster,' I commented. 'Monster?' he replied in bewilderment, and explained, taking care to get his Latin right, 'It is surely Venus after winning the beauty contest.' The female figure was naked and her long hair stuck out wildly. Her lower body and hips were oversized, while her legs tapered to tiny feet. In her right hand she held what I now realised was the apple that was her prize. In her right hand she held a mirror, except that she seemed to have dropped it. If this is the Britons' ideal of beauty I can only pity their men.

'Yes indeed,' I quickly replied, not wanting to offend my host, 'I was merely joking. And what fine, er, animals? The Fliery Lion, is that? And the mudderous bull? Your mosaicists were clearly remarkable.'

We dined for hours. Whatever was placed on the table, he swept it up in great handfuls: teats from a sow's udder and ribs from a pig, and a bird carved for two, and half a large fish, and a whole pike, and the leg of a chicken, and a pigeon dripping with sauce. He shoved hunks of meat into his mouth, all washed down with the vinegary water that passed for wine. At some point a troupe filed in. Our host propped himself up on his cushion as they began to recite verses from Virgil with such a heavy accent that it was some time before I could recognise the poet. 'Would you like me to explain what is happening in the story?' asked my host, and before I could summon up the words to explain tactfully that I was very familiar with the *Aeneid*, he continued, 'It is what is called an epoc and it tells the story of the fondling of Rome.' Thankfully he was then distracted when the cook carried in a boiled calf on an enormous platter. Eventually, when my head was almost dropping into my cup with tiredness, he announced that he had composed some verses, in my honour, in the manner of Virgil: 'O Falx,' he declaimed, 'I shall sing, not of arms and the man but of your great works ... ' and one hundred mangled verses later, he wrapped up: 'Nothing can last for all time,' (although his so-called poem came close), 'When the sun has finished shining it sinks to the sea / The moon wanes when it was just now full / And even the ferocity of Venus often calms to just a puff of wind.' Which seemed to prompt him to provide an unwitting blast of his own wind as an accompaniment to this finale.

This was my chance to escape and I jumped up and applauded him with great vigour, adding that this was the perfect end to a wonderful dinner and almost ran out of the room to my quarters before he could conjure up some other entertainment.

The arduous final leg of the journey came almost as a relief. My son commands an auxiliary regiment that mans the wall established by Hadrian. When I arrived at Cataractonium a letter was awaiting me from his wife, Claudia, welcoming me and inviting me to join her birthday party if I arrived in time. I stopped overnight at an inn in Vindolanda, where there was a heated public room and a small bath house in which to refresh myself. My son and his wife were currently staying at the fort of Vercovicium and I travelled there quickly on the military support road that supplies the whole length of the wall. Riding up the steep hill to the camp, I could only wonder at the power of Rome, that could bring defensive ramparts to so far-off and inhospitable a place. The only living things were the swathes of heather and occasional sheep. The fort is surrounded by a stone wall and ditch, with gates providing access. Inside, it contains a number of barrack blocks, a workshop, granary and bath house. In the centre is the large house where my son was staying. It was extraordinary to see him, my own flesh, living here at the extremities of the world. 'Here are your socks,' I said, 'And some extra underpants, too.' By the gods he will need them here in the winter.

He put on a good dinner, one to which I added various items I had brought with me: fowl, veal, pork, dried fish, cheese, olives and lentils. I asked about the barbarians who live further north and who constantly resist Roman forces. 'Why are the Caledonians so hungry for their independence?' I asked. My son replied, 'They believe us Romans are the robbers of the world who have plundered everything everywhere. They believe we are rapacious and power-hungry and that what we call empire is in reality theft, slaughter and rape. What we call peace, they call oppression.'

'And do you agree?' I asked.

'They know that if they lose we will take their women and children as slaves and their crops for our granaries. What else can they do but resist? And they have a point. Why should the Romans, who have seen the grandeur of Rome, want to conquer barbarian huts like these? Hadrian was right to stop here and draw a limit to Roman conquest.'

After dinner we walked on the north rampart of the fort. The whitewashed plaster of the wall gleamed in the evening summer sun and, as we looked towards the hills further north, it was easy to see that the glory gained by conquering such a barren land would never justify the vast cost. The wall allows us to scare them away, keep an eye on their movements, and tax the trade that comes to and fro through the gates. There are plenty of Roman traders who travel out into barbarian lands in search of gain. I have even heard of some who settled in Germania, in the land of the Marcomanni, because a special treaty allowed them to trade freely and make great commercial profit. Many thousands of Romans settled Dacia when Trajan conquered that province, pouring in from places as far as Dalmatia and Asia Minor, all seeking to benefit from the opportunities offered by Roman rule. But who would want to settle up here?

Romans have explored even further north, primarily in search of amber. At the time of the emperor Vespasian, an equestrian was sent to buy large quantities from the Baltic coast. Trade goes on with these northern barbarians along the rivers that penetrate deep into their lands. But that does not mean there is anything to be gained by attempting to conquer them. The further you travel from Rome the less civilised the world seems to become. Beyond the Rhine lies nothing worth having. I have noticed that of all the peoples we have conquered it is the Belgae who are the most courageous. This is because they are the farthest removed from the civilisation of Gaul and also because they are neighbours to the Germans, with whom they used continually to be at war. Similarly, the Helvetii outshine the rest of the Gauls in valour, because they had to struggle in almost daily fights with the Germans.

The Germans are, I believe, a pure-bred indigenous people. No people has ever tried to settle in their land and so mixed with them. Who would leave Asia, Africa or Italy to live in Germany, a hideous and rude place, with a harsh climate, that is dismal to behold? Their lands consist mostly of gloomy forests or nasty marshes. They have a tradition that Hercules visited their country and they sing songs to his honour as they advance into battle. Some of them also think that Ulysses entered Germany on his long and fabulous voyages, and that he founded a city, called Asciburgium, on the banks of the Rhine. I will leave it to you to decide whether you believe them.

The Germans count their wealth in the size of their herds, apart from those living adjoining the empire who have learned to value gold and silver for the purposes of commerce. They have little iron and so rarely use swords in battle but rely on spears, which they call framms, and which have a short, sharp, metal point. Armed with these, they can fight both at a distance or hand to hand. They have almost no cities and keep their houses detached from their neighbours, living apart in rows like trees in a wood. Every house has space around it. Their buildings are constructed of basic and uncut materials, lacking in all fashion and attractiveness. They often dig great holes in the ground that they cover with roofs made from manure and use these to shelter from the excessively cold winters. For clothing, they wear only a cloak. The wealthiest are distinguishable by the fact that they have a close-fitting vest, too. They also wear animal skins. The dress of the women does not differ from that of the men, except that the women wear a sleeveless linen tunic, embroidered with purple, that leaves the upper part of the breast bare.

The laws of matrimony are strictly observed and they are almost the only barbarians to be content with one wife. The children are brought up naked and rough. They are fed on their mother's milk and never handed over to nurses. They are all equally ill-mannered and you cannot tell the difference between a lord and a slave. For entertainment, the young men dance naked between the deadly points of spears. It has to be said, they become quite skilful at this and manage to display a certain gracefulness but it is all done solely to amuse the spectators.

The farthest lands are inhabited by even stranger barbarians than the Germans. There are certain tribes of the Scythians who feed upon human flesh and drink out of human skulls. There is also the country of the Abarimon, situated in a certain great valley of Mount Imaus, where the savage inhabitants have feet that face backwards, meaning that they can run incredibly quickly. This people cannot breathe in any climate except their own, for which reason it is impossible for them to travel. Then there is another race whose eyes are sea green in colour and who have white hair from early childhood and they are able to see better in the night than in the day. On one mountain lives a tribe who have the heads of dogs and clothe themselves in animal skins. Instead of speaking, they bark and live by catching birds. And I have heard of the Sciapods, who have only one leg but are able to leap with great agility. If it is hot, they lie on their backs in the shade of their one great foot. They live close to the Troglodytes, to the west of whom there is a tribe who lack necks and have eyes in their shoulders.

Why would one wish to leave the Roman empire? And why should the Roman empire wish to conquer these uncivilised peoples? But my musing was interrupted by the arrival of a letter-carrier to the fort, who had just managed to reach it before nightfall. He had clearly been riding hard and was directed to us as we stood on the wall in the twilight. We assumed that his letter was for my son. But it was for me. It was a message from the emperor, summoning me back to Rome.

·· COMMENTARY ··

The account of Boudicca's rebellion comes from Tacitus (*Agricola* 10–16) and Dio Cassius (*History of Rome* 62.6). Revolts often happened in provinces that had been relatively recently conquered, like Britain, before people had grown used to Roman rule. They can, in that sense, be seen as

reactions to the great tensions created by the process of
rapid acculturation that took place once the Romans
were in control – desperate attempts to return to local
rule before it was too late. Sometimes these tensions
were also reflected in the use of local religious traditions
to give a boost to morale in a way that the Romans
found hard to interpret, such as Druidism in Gaul (see,
also, *Augustan History*, Alexander Severus 60.6, on the
doom predicted by a Druid woman in the local language in 235 CE; and Tacitus *Histories* 4.54). The revolt
in Gaul also suggests what motivated these fighters,
where rebel leaders gave impassioned speeches about
the constant taxation, the burden of debt, and the brutality and arrogance of their Roman governors (Tacitus
Annals 3.40). When revolts did erupt, the rebels generally gave the Romans no quarter. Boudicca and her followers massacred the Roman troops and their families at
Colchester, London and St Albans. But such rebellions
were relatively rare during the empire. Roman military
might was such that most revolts were put down swiftly,
with a brutality that was carefully calibrated to deter any
other would-be rebels in the future. The Jews, as we saw
earlier, continued armed resistance for several generations, but they paid a heavy price for it. Most peoples
within the empire learned to put up with the Roman
yoke. The description of the geography of the British
Isles is based on Tacitus *Agricola*, Strabo and Diodorus
Siculus (*Library of History* 5.21–2). Tacitus discusses the
idea of his father-in-law, Agricola, to invade what is now
Ireland, in *Agricola* (24).

Villa Ventorum is the name given to the full-scale

reconstruction of a fourth-century Roman Villa at Hadspen House in Somerset, the first of its kind in Britain, complete with fine mosaics and frescoes. The characters are based on those used to recreate the experience of life on the ancient estate and can be found in the souvenir guidebook I have written. Approximately 130 curse tablets have been recovered from the spring in Roman Bath. Thrown into the waters to access the underground deities believed to lurk within the well, the tablets are highly formulaic and many were probably bought from a professional spell-writer. The text usually describes the offence in detail. Many seek the recovery of stolen property, which was a perennial problem at bath houses. Missing items include jewellery, money, household goods and, above all, clothes. The curses clearly reflect the powerlessness of most victims to do anything practical about their plight. No one in authority was going to be interested in a missing cloak. But it does also give a clear sense of the anger and injustice felt at the theft. The victim wanted revenge, often a violent one. A common tactic to try to achieve this was to transfer the ownership of the stolen item over to the god. Steal from a god and the thief is in trouble. The degree of punishment demanded is completely out of kilter with the scale of the offence but it goes to show how strongly the victim felt. The British curses are also very similar to others from all over the empire. There seems to have existed something of a universal language of the underworld that everyone recognised, and which shares something of the aggressive verbal violence of a modern internet troll. See John G. Gager (ed.), *Curse*

Tablets and Binding Spells from the Ancient World, Oxford University Press, 1992.

The Venus mosaic in the Roman villa near Rudston, in east Yorkshire, dates from the later third century CE. It is Roman but its naïve style suggests that the makers were Britons. In contrast to the snob, Falx, we can see this as enhancing its appeal. There are spelling mistakes: the lion is described as (LEO) F(L)AMMEFER, 'the fiery lion' and the bull is called TAURUS OMICISA, which means something like 'the murderous bull'. Some of the conventions and animals in the mosaic are reminiscent of north African works and it is possible that the design was copied from a north African pattern book. The poems by the host at Rudston are based on graffiti from Pompeii (*CIL* 4.9131 and 4.9123).

The tablets from the fort of Vindolanda, behind Hadrian's Wall, are thin wooden leaves that were used to write on like papyrus. The documents mainly record various military matters but also contain personal letters from people living at the garrison. Perhaps the most famous one is an invitation to her birthday party, sent by the wife, Claudia, of the commander of a nearby fort. Most of this text seems to have been written by the household scribe, with Claudia only adding some personal greetings at the end. Another of the tablets suggests that Roman soldiers in this part of the world had started to wear underpants (*subligacula*) to help keep the cold out. One asks to be sent some socks for the same purpose. And another refers to the local inhabitants as *Brittunculi*, a derogatory term meaning something like 'nasty little Brits'.

It is perhaps not surprising that many tribes fought tooth and nail to resist Roman domination. The comments about the Caledonians comes from Tacitus's account of the speech of their leader Calgacus (*Agricola* 29–32). Tacitus also provides the less than flattering description of the Germans (see his *Germania*), while Pliny the Elder describes some of the bizarre human beings who allegedly lived far beyond the borders of the empire (*Natural History* 7.2). In reality, the hard distinction that Falx maintains between Roman and barbarian never existed. The Romans themselves often granted citizenship to the people they conquered and to the slaves they freed, meaning that 'Roman' was always a permeable term, never linked solely to geography or ethnicity. Trade also encouraged cultural contact along the border areas, with the result that the border should not be seen so much as a sudden cut-off point but part of an area of differentiation between insiders and outsiders.

CHAPTER X

ROME-WARD BOUND

SPEED WAS PARAMOUNT. Leaving behind most of my retinue to travel back in their own time with the baggage, I rode with only a small party. By using the State Post to change horses regularly and maximise the amount of time we spent on the road, we could hope to cover fifty miles a day at a minimum.

Londinium took a week to reach, and a few days later, and a favourable sea, saw us passing through the land of the Belgae to Durocorturum, the capital of Gallia Belgica. From there we pressed on to Augustobona. The places became no more than names on our map and we saw nothing more than the inside of inns, and even those briefly. Eburobriga, Augustodunum, Cabillonum, Lugdunum, Vienna, all flashed by as we kept up our progress. Then we turned towards the forbidding slopes of the Alps.

The road becomes narrower as you start to climb and becomes not much more than six feet wide, but there are places for carriages to pass one another. The gradient is never excessively steep but is made manageable by the weaving of the road, and the turnings are broad enough to keep the road usable. Great bridges, tunnels, cuts and careful supports allow the road to pass through this inhospitable place. Thankfully we were travelling in the summer when the roads were free from snow. Winter would have seen us having to take the longer coastal route to Italy. It is possible to try the Alpine route at that time of year when the road is marked out with stakes, but these often disappear under the weight of snow and make it too dangerous. It is easy to walk unwittingly into an abyss or to be swept away by an avalanche. The narrowness of the roads means that you are often perilously close to a precipice and, when the roads are icy, it takes a strong head to make any headway. We continued our upward ascent and, towards the highest parts, the melting snow waters made the roads dangerously slippery and we had to dismount from our horses for some miles and walk. We passed wagons making their descent in the other direction and the carriages had to be bound together with enormous ropes, with men and oxen hanging on hard behind in order to try to hold them back and lower them down the mountainside safely.

Who could admire such a wild and savage scenery? A mountain can make an attractive background, in the way that a frame enhances a good painting, but the sombre monotony of its rock and ice gives no pleasure, just as the dry continuum of desert sands does nothing but terrify the human heart. When we see a mountain pass we see only difficulty and danger, a wilderness of ice and snow, and the fear of avalanche. The Alps are nothing but a horrifying barren desert in the sky. In Greece, at least, the famous mountains of mythology – Parnassus, Olympus, Pelion – can all be climbed in a single day, whereas the Alps take five days if not more. If we choose to ascend these sacred places in Greece it is to admire the panorama of the plains, and the cities and the sea beyond.

I suppose that habit can make us like any region we have lived in for a long time, even steep hills, but who can live in a mountain range? The snowy peaks and waving oaks and the mountains' firm gaze upwards to the heavens can indeed generate our admiration from afar. But our true admiration is for the fertility of the hills and plains: the corn, oil, and wine, the herds of cattle and flocks of sheep. It is only when a mountain is forced to reveal its hidden veins of gold and silver and its slabs of fine marble that we find it adding to the beauty of the world.

For Etna we may make an exception. All visitors to Sicily make the effort to go up to see the eternal snow so close to the showers of fire in the main crater. Even the emperor Hadrian ascended to see the rare sight of the sun emerging from the sea, which from the summit has the appearance of a long crooked streak. When the mountain is in action, the streams of lava rush down very nearly as far as the territory of Catana. It was on such an occasion that the famous act of filial piety of Amphinomus and Anapias occurred, when they lifted their parents on their shoulders and saved them from the doom that was rushing towards them. In an eruption, the fields of the region are covered with ash to a great depth, and, although it is an affliction at the time, the ash brings benefits later because it makes the land fertile and suited to producing fine wine.

Finally, we passed the summit and began the long descent towards Mediolanum. How my heart rejoiced to be back in Italy. Here, we find the highest magnificence of nature: the endless variety of vegetation fed by cool inexhaustible springs, clear streams with green banks, lofty vaulted grottoes, and limitless plains. And in Italy we find the finest cities and in the greatest abundance, too. Capua, Rhegium, Beneventum, Venusia, Nuceria, Hipponium – how I could continue. Here in Cisalpine Gaul, that part of Italy long ago occupied by the Gauls, we find such wealth and such fine cities: Verona; Ariminum; Cremona; Ravenna, built in the water on piles; Mediolanum; and Patavium, where some five hundred families have sufficient wealth to qualify for equestrian status, to say nothing of Aquileia, the great emporium of northern trade.

Italy is the parent of all lands, chosen by the gods to add its own emperors to the ranks of the deities. It is Italy that has civilised the world and has united the discordant and uncouth dialects of so many different peoples into one common language. One life is not enough to see Rome, let alone Italy. There are so many famous places that I am at a loss where to start. So blessed with natural beauty is it that it is clear that nature herself took delight in accumulating all her blessings in a single spot. How am I to do justice to it? There is the climate, with its eternal freshness, so full of health and vitality, the calmness of the weather, the fields so fertile, the hillsides so sunny, the groves so cool and shady, the fruitfulness of its fields, its vines, and its exquisite olives. Its numerous rivers and springs constantly refresh the land, and its surrounding seas bring trade from all over the world to its fine ports.

It is only when you return from a long journey that you fully appreciate your own land. How often do we take long journeys and cross the seas to examine curiosities, only to ignore those that lie before our very eyes? If they had been located in Greece or Egypt we would have rushed to visit them. I myself, a while back, was shown an Italian curiosity that I had never visited or even heard of before. My wife's brother had invited me to see his estates at Ameria. While I was walking round them he pointed out to me a sheet of water called Lake Vadimon. It is circular in shape, exactly like a wheel lying on the ground, and perfectly round. The water is crystal clear, with a sharp green tint, and it has a sulphurous smell and a medicinal taste, with properties that are, I am told, excellent for strengthening fractured bones. No boat is allowed on its waters because it is sacred and the many islands within it are all covered with reeds and rushes. Except that the islands are really masses of floating vegetation that are constantly driven by the wind against each other and the shore. Sometimes the islands are joined together in a string and look like one piece of land, other times they are dispersed by the winds in different directions, and occasionally they float alone and separately when the lake is perfectly still. It is not uncommon for cows to try to walk on to the islands when they are next to the shore, in the belief that they are firm land, only to find themselves falling into water.

But Italy has so many famous sites, too. At Laurentum, you can see the encampment where Aeneas first landed on these shores in flight from Troy. At Liternum, you can visit the olive trees planted by Scipio Africanus, and a huge myrtle overhanging a grotto, where a snake guarded over his coffin. At the bottom of the spring of Aponus near Padua, the dice thrown in by the emperor Tiberius can still be seen, while at Capri you can see the place from where he had victims hurled into the sea. The poet Horace's home can be visited at Tibur.

The rich flora and fauna of Italy have all been changed by its empire. Peacocks are in such demand for roasting that farms of them can be found on many small isles off the coast. Pheasants have reached here from Medea, as have flamingos, whose tender tongues were made popular by that great cook, Apicius. And what plants have come to our lands. It was the Greeks who first cultivated the vine and made Italy the favourite land of Bacchus. Olives, too, the Hellenes introduced, and the fig. Now even Syrian figs are grown here. The chestnut, once a foreigner to these climes, now adorns every well-kept table, as does the walnut. Plums are found in a multitude of varieties when they used not to grow here at all. Pomegranates, quinces and cherries were all once novelties on the Italian table, but have long since been grafted on to native stock. And what foreign flowers have brightened up our gardens. The rose travelled in with the Greeks, as did the lily, and were followed by violets and the difficult crocus. Italy has become the

garden of the world, a great orchard, which supplies
its inhabitants with a diet that is the envy of all. Everyday new delicacies are introduced. Peaches and apricots,
almonds and shallots have all recently arrived, as has the
pistachio nut, transplanted by the legate of Syria, Lucius
Vitellius, father of the emperor, to his estate near Alba.
Melons have even reached Naples from Oxiana. The
variety is such that nothing new seems possible.

And, of course, we have sent out these plants to the
furthest corners of the empire. The best cherry is that
which is grown in Belgica, or on the banks of the Rhine,
and the cherry tree has even made its way to Britannia.
The pistachio has already been transplanted westwards
to Hispania. So many places once thought too cold for
fruit trees now have flourishing orchards of their own.
Above all, the vine and the olive, those defining plants
of our empire, have spread to the very limits of our rule.
Where once the noble olive was confined to greater
Greece, now it has gone wherever the climate allows.
The vine has made it even further north, to the top of
Gaul and Germany, into the slopes of the Alps, Pannonia, and north Africa, even. The very Danube is now
shaded with vines. In Hispania, the people used to drink
beer and wine was rare, while olives grew only in the
south. How that has all changed. When Julius Caesar
conquered Gaul, only imported wine was to be found.
Now the province exports its vintages to every corner of
the empire, as the vine has relentlessly spread its tendrils
across the world. Italy is still the mother of all vineyards
but it has given birth to so many flourishing shoots.

Nearing Rome, I remembered that there was an

oracular cave near one of the lakes just off the route. I was confident that the emperor had summoned me back because he needed me for some important purpose, but our last encounter had left me nervous. Consulting the oracle would be a good way to know what was awaiting me. The priest handed me a special robe to wear, which reached down to my feet. I made the appropriate sacrifices and, holding cakes in my hand as an offering for the divine power, crawled on my hands and knees through the narrow opening of the cave. In the gloom I called out for the god to help me and repeated the sacred formula, then offered libations along with the cakes. I called on the spirit of my grandfather to visit me and for the god to speak to me through his shade. Then it appeared, an insubstantial shadow, difficult both to see and to recognise, yet endowed with a human voice and skilled in its prophecy.

'What is my fate?'

'Fear not, Falx, you are reaching your journey's end.'

And once it had answered, it vanished straight away.

I emerge squinting into the daylight. As we press on in our final stage, I feel confident that my exile is coming to a close. We gather speed as we near the capital. Before I see the eternal city, I hear it. Great roars are echoing out from the Circus Maximus during the chariot racing. Soon we will be back in civilisation: 'We'll soon be soaking in a hot bath house!'

But then this happened. Turning a corner, we were confronted by a centurion and a tribune, who had several other men with them. They stopped us and ordered us to dismount. They were still some distance away and Falx looked round to us, understanding what this meant. Clasping his chin with his left hand, as was his wont to do, he looked steadfastly at his assassins. His head was dusty from the journey and his hair unkempt. His face had thinned with fear but he walked steadily towards the centurion. He knelt and stretched out his neck, and the soldier almost succeeded in slicing off his head with a single blow. Once he had completed the task, by the emperor's command, he picked up the severed head to take back as proof that the deed had been done, and he also cut out the tongue that had offended the emperor so deeply.

·· COMMENTARY ··

The Romans may have loved nature but they drew the line at mountains, which they regarded as barren and dangerous barriers. They did, however, appreciate them from a distance and for the view they could afford of the broad plains and seas beneath, a way of seeing what they thought of as the best of nature on a grand scale. After the end of the Roman empire, it would not be until around 1350 that Petrarch would claim to be the first person since antiquity to have climbed a mountain solely to appreciate the view. As for a love of the wild, desolate majesty of mountains, that would have to wait for the Romantics.

Rome had an impact on the environment that lasts to this day. Deforestation occurred as a consequence of the clearing activities of Roman settlers in places such as the Germanic provinces. There was also heavy demand for wood as fuel, for use in shipbuilding and construction, and in mines for the smelting of metal ores. During the empire, the deforestation of the Apennine slopes increased because of the enormous charcoal demand of the imperial baths, despite the fact that firewood was being imported from north Africa. The island of Elba, which had rich deposits of iron ore, had its wood supply exhausted, making it necessary to transport the ore to the mainland for smelting. As we saw earlier, Roman gold mining practices included rerouting rivers to wash away the soil and making mountains collapse artificially to expose the ore. In the animal world, the wholesale capture of wild beasts for transportation to the hunting shows of the empire's amphitheatres had significant and even disastrous effects on the fauna of some regions. Elephants, rhinoceroses and zebras had become largely extinct in north Africa by the fourth century, while the poor hippopotamuses of Egypt were by then to be found mainly in the deep south of the country. There is no evidence of alarm at the depletion of such natural resources nor were any attempts made to redress the balance. Indeed, clearing provinces of dangerous animals was seen as evidence of the benefits that Roman civilisation could bring. The Christian writer Tertullian rejoiced that the Romans had turned woods and wildernesses into farming estates, that the cover of wild beasts had become grazing lands, and that marshes had been drained (*On the Soul* 30.3). And, as Falx describes, Rome's agricultural and horticultural practices led to the spread of all manner of plants and animals. Large-scale wine and olive oil production turned Mediterranean farming into the form that is familiar to us today. Ornamental plants such as pomegranates and flowers like lilies, roses, violets, poppies, marigolds and snapdragons decorated the gardens of the wealthy and left behind a legacy that is seen in garden centres across the world. In the neighbourhood of the villa at Chedworth, in the Cotswolds, even the large, pale edible Roman snail (*Helix pomatia*) still thrives.

The fourth-century historian Ammianus Marcellinus tells of travellers struggling over the Alps in winter (*Histories* 15.10). Strabo describes Etna (*Geography* 6.2). Pliny the Elder has a gushing account of Italy (*Natural History* 3.6), while his nephew writes in a letter about the strange lake Vadimo (*Letters* 8.20). The description of the oracle comes from Maximus of Tyre (*Dissertations* 26), while Falx's execution is based on Plutarch's account of the death of Cicero, whose severed head was displayed on the rostra in Rome from where he had so often criticised Mark Antony and Octavian, as were his hands, which had written so many vitriolic attacks against them (*Life of Cicero* 48).

No one now thinks that empire is a good thing because of the exploitation and oppression it inflicts on the conquered. How should we judge the Roman empire? We could draw up a list of the benefits: the roads, the great buildings, the development of law, trade, the assimilation of peoples, and, perhaps above all, centuries of peace for many areas that otherwise would have been stuck in the never-ending cycle of warfare that was the norm for international relations in the ancient world. But there were many terrible consequences: the brutality of conquest and the vicious oppression of revolts, the enslavement of millions, the arbitrary rule of an emperor, as Falx found out to his cost. But can we ever reduce such a complex and enduring phenomenon to a single judgement? And we will never know what most inhabitants of the Roman empire thought because their views do not survive. Rome was what it was. I love it and I hate it.

FURTHER READING

THE ORIGINAL LATIN AND GREEK texts are most easily accessed in the Loeb Classical Library, which has a facing translation. Good translations are also available in Penguin Classics. More thorough editions of the original sources can be found in the Teubner series. The best recent introductions to Roman history are Mary Beard's *SPQR* (Profile, 2015) and Christopher Kelly's *The Roman Empire: A Very Short Introduction* (Oxford University Press, 2006). Readers may also find useful my own *The Ancient World* (Profile, 2015). The three sourcebooks listed below also contain a range of textual selections relating to ancient travel and the Roman empire in general.

Lewis, Naphtali, and Reinhold, Meyer (eds), *Roman Civilization: A Sourcebook* (Harper Row, 1966).
Parkin, Tim G. and Pomeroy, Arthur J., *Roman Social History: A Sourcebook* (Routledge, 2007).
Shelton, Jo-Ann, *As the Romans Did: A Sourcebook in Roman Social History* (Oxford University Press, 1998).

General works on travel in the ancient world

Casson, Lionel, *Travel in the Ancient World* (Allen and Unwin, 1974).

Cioffi, R. L., 'Travel in the Roman World', *Oxford Handbooks Online* (Oxford University Press, 2016).

Or for more detailed studies:

Adams, Colin, and Laurence, Ray (eds), *Travel and Geography in the Roman Empire* (Routledge, 2001).

Scheidel, Walter, 'The shape of the Roman world', *Journal of Roman Archaeology* 27, 2014, 7–32.

Much fun can also be had on the Stanford ORBIS model, which allows journeys to be planned within the Roman empire: https://orbis.stanford.edu/

On ancient maps

Dilke, O. A. W., *Greek and Roman Maps* (Cornell University Press, 1985).

Talbert, Richard J. A., *Rome's World: The Peutinger Map Reconsidered* (Cambridge University Press, 2010).

On transport and its cost in antiquity

Adams, Colin, 'Transport', in *The Cambridge Companion to the Roman Economy*, Scheidel, Walter (ed.), 218–40 (Cambridge University Press, 2012).

Meijer, Fik, and van Nijf, Onno, *Trade, Transport and Society in the Ancient World* (Routledge, 1992).

Scheidel, Walter, 'Explaining the maritime freight charges in Diocletian's Prices Edict', *Journal of Roman Archaeology* 26, 2013, 464–68.

On road travel

Adams, Colin, *Land Transport in Roman Egypt: A Study of*

Economics and Administration in a Roman Province (Oxford University Press, 2007).

Laurence, Ray, *The Roads of Roman Italy: Mobility and Cultural Change* (Routledge, 1999).

On travel by sea and river

Arnaud, Pascal, *Les routes de la navigation antique: Itinéraires en Méditerranée* (Éditions Errance, 2005).

Campbell, Brian, *Rivers and the Power of Ancient Rome* (University of North Carolina Press, 2012).

Casson, Lionel, *Ships and Seamanship in the Ancient World* (Princeton University Press, 1995).

Hohlfelder, Robert L., *The Maritime World of Ancient Rome* (University of Michigan Press, 2007).

On pilgrimage

Dillon, Matthew, *Pilgrims and Pilgrimage in Ancient Greece* (Routledge, 1997).

Elsner, Jaś, and Rutherford, Ian, *Pilgrimage in Graeco-Roman and Early Christian Antiquity: Seeing the Gods* (Oxford University Press, 2005).

Rutherford, Ian, *State Pilgrims and Sacred Observers in Ancient Greece: A Study of Theōriā and Theōroi* (Cambridge University Press, 2013).

Wilkinson, John (ed.), *Egeria's Travels to the Holy Land* (SPCK, 1971).

On ancient travel guides

Alcock, Susan E., Cherry, John F., and Elsner, Jaś (eds), *Pausanias: Travel and Memory in Roman Greece* (Oxford University Press, 2001).

Arafat, K. W., *Pausanias' Greece: Ancient Artists and Roman Rulers* (Cambridge University Press, 1996).

Matthews, John, *The Journey of Theophanes: Travel, Business, and Daily Life in the Roman East* (Yale University Press, 2006).

Pretzler, Maria, *Pausanias: Travel Writing in Ancient Greece* (Duckworth, 2007).

INDEX